Understanding Human Life through Psychoanalysis and Ancient Greek Tragedy

Drawing parallels between ancient theatre, the analytic setting, and the workings of psychic life, this book examines the tragedies of Euripides, Sophocles, and Aeschylus through a psychoanalytic lens, with a view of furthering the reader's understanding of primitive mental states.

What lessons can we learn from the tragic poets about psychic life? What can we learn about psychoanalytic work from ancient tragedy and playwrights? Sotiris Manolopolous considers how the key tenets of ancient Greek theatre – passion, conflict, trauma, and tragedy – were focussed on because they could not be spoken of in daily life and how these restraints have continued into contemporary life. Throughout, he considers how theatre can be used to stage political experiences and shows how these experiences are a vital part of understanding an analysand within an analytic setting. Drawing on his own clinical practice, Manolopoulos considers what ancient playwrights might teach us about early, uncontained agonies of annihilation and primitive mental states that manifest themselves both within the individual and the collective experience of contemporary life, such as climate change denial and totalitarian politicians.

Drawing on canonical works such as *Hippolytus, Orestes, Antigone,* and *Prometheus Unbound*, this book continues the legacy of research that shows how contemporary analysts, students, and scholars can learn from ancient Greek literature and apply it directly to those negatively impacted by the trauma of 21st-century life and politics.

Sotiris Manolopoulos is a child analyst and training analyst based in Athens, Greece. He was trained in the Canadian Psychoanalytic Society and is a member of the Hellenic Psychoanalytic Society, where he was previously president and director of training.

Sotiris Manolopoulos' work wells from a profound psychoanalytic understanding of the child's interaction with the early maternal environment containing a tragic dimension from the very beginning. Without the mother's silent work of mourning, it would possibly result in destructive consequences both at the individual and social level. The author's linking this constellation to the ancient Greek tragedy in a creative way is a major achievement.

– **Simon Salonen, M.D., Ph.D.**, *Emeritus Adjunct Professor of Psychiatry, University of Turku, Member of Finnish Psychoanalytical Society. Author of "Metapsychological Perspectives on Psychic Survival".*

Deeply familiar with Greek mythology, and well versed in philosophy and psychoanalysis, Sotiris Manolopoulos throws a wide net to capture and bring together the individual, the clinical, the social and the political in their intricate connectedness. His thoughtful exploration of tragic theatre illuminates psychic life between passion and order, despair and resolution. A greatly enriching journey through the lands of ancient drama from the vantage point of contemporary psychoanalysis.

– **Cordelia Schmidt-Hellerau, Ph.D.**, *Chair of the IPA in Culture Committee.*

In this book Sotiris Manolopoulos takes the reader on a psychoanalytic Odyssey to explore some of the key Greek tragedies. Through a psychoanalytic lens familiar Greek characters are analysed to highlight the depths of the human psyche. It is an impressive endeavour that offers a compelling integration of both theatre and psychoanalysis.

– **Jan Abram**, *Author of* The Surviving Object: psychoanalytic clinical essays on psychic *survival of-the-object (2022) New Library of Psychoanalysis, Routledge.*

Sotiris Manolopoulos unpicks with mastery the thread of the souls of the heroes from Ancient tragedy, analysing their words and actions in the light of modern psychoanalysis and his clinical experience, displaying through the function of the chorus the connection between the collective and the individual at the point where the personal psyche, in order to be woven, consistently relies on the social and the sequence of passages through the Other, and the others, to the sufferer and the living subject.

– **Thanassis Hatzopoulos** *is a child psychiatrist, psychoanalyst (member of the* Société de Psychanalyse Freudienne, Paris, *of the* International Winnicott Association, *Sao Paolo, and president of the* Hellenic Psychoanalytical Space D. W. W, *Athens) and a poet.*

Understanding Human Life through Psychoanalysis and Ancient Greek Tragedy

Explorations of Euripides, Sophocles and Aeschylus

Sotiris Manolopoulos

Translated by Hector Tsougarakis

LONDON AND NEW YORK

Cover image: Delphi, the circular temple of Tholos.
Stefan Cristian Cioata, Getty Images: 1089241248

First published 2025
by Routledge
4 Park Square, Milton Park, Abingdon, Oxon OX14 4RN

and by Routledge
605 Third Avenue, New York, NY 10158

Routledge is an imprint of the Taylor & Francis Group, an informa business

© 2025 Sotiris Manolopoulos

The right of Sotiris Manolopoulos to be identified as author of this work has been asserted in accordance with sections 77 and 78 of the Copyright, Designs and Patents Act 1988.

All rights reserved. No part of this book may be reprinted or reproduced or utilised in any form or by any electronic, mechanical, or other means, now known or hereafter invented, including photocopying and recording, or in any information storage or retrieval system, without permission in writing from the publishers.

Trademark notice: Product or corporate names may be trademarks or registered trademarks, and are used only for identification and explanation without intent to infringe.

British Library Cataloguing-in-Publication Data
A catalogue record for this book is available from the British Library

ISBN: 978-1-032-71285-7 (hbk)
ISBN: 978-1-032-69920-2 (pbk)
ISBN: 978-1-032-71286-4 (ebk)

DOI: 10.4324/9781032712864

Typeset in Times New Roman
by Apex CoVantage, LLC

Dedicated to Jason and Sophia

Contents

Acknowledgments — xi
Acknowledgements for permissions — xii
Preface by Michael Parsons — xiii

Introduction — 1

1 The dramatic point of view — 11

2 Euripides' Hippolytus: drives unleashed — 26

3 Euripides' Medea: the barbaric reality — 41

4 Euripides' Orestes: the contamination of the city — 57

5 Euripides' suppliant women: mourning and femininity — 65

6 Euripides' Alcestis: narcissism and anti-narcissism — 82

7 Euripides' Iphigeneia in Tauris: bringing the stranger back home — 94

8 Euripides' Iphigeneia in Aulis: triumph in sacrifice — 104

9 Sophocles' Philoctetes: from somatic pain to trading — 113

10 Sophocles' Antigone: the tragic staging of the political — 119

11 Aeschylus' Prometheus Bound: from suffering to thinking — 126

12 A plea for a new political subject — 135

Index — 151

Acknowledgements

This book was originally published in Greek in 2021 in Athens by Armos Publications. In the present English version, I have added an introduction and an epilogue in which I develop some ideas on the political dimension of ancient tragedy. I made some changes of emphasis in the existing chapters, and I added a chapter on Sophocles' *Antigone* and on Aeschylus' *Prometheus Bound*.

I would like to thank the editor of the Greek versions of the book, Thanasis Hatzopoulos, and my colleagues, Petros Kefalas and Eliza Nikolopoulou, whose thoughtful comments helped me further develop my ideas.

My grateful thoughts also go to the members of the 10th International Psychoanalytic Delphi Symposium (Evy Zacharakopoulou, Dimitris Jackson, Maria Chatziandreou, Ariella Asser, Eliza Nikolopoulou, Marina Perris) whose aporias helped me enrich my ideas in the new English version of the book.

I am grateful to Zoe Meyer for her guidance and to Jana Craddock and Priya Sharma for their editorial assistance, which made the process of preparation of this book an enjoyable learning experience. I also wish to thank Lena Zouridi, who helped me organise my work.

Acknowledgements for permissions

With gratitude, I acknowledge that:

Armos Publications (Athens, Greece) allowed me to translate the original Greek version of the book and publish it in English with some alterations.

Taylor and Francis Group has granted me permission to use the material from my book *Psychoanalysis and Euripides' Suppliant Women. A Tragic Reading of Politics* (2022, Routledge/Focus) for Chapter 5. Euripides' Suppliant Women. Mourning and Femininity.

The Psychoanalytic Quarterly granted me permission to use my paper "Medea by Euripides: Psychic constructions for preverbal experiences and traumas"©, The Psychoanalytic Quarterly 2015, 84 (2), 441–461, with a few minor changes, for Chapter 3. Euripides Medea. The Barbaric Reality, which is reprinted by permission of Taylor & Francis Ltd, www.tandfonline.com on behalf of *The Psychoanalytic Quarterly*.

Preface

This book has an ambitious title. Sotiris Manolopoulos does not just want to use psychoanalytic ideas to understand more about Greek tragedy, nor just to see how the themes of Greek tragedy link to psychoanalysis. He wants to understand human life. Psychoanalysis and tragic drama are both, in their own way, investigations of human life, and running through the book is the question of how far their distinctive sources of inspiration lead to similar or different discoveries.

One thing both tragedians and psychoanalysts would certainly recognise is "the struggle between the need to make meaning and the irrational forces that destroy the links of meaning" (p. 22). But what kind of meaning, and what sort of irrational forces? Tragedy may seem to be concerned with external violence and the way hubris produces political as well as personal catastrophe, while psychoanalysis looks inward, dealing with an unconscious internal world. There is a boundary between inner and outer, but Manolopoulos shows the impossibility of separating them. All the time, they bleed into each other. The ten tragedies examined individually in this book explore in various ways what Manolopoulos calls the "unknown lines of meaning between the psyche and society" (p. 22).

Putting psychoanalysis and literature together is risky. Their relationship has always been uneasy. Even though Freud said great writers had understood unconscious processes before he arrived on the scene, psychoanalytic commentaries on works of literature have often been criticised, as when Lionel Trilling said that Freud's and Ernest Jones' accounts of *Hamlet* revealed that they did not understand the nature of artistic meaning (Trilling, 1951, p. 48, p. 52). This negative view of psychoanalysis has been especially evident where classical literature, and Greek tragedy in particular, is concerned. Freud's use of the *Oedipus Tyrannus*, for example, as a foundational text for psychoanalysis has been seen as an illegitimate appropriation of classical culture, and classicists regularly denigrate psychoanalytic commentary on Greek tragedy (e.g., Lloyd-Jones, 1985; Goldhill, 1997).

There are welcome exceptions to this, but the frame of reference for those academics who do make use of analytic ideas tends to be limited. Psychoanalysis may be employed as an intellectual method, but there is seldom any allusion to how analysts think clinically. Miriam Leonard, for example, Professor of Greek Literature at University College London, strongly affirms the value of psychoanalysis in her paper on Sophocles' *Antigone* (Leonard, 2003), but her analytic references are virtually confined to Lacan and the feminism of Luce Irigaray, with Hegel as a strong background presence.

Manolopoulos also writes about *Antigone*, and his chapter on the play makes for an interesting comparison. He, too, refers to Hegel, and, like Leonard and Irigaray, he insists that Antigone's personal conflict does not displace the political dimension of the play. He, too, asks what kind of ethical dilemma it is that confronts Antigone: political, religious, or psychological? He is a clinician, however, as well as a classicist, and his discussion of these issues is not simply conceptual. It is always related to ideas that analysts use in their clinical work, including the loss of omnipotence, the working through of grief, and the significance of object relationships, both infantile and adult, external and internal.

> The tragic and the political begin when the subject emerges from the primary union and the boundaries between phantasy and reality begin to form. In the area of transitional objects contradictions are not resolved through compromises. They become paradoxes that are connected with the tragic and the political action.
>
> (p. 120)

The discussion of Euripides' *Orestes* in Chapter 4 exemplifies this focus of the book especially well. Orestes has murdered his mother, Clytaemnestra, in revenge for her killing his father, and the citizens of Argos are threatening to execute him. Manolopoulos explores the ways in which the ancestral curse of the House of Atreus, the individual psychological catastrophe of Orestes, and the breakdown of social order all intertwine. The play shows how lost objects that cannot be mourned refuse to die but return, creating political as well as emotional disruption. Political disaster and moral iniquity, for their part, cannot be made sense of without understanding the unconscious internal world and infantile experience of the characters concerned.

The nature of tragedy is to show the darker aspects of life, but this is only one side of a coin. Manolopoulos emphasises that the darkness is necessary as a backdrop to light. All tragedies, he says, are illuminated by a faith in human life.

> Sophocles' Antigone gives a moving hymn to civilisation. Aeschylus' Prometheus dedicates a profound scene to human progress. In Euripides' *Suppliants*, Theseus speaks of his love for his city and praises its democracy and its politics in a profoundly moving manner.
>
> (p. 20)

Besides his dominant emphasis on Greek tragedy, Manolopoulos makes reference to poets of our own age, such as Seferis and Heaney. He makes clear all along that, as well as the ancient world, he is writing in relation to the present day, with its current emotional stress and political challenges. Manolopoulos is a deeply humane psychoanalyst and writer, always wanting to shine a light on the most intractable of contemporary global problems. Not for nothing is the final chapter called "Plea for a New Political Subject".

by Michael Parsons

References

Goldhill, S. (1997). Modern critical approaches to Greek tragedy. In P. E. Easterling (Ed.), *The Cambridge companion to Greek tragedy* (pp. 324–347). Cambridge: Cambridge University Press.

Leonard, M. (2003). Antigone, the political and the ethics of psychoanalysis. *Proceedings of the Cambridge Philological Society, 49*, 130–154.

Lloyd-Jones, H. (1985). Psychoanalysis and the study of the ancient world. In P. Horden (Ed.), *Freud and the humanities* (pp. 152–180). London: Duckworth.

Trilling, L. (1951). *The liberal imagination: Essays on literature and society* (Uniform ed., 1981). London: Secker & Warburg; Oxford University Press.

Introduction

Psychoanalysis and ancient Greek tragedy do not have a worldview. However, they examine how we are in the world. Human life is how human nature is in the world. Human life is psychic and social. Human nature is the same in every period of history in every culture. Human life is constantly changing. In times of transition, like today, in the epoch of the 4th technological revolution, human life changes dramatically. Our identities are shaken. We often defend our sense of self with many faces of Hubris: arrogance, populism and authoritarianism, exploitation of natural resources, excess of wild passions, craziness, violence, attacks on thinking, fragmentation of self and society. In such times, we turn to ancient drama and psychoanalysis to help us understand human life and restore its multiple meanings and our belief in its value.

Reality is a finding and a creation, a making (*poesis*).[1] Playing and fantasy assign meaning to our experiences. We live our experiences when we are in the intermediate area – between internal and external reality – of transitional objects and phenomena. We give meaning to experiences with our unconscious fantasies. With every translation of an experience, we create a new original one (Freud, 1914, 1915, 1916–1917, 1920; Winnicott, 1971).

The tragic poets have an interpretation to give us with each of their plays, a kind of meaning that is based on their theories of the mind and brings about a change in our capacity to think and understand. It has an echo effect. It creates a corresponding realisation on stage. This is a realisation of an emotional experience that is created and shared between the characters in the drama and the spectators (Bion, 1962/1967, 1962/1977, 1965/1984). From this experience, we can understand something about the unknown depths of human life. We can think psychoanalytically about the works of the poets, but we should not reduce them to psychoanalytic categories. We are all invited by the poets to watch a play. We do not know their primal themes. However, their themes are universal. They explore the core unconscious issues of human life.

Aristotle, in his *Poetics*, defines tragedy by the effect it has on the audience. Ancient tragedy is an emotional experience we live when we read a play or watch it on stage. What do we learn about human life from this experience? How do the psychoanalytic explorations of Euripides, Sophocles, and Aeschylus enable us to understand how our psyche and our culture work?

Psychoanalysis takes from the tragic poets the painfully accurate diagnoses of human life. It also takes the recognition of men's need to express themselves in the presence of others; to access the stranger, the other, inside through the other outside; to present their private suffering in public; to be alone with themselves in the presence of the other; to have a witness of the suffering of their experience, in order to reflect on it. Psychoanalysis borrows from the poets the idea that humans struggle to create and suffer their experiences in order to represent and integrate them psychically. The discovery and exploration of the unconscious was the essential work of Freud. The poets, however, had also made important contacts with the unconscious. In their works, Freud sought proof for his theories and also their insight into how the psyche and culture work.

We do not analyse tragedy. Through the poets' insights, we reinterpret psychoanalytic insights. The tragic plot is our analyst. It highlights transference situations that we encounter in analysis and in everyday life. Through the plot of a tragedy, we recognise the psychic process, a series of changes that unfold successively in time before finding après coup their meaning, and place them in subjective history. We assume that the psyche knows the way in which it functions and reconstructs this knowledge.

Tragedy was born when myth encountered logos. It was not a random encounter, and it would not have had an ecumenical resonance had it not registered in the processes (i.e., dream, playing, mourning, transference) with which the psyche struggles to face an intolerable reality (the loss of omnipotence).

Alford (1992) follows Nehamas' (1990) insight that for the poets, humans neither know (nor) control their basic nature and desires (Alford, 1992, pp. 142–143). Tragedy shows the dark side of life: the irrationality, the incoherence, the devastating passions, the grief, the rage, the violence, and the lack of resolution and settled outcome of our struggles. In ancient drama, there is a constant tension between despair and celebration of human life. We struggle to create links of meaning, to bridge the splittings inside ourselves and our societies.

A faith in human life illuminates all tragedies. De Romilly (1970) concludes that in all tragedies, the suffering is presented under a special light that compensates for the darkness. Sophocles' *Antigone* gives a moving hymn to civilisation. Aeschylus' Prometheus dedicates a profound scene to human progress. In Euripides' *Suppliants*, Theseus speaks of his love for his city and praises its democracy and its politics in a profoundly moving manner. There is always a light that comes through the darkness of a tragedy. It is the reassuring light of the dawn that life goes on: when a child, our original poet, wakes up from the night and begins to narrate to her/his mother or father the night's dream. The child feels full of creative thoughts, feelings of safety, and pleasure that she/he did not really murder them and did not commit incest with them, like it happened at night in the dreams. They actually survived; here they are, real, alive, and present, to listen to the story, acknowledge, and confirm her/his investments. The story and the creative thinking mean that the internal listener and respondent have survived. The darkness of despair has become a night of dreams and a new dawn. A Catharsis, a clarity, has been achieved.

The spectators leave with a deep sense of realness, aliveness, presence, and a convincing authority, authenticity, of the self.

Ancient Tragedy, and Psychoanalysis, have no words of comfort to offer. They only offer their sympathy to the human struggle. We struggle day and night with our psychic constructions to build our cosmos – a human world, an order with meaning – out of the inhuman universe. The poets tell us the stories of these struggles.

Ancient tragedy and psychoanalysis pose the question: How does one act responsibly in the absence of freedom? We become responsible for (we bring under our ego's control) the past devastating traumas in which we split off our emotions and, therefore, were not present to live the experience (Winnicott, 1960). We compulsively repeat these traumas. The freedom we have is to create new experiences in the present, to feel and express our feelings, and to choose the meaning we give to our past. The way we register our experiences is our responsibility.

In order for the primitive emotional experiences to be translated, it is necessary to access the work of our primary processes, which form the autoerotic soundtrack of the psyche from which words and fantasies emerge. The psychoanalytic process and tragedy are co-productions of the unconscious fantasies that are shared by the ego and the external object. We struggle to make meaning.

The analysts process what their patients hand out to them. In their listening, the patients find a stage, a space that can hold them and contain their story. If the patients were not talking to someone who had meaning for them, if they were not talking to their object, if there was no transference, how could their investments be recognised, responded to, or confirmed?

The myths, the child's playing, the transferences, and the tragic plots are transitional spaces in which we struggle to link internal with external reality. However, this creative work is accompanied by catastrophes. Irma Brenman Pick argued that a new tragic position is needed alongside the paranoid-schizoid and depressive positions to describe situations where defences mounted have led to real harm to the world (Weintrobe, 2023).

I think that we reach the tragic position when we emerge from the primary union and face the shock of the loss of omnipotence with the help of transitional objects and phenomena (Winnicott, 1971). The loss of omnipotence is compensated by the creation of intermediate areas of playing, myth, tragedy, and politics.

Following Bernard Williams (1993) we can think that central to any tragic plot is the shattering of the omnipotence of Hubris and the emergence of a tragic subject who "yokes the yoke of necessity" and personally accepts that what will befall it has to happen because of an ageless planning of mysterious forces. As psychoanalysts, we can say that these forces are unconscious. They come from an unknown past. They are presented as a compulsion to repeat, a fate (moira). With the loss of omnipotence things begin to happen in reality. Then the tragic position begins to be formed.

I hypothesise that there are unknown lines of meaning between the psyche and society. With caution, I make links between what we think psychoanalytically about an infant's psyche and what we can think about the politics and the function of a society.

Zajko and O' Gorman (2013, pp. 11–13) say:

> Like the study of the myth . . . psychoanalysis attempted the imaginative construction of a group subjectivity, based on the analogy of the individual; the psychoanalytic model of the collective is clearly based upon the model of infant development.

The infant and society have in common the struggle for survival.

For Meg Harris Williams (2013, p. 235), both the poets and the psychoanalysts are myth makers. The poet often makes references to myths to interpret the present experiences acted on stage. The psychoanalyst makes references to infant development for the same reason.

In Chapter 1, I examine what we call in psychoanalysis 'dramatic point of view'. I draw analogies between the psychoanalytic process, tragic theatre, psychic life, and politics. What can we learn about human life from the psychoanalytic explorations of ancient drama? Ancient drama presents the struggle between the need to make meaning and the irrational forces that destroy the links of meaning. It presents the extreme situations of disorder and violence caused by wild passions of love, hate, and revenge.

In Chapter 2, Euripides' *Hippolytus* invites us to examine how primary creativity meets the learning from experience in order to face the unconsciousness' negativity (castration, separation, and death anxiety) through symbolisation. The subject emerges from a breach of the narcissistic union. This discontinuity is introduced by the primal scene, which Freud considered a basic order of meaning, a logos. What kind of a helmsman was Hippolytus? His name indicates rebellious adolescent freedom but also the loss of mastery – his powerlessness in the face of the object's influence. His play reminds us of early trauma that leads to insufficient fusion of the drives, weak object cathexes, deficit of primary narcissism, and primary masochism. The loose drives are those which are not well represented and held so that they can be part of a story, contained in a meaning. Hippolytus avoids a full commitment to this world. He is an illegitimate son; he is not a full member of his world. His mother, the Amazon Hippolyta, is absent from his drama. His stepmother, Phaedra, overwhelms him with her passions. He reminds us of the infant that is precociously introduced to an object (of the drives) mother; it is deprived of an environment mother who makes the nursery a safe place full of meanings, thinking, and pleasure; it is deprived of its primary legitimate illusion (Winnicott, 1965/1990).

The first (classical) tragedies of Euripides are dominated by a tragic figure (Medea, Phaedra, Hecuba). Behind the passions and the violence, there is a woman we fear. Hecuba, in the limits of despair, feels a deep pleasure when she plots and realises her horrible revenge. She kills the children of Polymestor and blinds him. And then, in triumph, she says to him that he can strike on and burst the doors since he can never again put the bright light in the pupils of his eyes, and he can never see his sons alive since she herself has killed them.

In Chapter 3, I use Euripides' Medea as a metaphor for the psyche's struggles to express and symbolise preverbal, unrepresented experiences and wounds visited upon it before there was any word for trauma. Medea betrayed her motherland, her father, and her brother for the words of a Greek. From then on, she can never find a place to contain her. Medea, the wild stranger whose murderous magic is unleashed when the holding environment betrays her, could be thought of psychoanalytically as the uncharted realms of a traumatised existence yearning to find a way to represent itself on the stage of language and reality.

When we work through our mourning, a fog is lifted, and we can see clearly the traumatic reality of painful losses (Winnicott, 1963/1990). Catharsis, in ancient Greek tragedy, does not mean purification. Our emotions are clarified. Our view of reality becomes clear. It means clarity (Nehamas, 1992). It means that we have gone through a piece of work of mourning.

In Chapter 4, Euripides' *Orestes* discusses the illness of the individual that contaminates the city. In Argos, the heroes of Euripides' tragedy are besieged. They live in fear of the impending reality, a horrible end. After the matricide, the violent final eviction of his mother, Orestes is withdrawn. He stays at home, sick, lonely, and asleep. A hypnotic lethargy depersonalises him. His psyche ceases to live in his soma; it is elsewhere, dissociated, like a ghost that wanders around. What we, the spectators, see on stage are actors imitating real people who have been possessed by ghosts (unresolved losses, un-dead lost objects, un-mourned traumas, transgenerational curses) that commit real crimes in real time. The ghosts do the casting. What we see on stage are actors imitating the actions of real persons who have been taken over by ghosts that seek to drink real blood and kill real people.

Freud (1916) examined a type of character pathology in which the individual commits a crime in order to give reality, substance, and reason to his not well-represented and integrated sense of guilt. The scene of the crime becomes the theatre that stages the time, place, and aetiology of a missing link. It makes it a living occurrence. The crime revives and gives reality to someone who was unjustly killed and became a ghost because no one became the subject that would undertake the responsibility of the crime.

Such ghosts come to life, but the real people who bear them do not feel alive until the time at which they relive in the present the experience of the past and work through the mourning. Then, they feel alive. They separate fantasy from reality, past from present, the dead from the living, the private family from the public space. You cannot capture and kill a ghost. You can only mourn it. The dead have to be buried and mourned and become a past. Otherwise, a cycle of revenge opens; it never ends. Blood for blood, murder for murder.

Carson (2006, pp. 8–9) takes grief lessons from Euripides. She says that there is tragedy because there is rage, and there is rage because there is grief. The Athenians are at war and live the pain of destruction and grief.

'Why war?' was still the question 2,500 years later in the correspondence between Freud and Einstein (Freud, 1933). We ask the same question today. Politics and the rule of law provide a refuge of containment for man. However, the rule of law in its origins is violence deferred, displaced, and reassigned to the Community. The Community is held together, said Freud, by the force of violence and the ties of identification between its members.

In Chapter 5, I examine Euripides' *Suppliant Women*. In this tragedy, mourning and femininity form the core of existence. This tragedy is a tragic reading of politics. *The Suppliants* present the unconscious conflicts involved in forming and maintaining a democratic polis. Euripides' painful diagnosis is that politics is a struggle to integrate split-off forces of the past that lie beyond the order of politics, words, and reason. The laws of the polis do not replace mythical and religious beliefs but are instead linked to them. Our societies should have a sense of tragedy. We need a transitional space of politics where contradictions are tolerated and can co-exist without being split off or covered up with compromises.

We should think about the role of the feminine element and of the mourning work in the constitution of the primal matrix of human existence and society. Apart from the mother's dream work (reverie), we should also consider the mother's silent work of mourning, containing and binding the drives, defending against them from devastating our inner world and our societies. Instead of ghosts, the work of mourning creates links between the living and the dead so that death is not an evacuation of all meaning in human life but instead a new beginning.

Arvanitakis (2019, p. 35) believes that both the birth of human society and the birth of the individual are indissociably linked with the primal scene, violence and death. "We posit here that behind the various fantasy scenes that tragedy imitates there is, ultimately the fantasy that relates to the very identity of the hero . . . the Ur-szene of the birth of the individual".

In Chapter 6, I examine Euripides' *Alcestis*. This play shows the struggle to confront death. It shows narcissism and anti-narcissism of the subject, the couple, and the city. There are three ecumenical tragic movements that permeate the drama. First is the question of inescapable Necessity: How death (a law of nature) becomes integrated as a personal experience. Second is the question of what constitutes reality: How the work of mourning lifts the fog of depression that covers the reality of the object. And third, and most tragic, is the question of anti-narcissism: Why is it that by loving the object, the subject must die? Alcestis' drama is played between the primal scene (marriage) and death. In the wedding of Admetus and Alcestis, death is already present. Heracles is the mad guest that celebrates maniacally while Alcestis dies. In the end, from death, a new subject is born, a stranger – Alcestis, who Heracles brought back from the dead – finds a home (self).

Recognition is how the self is at home and how the self opens as a home for the stranger to return to. Homer's *Odyssey* was the poem that introduced the recognition of the stranger as a dramatic act. The ultimate moment of recognition concerns the coupling of two sexual bodies. Athena delayed the dawn and prolonged the night. The two lovers, Odysseus and Penelope, were given more time together. They derived pleasure, and conviction, by making love and then by talking with words.

The strangers persuade and recognise each other when they create an emotional experience together, be present as subjects to live it and meet – not split the affect. Only then does the sun rise and the new day, time begin. Tragedy used recognition as a very important turn in the course of the plot. Orestes' recognition by Iphigeneia is an important example of recognition according to Aristotle's *Poetics* (Nehamas, 1992).

In Chapter 7, I examine Euripides' *Iphigeneia in Tauris*. In this play, bringing the stranger back home is linked to the catharsis of the city. Euripides presents the discovery of otherness as a traumatic rupture in human development. He presents uncanny horrible scenes of massacre that offer us an acute sense of the self. He stages the work of mourning the sense of omnipotence, which is brought on by the shock of discovering the otherness of the object. Like the seismic shock that Iphigeneia saw in her dream, she now mourns with profound grief the fact that she is a stranger in Pontus, deprived of a polis, a husband, and children, and is forgotten by all. Nobody awaits her return. Nobody believes in her nostos. Instead, she blesses the slaughter of the strangers, covered in blood and tears. The Athenians, in the middle of a war, needed to bring the statue of Artemis back and found their city once more. They needed to shoulder the responsibility for the continuation of its traditions. They needed first to recognise their fears of persecution, and the bloodshed of sacrifice, that constituted the city's war situation as defences against their sense of guilt.

Alford (1992, p. 135) writes: "Expressed in the language of the poets, each of us achieves authenticity to the degree that we accept our moira (fate) and our demon". Our moira is our compulsion to repeat. Our demon is the 'infantile', the sexual and aggressive drives that push the psyche and the object to work, to represent and integrate them (Guignard, 1995). We are acted upon by our passions; we are not the centre that controls them. The belief that the subject is a centre of free will is a defence against recognising and tolerating our violent passions. Plato, the Enlightenment, and Christianity sanctified this defence and made it difficult to recognise.

In Chapter 8, I explore the triumph in sacrifice in Euripides' *Iphigeneia in Aulis*. This tragedy is a depiction of the sacrifice of the individual that fantasises about uniting with the entirety of the large group in order to both 'be saved' and 'save' it from the dissolution that threatens it at the moment when the individual and the group are integrated as a unit. At the same time, it is a depiction of the sacrifice of a primary union (with the primary mother and the large group) in order for the individual to emerge as a unit. Iphigeneia is summoned to Aulis, unaware of the fact that she has been selected to be sacrificed. However, she decides to recognise her emotions, not to deny them, to be present at the beginnings of her violent primal experiences. She decides to sacrifice herself for the sake of her large group, her country.

In Chapter 9, I discuss Sophocles' *Philoctetes,* who clings to his physical pain uncompromisingly. He defends his existence with a pain that reaches the human limits. Philoctetes struggles with his physical pain to unify his fragmented self. However, his pain unmakes the world of meanings that contain the self. Philoctetes lives in exile. He is deprived of his polis. He is deserted by his comrades with no world (meaning, order) to envelop him and be his fate. He is literally without a fate. The scream of pain is an aggressive act that defends (unifies) the self. At the end of the play, a unification of his containing world is proposed. Out of nowhere, a merchant appears, echoing Odysseus' negotiating powers. The merchant, by definition, travels the world, and with his journeys, he charts and unifies it. A solution is proposed through negotiation and thinking on both sides of the fence. The hero's containing world is created through political negotiations and collaboration. The negotiations put him on the map of a world where he can live; they give him a fate, a history.

In Chapter 10, I study the tragic staging of the political in Sophocles' *Antigone*. Death is a necessity, determined by nature. Mourning is a human need. It is a psychic work that must be done. It is a personal, profound, internal, painful process, and it is also always a public affair. Creon obstructs this process for the next of kin of Polynices and for the community. Antigone goes out into the agora and clashes mortally with Creon, who expresses the law of the state. Antigone expresses the 'morality of common blood', the unwritten law. The poets took the position that seers had in the polis in order to speak about the areas of human experience that lie beyond the order of politics, written law, and reason. It is horrible when your environment does not give you signs of mutual recognition. Signs to construct a meaning that will contain your story, signs with which you can construct a world where you can live. The conflict between the untamed sexuality and aggressivity of a young virgin and the unyielding authoritarianism of the older leader is relentless. The outcome is not a compromise. Justice belongs to both sides of the confrontation. The tragic and the political begin when the subject emerges from the primary union, the omnipotence is shattered, and the transitional space begins to develop.

Aeschylus craves justice. He believes in divine and human justice. The essence of the tragic in Aeschylus is 'pathei-mathos'. We learn from the experience we suffer. *Prometheus Bound* lives in a pre-political era and seeks politics, where the persecutory anxieties that are felt as unforgivable are mediated by group concern.

In Chapter 11, I examine Aeschylus' *Prometheus Bound*. The Titan suffers violent passions that unfold on stage. *Prometheus Unbound* follows. We assume that this sequence produces a transformation. Heracles sets Prometheus free. Omnipotence is internalised, and a forgiving paternal authority prevails. Aeschylus created a play of apocalypse. Bound on the rock, Prometheus presents the drama of his torture in front of himself and others. He asks for a response from the external object in order to not fall into the abyss of annihilation. At the end of *Prometheus Bound,* the Earth is shaken by Zeus' thunderbolts. Prometheus, along with the chorus of the daughters of Oceanus, falls into the farthest depths of Hades. Prometheus' Hubris was that he gave a gift to humans before they were capable of conquering it. Prometheus is split. He is a benefactor, omnipotent, good. He has nothing to do with violence, weapons, and war despite being a revolutionary. With Heracles' weapons, he breaks free. The splitting is lifted. Prometheus can now imagine the suffering, the challenge, the effort. He undertakes the struggle. He internalises his omnipotence. Aeschylus is a democrat. He uses Prometheus' disobedience as a trigger for the conflicts that will lead to transformations regarding authority, justice, and personal responsibility. Finally, when Heracles slays the Eagle with his bow, Zeus frees Prometheus but asks him to wear a ring of loyalty made of the chain and the rock on which he was bound. Obedience becomes commitment. The chain becomes a ring, an endless cycle.

In Chapter 12, I hear the ancient tragedy making a plea for a new political subject. Ancient tragedy developed in Athens over a span of 80 years, a time of destruction and a spring of creativity. It was born after the victory against the Persians and died after the war against Sparta ended with a devastating defeat. Greek tragedy offers an extremely realistic image of the unreliable, incomprehensible, incoherent, violent world in which we live. In the end, we feel that a catharsis occurs. We see clearly the reality, and we believe deeply in the struggle for human life.

Note

1 For the translation of Greek words, I have used *The Cambridge Greek Lexicon*. Cambridge: Cambridge University Press.

References

Alford, C. F. (1992). *The psychoanalytic theory of Greek tragedy*. New Haven, CT and London: Yale University Press.
Arvanitakis, K. (2019). A psychoanalytic perspective of tragedy, theatre and death. In *Tadeusz kantor and the ontology of the self*. London and New York: Routledge.
Bion, W. R. (1967). A theory of thinking. In *Second thoughts. Selected papers on psychoanalysis*. New York: Jason Aronson. (Original work published 1962)
Bion, W. R. (1977). Learning from experience. In *Seven servants*. New York: Jason Aronson. (Original work published 1962)
Bion, W. R. (1984). *Transformations*. London: Karnac. (Original work published 1965)
Carson, A. (2006). *Grief lessons: Four plays*. New York: New York Review of Books.
De Romilly, J. (1970). *La Tragedie Grecque*. Paris: Presses Universitaires de France.
Freud, S. (1914). Remembering repeating and working through. *S. E.*, *12*.
Freud, S. (1915). The unconscious. *S. E.*, *14*.
Freud, S. (1916). Some character types met with in psychoanalytic work. *S. E.*, *14*.
Freud, S. (1916–1917). Introductory lectures of psychoanalysis. *S. E.*, *16* & 17.
Freud, S. (1920). Beyond the pleasure principle. *S. E.*, *18*.
Freud, S. (1933). Why "war"? *S. E.*, *22*.
Guigniard, F. (1995). The infantile in the analytic relationship. *International Journal of Psychoanalysis*, *76*, 1083–1093.
Nehamas, A. (1990). The rescue of humanism. *The New Republic*, *203*(20), 27–34.
Nehamas, A. (1992). Pity and fear in the rhetoric and the poetics. In A. O. Rorty (Ed.), *Essays on Aristotle's Poetics*. Princeton, NJ: Princeton University Press.
Weintrobe, S. (2023). From illusion to delusion: Reflections on the rising crazy. *EPF Bulletin*, *77*, 254–277.
Williams, B. (1993). *Shame and necessity*. Berkeley and Los Angeles, CA: University of California Press.

Williams, M. H. (2013). Playing with fire: Prometheus and the mythological consciousness. In V. Zajko & E. O' Gorman (Eds.), *Classical myth and psychoanalysis*. Oxford: Oxford University Press.

Winnicott, D. W. (1960). The theory of the parent-infant relationship. *International Journal of Psychoanalysis, 41*, 585–595.

Winnicott, D. W. (1990). The development of the capacity for concern. In *The maturational processes and the facilitating environment*. London: Karnac. (Original work published 1963)

Winnicott, D. W. (1990). *The maturational processes and the facilitating environment*. London: Karnac. (Original work published 1965)

Winnicott, D. W. (1971). *Playing and reality*. London: Tavistock.

Zajko, V., & O' Gorman, E. (2013). *Classical myth and psychoanalysis*. Oxford: Oxford University Press.

Chapter 1

The dramatic point of view

In addition to the established psychoanalytic viewpoints (dynamic, economic, topographical, genetic), we also need a dramatic (poetic, dialectical, situational) viewpoint of psychic life (Bleger, 1967, 1969; Baranger & Baranger, 2009). I think that the dramatic point of view describes a field where samples of human life are played out, forming links between internal and external reality and drawing temporary lines of orientation. Such a field is our object of observation. The concept of the field describes the psychoanalytic situation as a spatial and temporal structure with specific transference experiences and fantasies that the participants share.

Transference is a repetition. It is also a new creation. It is by itself 'therapeutic'. It presents, organises, and assigns meaning to experiences that have not been adequately represented, differentiated, and internalised. In the relational field of transference, emotional experiences are created and shared between the participants. A fantasy is co-constructed by the participants. It gives meaning to the shared experience (Baranger & Baranger, 2009 ; Ferro, 1999).

Transference creates the matrix of the frame, a womb where experiences are gestated and transformed. In an analysis, as in everyday life, we transfer experiences. We place them in time; we eventually make them our past. Through interpretations/constructions and also through playing, to some degree, the roles we are assigned, we make the analytic situation an occasion for psychic work. We make it a dream workshop that creates and transforms the raw somato-psychic elements into a psychic tissue of alpha elements that are stored in memory with successive layers of links of meaning.

In line with the dramatic viewpoint, we regard the psychoanalytic interpretation as implicit (inherent) with the material on which it acts. It is not a one-off act of speech. It is a process. The tragic plot is also an interpretation that is implicit in the emotions and fantasies of the audience on which it acts. Finally, in everyday life, we address the discourse of interpretation to the other person so that she/he will, in turn, reinterpret it and return it to us. The work of culture is a lifelong debt – which we undertake after we emerge from the primary union – to work day and night in order to construct links of meaning between the internal and the external reality (Winnicott, 1971). Theatre is a supreme sample of such work.

Freud liked theatre more than any other literature genre (Green, 1969). There are analogies to be drawn between psychic transformations of analytic process, theatre, and everyday life. The thread that runs through the poetics of dramatic art, analysis, and life consists of the work that aims at restoring the psychic quality of the elements of an experience. Psychic quality refers to meaning. It is a result of the work that unifies and expands psychic space and history by representing and integrating raw, unprocessed traces of experience in associations of thing and word representations (Freud, 1900). However, every psychic formation has a core of traumatic elements of untransformed reality. This is a grain of historical truth around which the psyche weaves a meaning, much like a pearl is formed around a grain of sand (Freud, 1916–1917).

Our thought that is subject to language (secondary processes) makes us aware of unconscious thing representations and sensory, motor, and perceptual impressions and proto-emotions without them losing their primitive origins in the translation. We speak in order to transmit meaning to ourselves and others. But words fly with the wind; you never know their direction, course of action, and effect. Their preverbal sensory-motor and proto-emotional elements transmit meanings and connect unexpectedly remote areas of our psyche. The hallucinatory realisations of these elements create scenes. Freud (1900, pp. 546, 595) observes that in the frame of the pleasure principle, childhood sexuality gives birth to psychic acts that occur in an unconscious infantile scene. This visual memory of the object of desire is the first theatre stage of the psyche. The poetics of dramatic art help us comprehend how our psychic constructions transform the traces of experiences that are accessed through regression and identification. We collect them on the basis of common meaning (alpha elements) and historical truth (beta elements). We present them to ourselves and others through hallucinatory realisations in the language of actions and the body. Then, a new experience is created in the here and now as an act in which they find a place. Our constructions are convincing because they use the language of action and the body; thus, they ensure the consent of the other subject with which we converse.

Tragedy borrowed the art of persuasion from the Rhetoric that was taught by sophists in Athens in the 5th century BC to be used in courts and assembly meetings. A court, an assembly, and a theatre are spaces where people and their experiences come together to make a persuasive story. Austen (1817/2007) acknowledges that persuasion is an integral part of the stories that make us humans exist in the world with others. Many actions, movements, and changes of space and time occur until all favourable persons are together at the same time at the same place. Being together means that the different parts of a whole are alive, real, in the present, linked with common threads of truth that hold them together in a coherent world. The state of 'being together' is what makes a situation persuasive. The ancients called this state 'Kairos' (appropriate measure, favourable time, time). This: 'being together' can also be called 'a selected fact' in Bion's terms. Analysis, poetry, and drama are experiences that happen in real time.

The meaning envelops the story and not the other way around. There is an appropriate metre, a favourable time. Metre has the same etymological root as

Metis, which represents primary creativity, an innate capacity for self-teaching, and a deep intelligence before any knowledge.

Across from Ithaca is the coast of Scheria, from where Phaeacians escorted Odysseus to his homeland. Odysseus was asleep, and his sleep surrounded his dreams. The Phaeacians' ships were said to have a deep intelligence to find their way. This deep intelligence may represent the primary creativity of dreaming in which the metaphors (transferences) link opposite coasts between body and psyche, unconscious and conscious, internal and external reality, self and object, past and present. In analysis and in poetry, we do not seek a real past event. Historicity creates the truth and not the other way around. Through psychic constructions, our experiences are documented as subjective history in the context of their era. We restore their historicity (Freud, 1937; Green, 2005; Parsons, 2007). In Conrad's (1902) *The Heart of Darkness*, the meaning envelops the story and not the other way around. Truth is the gathering and the ordering of our elements of experience.

We create and share an emotional experience and a fantasy every time we meet. We meet in a situation of intersubjectivity, with a biological need, similar to hunger and thirst, to seek another self. There, we sense the breath of human life, our primordial ethics, and the mutual recognition in a visceral level of human similarity with the other, in spite of our differences (Dupond, Balint, & Jackson, 1988; Ogden, 2004; Miller, 2019).

When a child enters a playground, an analysand a consulting room, or a spectator a theatre, they resemble a character in a drama who enters the stage. They do not enter a place. They enter a moment, a living occurrence. This is a dramatic situation where action occurs in real time. Dramatic arts tell stories on stage through action. The inescapable presence of the past and future and their uncanny ruptures now create a strange experience. The visit to a theatre creates a radical attention to the realness of the place. The subject exists acutely; she creates and lives an emotional experience; she becomes present and real; she lives fully in a timeless moment, a pregnant moment, where present, past, and future meet. The object that inscribed the trace of experience in the past and the self that interprets it now meet and live together an experience and share a fantasy that interprets the experience. They are together now on stage. History becomes a performance. The present is a timeless moment. A mystery that we attend.

Zajko and O'Gorman (2013, p. 9) observe that the myth is timeless. In Homeric poetry, some speeches are pregnant with what is not said. These moments give us a profound sense of internal life.

When a meaning encounters a sound

Tragedy was born when a myth encountered words. Words not only express but also shape our thinking (Vygotsky, 1934). According to Aristotle, tragedy came from improvisations, lyrical forms, dithyrambs, and choral songs sung in honour of Dionysus, the god of disorder. The religious celebration of Dionysus created tragedy, and epic poetry made it a literature genre (De Romilly, 1970; Zimmermann, 1986/1991, p. 7).

The language of the ancient tragedy is the language of emotions. Almost all the plays that we know today, with the exception of two, draw their material from the same myths that the two epic poems used. The tragic poets took from Homer's epic poems the art to create persons and scenes that could move the spectators. They also took the crucial function of recognition.

Jacqueline De Romilly (1970) writes: Tragedy encompasses two separate elements: the Chorus and the persons of the drama. Dithyramb was indeed a dialogue between a person and the Chorus. The ancient Greek tragedy was played in two distinct places at the same time. The spectators were sitting on the benches of a huge amphitheatre. Across the seats was the acting area, a stage, a place where the persons of the drama acted. The 'skene' was the background of the acting area. On top of the skene was a balcony from which gods could appear. Then there was the 'orchestra', a wide circular space in the centre of which there was an altar dedicated to Dionysus. This was the space in which the Chorus moved.

The double limit (separation), on the one hand, between the stage of the drama and the orchestra of the Chorus, and on the other hand, between those and the city, who is present on the benches of the theatre, reminds us of the double limit between conscious and unconscious on the one hand and between internal and external reality on the other We, the spectators, sit on the benches with double attentiveness. On the one hand, we let ourselves be immersed in (we feel) the experience of the play, and on the other hand, we think, and we make links of meaning.

There were steps that joined the two spaces, the stage and the orchestra that were clearly separate. Apart from the steps, there were threads of speech and waves of emotion that joined the two spaces. The emotions were carried by the music of words. The kommos was a song of lament that was shared by the Chorus and actor(s), creating a symphony. The actors expressed themselves in iambic trimetres, and only under the impact of a strong emotion would they use lyrical forms. The Chorus expressed itself with metres clearly lyrical. The Chorus maintained its independence from the acted plot on the stage. It had a dialogue with the persons of the drama, but it was separate. Separateness was the condition of the dialogue. There were voices between the members of the Chorus and the persons of the drama. However, the main role of the Chorus was lyrical. It sang and danced.

"A tragedy consists . . . of alternating sung, recited, and spoken parts. We may get some sense of the music to which verse was set by studying its various meters" (Zimmermann, 1986/1991), p. 18). De Romilly (1970) explains: The ancient poetry was based on the length of syllables that were ordered in predetermined rhythms. In every 'strophe' (turn), there was an 'antistrophe' (turn to the opposite), and from one to the other, the rhythmical shapes were repeated, metric foot to metric foot, syllable to syllable. Symmetrical pairs, as well as more complex sets, follow an austere metrical order. All this art has been lost in the translation today. It is said that Euripides was an excellent composer. His lyrical songs were deeply moving. We do not have his music today, but we can imagine the moving effect his lyrics had.

In psychoanalysis and in ancient tragedy, the music of the words refers to affects. When separating from its mother's body, the child develops a 'melodic line', a transitional phenomenon. When the sound meets the meaning, poetry is made. A child, frightened in the dark, speaks to get a response, to hear someone from the next room speaking. The child cannot see the other person, but if anyone speaks, it gets brighter. Freud (1905) heard this as an expression of separation anxiety and as an address to the object in search of a witness for its experience and a meaning for it. In ancient tragedy, we can see a crack of light in the middle of the darkness, the necessity of death. The source of this light is the voice of the words, the music of language that is poetic. Prometheus is immobilised, but his words fly all over the world, like Io.

The sound – and not only the content – of speech, the prosody and music of words, has its own rhetoric that conveys meaning. It also carries the sense of self. Freud (1920) comprehended the relation between the sounds of the voice and emotions that are set like scenes in the psyche: the child expresses his sadness for the disappearance with a long 'o – o – o-oh' (gone), and the joy of reappearance with the short 'da' (here) as he plays the separation and reunion with his mother with his reel (Green, 2005).

In analysis and poetry, we listen to the music, the rhythm of speech that divides time. The processes of making (poesis) our world in the springs of the psyche are governed by musicality. The infant's (the original poet's) internal rhythms resonate with its environment. They form islands of experience from primary materials: contacts of skin, heartbeats, breathing, alternations of day and night, sleep and awakening, hunger and satiation, muscle relaxation, and tension. An environment mother allows the infant's autoerotism to develop and manages the ego needs as a guarantee for its psychosomatic unity, an invisible sponsor, a primitive knowledge predating comprehension, a silent language from which words emerge (Winnicott, 1965/1990, 1988; Botella, 2002, pp. 79–86; Denis, 1995, pp. 1109–1119).

Freud (1905) referred to the role of rhythm in the formation of autoerotism and the object. He invented the analytic frame, whose rhythms are defined by continuities and discontinuities and require investment in time and patience. Through such continuities and discontinuities, the ability to create representations is facilitated. Winnicott (1971, 1988) discovered that babbling, as a transitional phenomenon, helps the infant in its course of emerging from the enmeshment with its mother. Anzieu (1979, pp. 23–36) talked about a sound mirror and an audio-phonic skin of morphological signifiers that defines the ability of symbolisation. Children rock to the sound of a lullaby, reinforcing the sense of rhythm that renders them capable of being patient, waiting, and thinking. The exchanges of sound images unite and separate the infant from the mother. Their words hold their bodily rhythms. Aristotle considered rhythm to be the most important medium of *mimesis* (imitation) after myth. It is a profound need of the psyche (Sykoutris, 1937/1991). Rhythmicity is an integral part of parent–infant interactions.

The parents' voice transmits meanings that the infant absorbs through primary identification and thus composes its core sense of self. Speech expresses affect. Sounds are associated with emotions from the preverbal period. Ogden (1999, p. 974) studied how the foundation of both poetry and psychoanalysis attempts to increase the width and depth of the things we can experience. Parsons (2007, pp. 1446, 1451) suggested that when we listen to a poem, instead of abstracting the meaning, we hear the meaning; we let the poem inside ourselves and then see what happens inside us.

The true speech, the speech that signifies, frees the meaning that is captive in the thing (Merleau-Ponty, 1960/1964, p. 44). The mother that speaks to her child with her voice also transmits the flesh of words, the preverbal things. Thus, the maternal voice becomes persuasive (Taiana, 2022, p. 66). The sense of words depends on their connection to primitive forms of thought. The word shapes thought. We do not distinguish the words from the emotional experiences in which they have been woven. We find memories in feelings and the senses (Freud, 1914; Klein, 1948/1975).

Green (2005, pp. 206–209) noted: Language is the medium for the recognition and the self-recognition of psychic movements. In analysis, we have a double transference concerning 'discourse' on the one hand and the 'object' on the other. Analysis of the preverbal is performed by referring to that which is verbalised through transformation into speech. However, language is not the only medium that expresses meanings. The non-verbal sign systems convey meaning by themselves.

The sound (affect) and the meaning comprise an original somatopsychic link at the heart of existence. This link lies at the foundations of primal scene fantasy, which is the origin of the subject. The primal scene fantasy is a theatrical time and space and a story-theory that narrates it. Prometheus becomes a subject in the time and space between the cry and the silence, where language (in the form of his visitors: the Chorus of Oceanides, the daughters of Oceanus, then Oceanus, Io, and Hermes) finds him. Prometheus, the messenger, becomes the message, thinking. From suffering from being bound, he transitions to the passion – binding and commitment – to thinking together with an object. Language makes this possible. In ancient tragedy, as the role of the Chorus progressively diminished, it was replaced by the agon, an organised dialogical conversation. Euripides developed this technique of confrontation, where each person on stage speaks to defend and own their feelings and ideas. Euripides borrowed this technique from the rhetoric of the Sophists. Aristotle linked both Poetics and the Rhetoric with emotions (pity and fear) (Nehamas, 1992).

The poetics of the analytic process and ancient tragedy are substantiated at the level of the smallest units of language, especially in their relation to the voice, where the connection of meaning and affect is inherent. Sound and meaning comprise an indivisible language core. When people gather together and converse, a shared emotional situation is activated. Then, the participants feel as if they always knew each other very deeply.

Jakobson emphasised the emotional function of language. He established the research of phonology that was based on the concept of the phoneme as an inseparable bond between sound and meaning. The phonemic contrasts play a mediating and differentiating role in regard to grammar that has a specific meaning. They also have their own direct, albeit latent, significance that affects how language is organised (Jakobson & Pomorska, 1983).

Unconscious processes become known under the condition of dreaming (Freud, 1900; Bion, 1962/1967, 1962/1977). In poetry and the psychoanalytic process, the creation of a symbolic representation opens new horizons in the ego's future. The symbol is not an object but rather a regulatory framework that frames in a variety of ways that Peirce calls "*occurrences*". The verbal symbol is the regulatory framework, a condition for all things that will happen in the future. In the context of every sequence of events, the constant of the verbal sign – its general meaning – acquires a new specific meaning. The context changes, and with every new context, the word is subject to a renewal: herein lies the creative force of the verbal sign (Jakobson & Pomorska, 1983). We leave the theatre with a sense of light in spite of the darkness of the tragic story. This light is the sense of the future, which promises us new occurrences. We do not despair. We have a future. We will not be extinct.

Theatre is a reflection of nature (Rustin & Rustin, 2002). We can conceive the dramatisations of a theatrical piece as a transferential acting out and psychoanalysis as a form of dramatic act (Nuetzel, 1999). The actor plays her/his 'pieces' – pieces of the self, genuine emotional experiences that she/he shares with other actors and with the audience. She/he plays like a child, risking that, in doing so, they will lose control (Fenichel, 1946 pp. 149–152). She/he plays seriously with a sense of responsibility.

Drama represents 'actions', 'pieces of emotion' that contain archaic codes, unknown forms, and latent links. These actions condense universal truths in which internal and external reality have met. They salvage the original encounters of the infant with maternal care. The skene (stage), the thymele (altar), the koilon of the theatre, and the orchestra represent the maternal space. Drama uses drastic language, that is, "words of persuasion (that) pierce the soul: they cause anxiousness and hope. Anxiousness that all will be emptied, and hope that not all is lost" as Austen (1817/2007) said.

In creating meaning, we enter historical time and undertake the responsibility for our world and its interpretation. In *Poetics*, Aristotle expresses the opinion that man seeks the creation of conjunctures with curiosity.

Psychic staging

Breuer (Breuer & Freud, 1895) coined the phrase "private theatre" referring to Anna O's internal world, where the production of her fantasies occurred. The analysis of transference is life-like, as is good theatre (Bion, 1977). It unfolds like the dramaturgy of the unconscious on the analyst's couch. In psychotherapy, children set stages using play materials. The first week of Richard's analysis by Klein opens like a scene from Chekhov, with all the actors on stage (Meltzer, 1978).

The space of a dream is a theatre where meaning is created (or destroyed) (Freud, 1900). The analytical context, like the dream, is also a stage. Analysis is performed on two different stages (Freud, 1937). The production of fantasies constitutes an internal theatre. In *Totem and Taboo*, Freud (1912–1913) understood tragedy as a dramatic enactment on the stage of the primordial crime. The protagonist of the ancient drama is the pharmacos (scapegoat), who shoulders the guilt on behalf of the whole community.

Pontalis (1974, p. 455) found traces of Freud's discovery of the psychoanalytic concept of space by following the path that began from Charcot's theatrical stage. Freud captured the structure of the psychic apparatus and invented the psychoanalytic situation, realising that he had to begin with the organisation of the fantasy and its special coordinates of time and space, in which the changes happen, the movements that hide identification positions.

Pedder (1977, pp. 215–223) followed Winnicott in studying psychoanalysis, play, and theatre as transitional spaces. In Pirandello's play *Six Characters in Search of an Author,* the internal drama is externalised. An action does not merely express but also shapes the fantasy with memory traces of experiences that seek life. The character/father expresses, formulates and accomplishes the desire "to live for a moment inside of you". In everyday life, day and night, the psyche constructs persons and things in a plot, which it interprets. Thus, it undertakes the responsibility of interpreting the world as a stage director of its fate. Our ego stages scenes with unconscious productions that inform the conscious (Freud, 1915).

The psyche's work is performed in psycho-somatic scenes (fantasies) that have both content and form, defined by the drives and the defensive compromises. The poetics of psychic work set a dramatic plot of object relationships, with the function of the psychic stage separated by clear permeable boundaries from the backstage area of the unconscious and from the external reality.

Theatre is based on the function of playing. When playing, the child separates internal from external reality so as to feel safe to experiment with real objects and to truly – not as if – play with pieces of dream thoughts and experiences. What happens on stage is real, provided that we know that the stage is not real life (Parsons, 2000). The persons of the drama and the spectators are real, provided that they play with subjective objects in the area of illusion. The area of illusion, like the core of the true self, is not for communication with – it is protected from the intrusions of – the external objects. The illusion of the play must go on. The spectators, Chorus, and actors play their roles. They sing, dance, and act or watch the mimesis of action played on stage. They do not actually and concretely invade the stage or the orchestra. Gorgias, in the 5th century BC, said something similar. He said that being able to be deceived (live an illusion) makes you wiser (enables you to know reality). I will come back to that at the end of the book.

Aron and Atlas (2019, pp. 249, 258–260) write: Ferenczi's (1931) and Dupond et al. (1988) clinical experiments allow us to think of the psychoanalytic process as a live dialogue in the here and now, where, "internal object relations and multiple self-states are unconsciously dramatised and brought to experiential life on the analytic stage". We can use "the metaphors of playing, dramatizing, dancing and dreaming with the patient" in order to describe the analytic co-participatory enactments. The notions of generative enactment, the prospective function, and dramatic dialogue describe the analytic couple at work. Loewald (1975) states that language is a form of action. In the session, in everyday life, and on the stage of a tragedy, we find, create, and share reality and meaning in a deep, participatory way. The analyst, like a Chorus, participates in the dramatic dialogue, the drama of the patient's inner life. In analysis, like in the theatre and in a dream, we observe "characters and personifications of self-states and object-relations in symbolic and pre-symbolic, verbal and nonverbal, enigmatic and pragmatic registers" (Loewald, 1975, p. 298). However, these characters are moved by unknown, mysterious forces that come from the past. The dramatic point of view is interactive. Bleger (1969/2012) suggested that we use a dramatic point of view in which "human beings with their human characteristics, life and behavior" acted on the stage of the session.

We can think of the session as a performance of a tragedy, in which the persons of the drama, the Chorus, and the audience dream together, the plot, in Ferro's terms. An analytic session and a performance of a tragedy work like a dream and construct a field of ambiguity (in Barangers' terms) in which each element is understood as something else.

Psychoanalysis encounters tragedy on the level of staging a transference experience that aims at symbolising and integrating unassimilated experiences. When the on-stage protagonists of the drama became two, the primal scene of the parental couple became a reality and turned into an action that had a plot and an outcome. The spectators, with curiosity, dare to participate in a peripeteia with its sudden changes and unexpected turns: they enter the corridors encircling the chamber of the primal scene, and in doing so, they allow their fantasies, affects, and thoughts to unfold. The truth does not lie in events but rather in the way in which they are intertwined.

In the beginning, the Chorus, with its dances and its songs, was the most significant ingredient of tragedy. Gradually, the plot and the dramatic action on stage became more important. De Romilly (1970) observes that Euripides was indeed the poet who invented what we call today a plot. His plays are full of schemes, surprises, unexpected mis/understandings and mis/recognitions. Out of nowhere, suddenly people appear and meet, and things begin to happen. More persons began to take part in the action. The scenic development became more diverse.

De Romilly observes that Euripides knows how to give movement to action and heighten the tension of the rhythm, which enriches the human echo of the drama. He knows how to transmit fear and cause the heart to beat fast. Someone is expected to come as saviour, but he is late and causes despair to those that expect him. And when all hope is lost, he suddenly appears. Very often, the person in the drama is led to perish because of his effort to avoid it. In Euripides, the long monologues as well as dialectical arguments of agons, the sudden changes of action, the ideas, and the emotional scenes are used to express strong passions.

Tragic poetry and history are of the same order; they are both research (Sykoutris, 1937/1991). Curiosity and research begin in infancy. The child solves the riddles of creation in play (Freud, 1908). Through fantasies, the child interprets the experiences it creates. Action of play and the storytelling of fantasy are deeply connected. The child experiences in the here and now the action of playing and tells a story to trace the origins of the riddles of life in early experiences. It creates a past and makes a future. Telling a story allows the truth to emerge. Money-Kyrle (2015) describes 'the facts of life' that are hated because they bring us the trauma of contact with reality: the difference between generations, the difference between the sexes, and the reality of the passage of time. There is a good object, the mother's breast, that we envy because we depend on it, and its separate existence threatens our omnipotence. We originate from a couple's sexual dimension, from which we are also excluded. Finally, we realise that time passes. Our mortality is a painful fact. To be able to live in the world inside time (history) is a major achievement of development.

The primal scene is where we start from. It shapes the plot of a tragic story, the "composition of things" (Sykoutris, 1937/1991). It is a lens through which the child reads and recognises reality (Laplanche & Pontalis, 1973). The child is born with pre-conceptions that become conceptions with realisations (Bion, 1962/1977). A major realisation is the child's ability to connect to links of meaning and of relations, to belong and be related to the world, and not to feel alienated, redundant, and irrelevant. The child's true descent is at stake: true participation and access to authentic rather than false experiences. The subject's originality is at stake: authenticity, autonomy, and contact with innermost experiences.

Aristotle, in *Poetics*, discussed tragedy as a type of imitation (mimesis) that is inherent to humans. We have to double what we experience on the basis of likeness. Imitation can be thought of as a basic transformation work that happens on many levels, from beta to alpha elements, from soma to psyche, from unconscious to conscious, from the pre-psychic to the psychic quality, from psychic to external reality, from self to object, etc. The tragic plot that is acted on the stage in the present is a realisation of a primal mythical scene. For all arts, imitation means that the artist provides his audience with the capability to draw connections between what they are experiencing now and previous personal experiences. Thus, the forms that emerge are placed inside the story that the spectator makes, with a tragic sense of this historicising process.

The tragedians organised their material in such a manner as to offer opportunities for the realisation of emotions (Sykoutris, 1937/1991; McLeish, 1998/2001). The emotional context of these moments allows us to realise the wider significance of events and the complexity of the world. We experience the passions, and then we enjoy the passion of thinking about them and learning from the experience. According to Aristotle's *Poetics* and *Rhetoric*, by participating in the acts of a tragedy, we draw pleasure from learning (Sykoutris, 1937/1991; Eliou, 1974).

Taplin (1988) argued that tragedies were not written to be read but rather to be presented as actions on stage. He cites T. S. Eliot, who noted that behind the words of a tragedy are actions, and behind those are the emotions. After having prepared the audience with words, the realisation occurs with the appearance of Oedipus wearing the mask with the bloody, gouged-out eyes: *Ecce szene*. When the psyche has invested in perception, this perception appears, is presented, and acquires substance. Our psyche 'creates' forms that suffice and satisfy because they bind the excitations. The failure to give form to emotions causes a feeling of being unsatisfied and fearful because of the regressive stripping of affect that has lost its ability to mean and contain.

The sounds of voice comprise scenes with dimensions of space and time. Talking makes things happen (Enckell, 1999, pp. 219–238; Hughes, 2004, pp. 153–165). The sensory images offer their magic (deceptive protean sudden presence, transformations, and sudden disappearance) to the fantasies in which they are composed (Rolland, 2005, pp. 7–23).

Coexistence and change are inextricably connected in transitional spaces. Transformations occur with an internal rationale, not towards progress but based on points of convergence and divergence (Jakobson & Pomorska, 1983). Changes are defined by convergence and deviation of context elements that stem from unintegrated and integrated areas. The history of our subjective experience does not move in a linear course. We have learned this from the poets, dating back to Homer.

The awareness of the time that intervenes between perception and the meaning that perception acquires is the sense of transience (Freud, 1916; Manolopoulos, 2003). The sense of self is born in this space. The awareness of the sense of transience, the fact that time passes, is the solidification of the creation of a world to live in, an ethos, a habitat, which begins with the experience of a loss. The spectacle of the primal scene, the theatre, brings the death and the birth of the new. Saint Paul the Apostle writes: "For I think that God hath set forth us apostles last, as it were appointed to death: for we are made a spectacle unto the world, and to angels, and to men" (1 Corinthians 4:9).

In the face of the calamities of child development and of the threat of personal death, we become fervidly optimistic with a passion for life, a passion for being a thinking subject. All of these have the beauty of transience and clarity, the result of the work of mourning (Freud, 1916). The experience of watching a tragedy, particularly one of Euripides', the most tragic and, I would add, the most musical of the poets, is full of illusion, musicality, and evanescence, like the experience of listening to music. Grier (2023, pp. 986, 987, 999) writes: "(You) go to a concert, you hear the music and – it's gone!". However, "The fear that the music is quite gone, lost forever oscillates with a sense that is suddenly over, which leaves room for the possibility that something might be remembered". Iphigeneia suddenly leaves Aulis and flies in the air like Io, leaving room for something new. "Yet, we feel, that we really, were onto something, and we will try for it again". We can feel that all is an illusion and become nihilistic. Or we can accept that "much in the world and our attempt to grasp it will always be illusory, yet to know that reality is always covered with a cloak of illusion, may begin to make at least certain qualities of illusion quite precious". Creative artists "undertake the same task over and over again". Prometheus' gift of "flashing fire, source of all arts" helps us undertake such a continuous effort.

We use theatrical scenes, attributing to them our inner contradictory feelings and thoughts. This is the source of our encounter with the world, which is not a reproduction of reality but a co-production of our own and the others' unconscious. McDougal (1985, 1989) studied the theatrical dimension of psychoanalysis. She discovered that access to unelaborated traumatic areas can be obtained through the somatic expression of emotions. Elements of communication convey meaning. The child's play is the first theatre, a comprehensive activity, a trial with which the ego takes a sample of a dream out in the external reality and plays it out with material objects (Freud, 1920; Winnicott, 1971; Mahon, 2004).

When we act out, we utilise perceptions as gateways for time travelling, not in the traditional après coup order, but as visits to traumatic pre-representational areas (Botella & Botella, 2005). Acting out constitutes scenes of 'theatre within theatre' that place life inside theatre and theatre inside life. It is – like a 'dream within a dream' – a stage presentation through which we can visit trauma.

Children, through play, appropriate both their own history and that of their parents. They experience, play, act, talk, and imitate a conversation between the self and the object while learning to manage their body's excitations. Initially, the mother manages the emotional reactions so that the internalisation processes will continue. Her speaking is a framework of the child's emotional experiences and actions. Her imagination is the first stage, where traces and investments are collected to construct an experience and a story.

In tragedy (like in infant development and analysis), we require a full, real, and alive presence and participation in the plot, in the context of which passions are revived. We want a full commitment, as Aristotle (1996) stated in his Poetics. We prefer for passions to be moderate, but we mostly fear impassivity, apathy, and indifference. We want to be able to endure being subjected to passions, conflicts, and trauma. To not be terrorised, to not withdraw behind narcissistic walls, and to fully participate in the awareness of the experience.

References

Anzieu, D. (1979). The sound image of the self. *International Review of Psycho-Analysis*, 6, 23–36.

Aristotle. (1996). *Poetics. Translated with an introduction and notes by Malcom Heath.* New York: Penguin Books.

Aron, L., & Atlas, G. (2019). Dramatic dialogue & drama in contemporary clinical practice. *Psychoanalytic Perspectives*, *16*(3), 249–271.
Austen, J. (2007). *Persuasion*. New York: Vintage Classics. (Original work published 1817)
Baranger, M., & Baranger, W. (2009). The work of confluence. In *Listening and interpreting in the psychoanalytic field*. London: Karnac.
Bion, W. (1977). *Two papers; The grid and caesura*. London: Karnac.
Bion, W. R. (1967). A theory of thinking. In *Second thoughts. Selected papers on psychoanalysis*. New York: Jason Aronson. (Original work published 1962)
Bion, W. R. (1977). Learning from experience. In *Seven servants*. New York: Jason Aronson. (Original work published 1962)
Bleger, J. (1967). Psycho-analysis of the psycho-analytic frame. *International Journal of Psychoanalysis*, *48*, 511–519.
Bleger, J. (2012). Theory and practice in psychoanalysis: Psychoanalytic praxis. *International Journal of Psychoanalysis*, *93*, 993–1003. (Original work published 1969)
Botella, C., & Botella, S. (2005). The work of psychic figurability. In *Mental states without representation* (Michael Parsons, Introduction.). Hove and New York: Brunner-Routledge.
Botella, S. (2002). Une approche psychanalytique de la langue maternelle. In *Penser les limites. Écrits en l'honneur d'André Green. Sous la direction de Cesar Botella*. Paris: Delachaux et Niesle.
Breuer, J., & Freud, S. (1895). Studies on hysteria. *S. E. 1*.
Conrad, J. (1902). *The heart of darkness*. London: Penguin Books.
Denis, A. (1995). Temporality and modes of language. *International Journal of Psychoanalysis*, *76*, 1109–1119.
De Romilly, J. (1970). *La Tragedie Grecque*. Paris: Presses Universitaires de France.
Dupond, J., Balint, T. M., & Jackson, N. Z. (1988). *The clinical diary of Sàndor Ferenczi*. Cambridge, MA: Harvard University Press. (Original work published 1932)
Eliou, E. (1974). Comments Aristotle's rhetoric. In *Greek* (E. Eliou, Trans.). Athens: I. Zacharopoulos Publications.
Enckell, H. (1999). Transference, metaphor and the poetics of psychoanalysis. *Scandinavian Psychoanalytic Review*, *22*, 219–238.
Faculty of Classics, University of Cambridge, & Diggle, J. (2021). *The Cambridge Greek lexicon*. Cambridge: Cambridge University Press. doi:10.1017/9781139050043
Fenichel, O. (1946). On acting. *Psychoanalytic Quarterly*, *15*, 149–152.
Ferenczi, S. (1931). Child analysis in the analysis of adults. *International Journal of Psychoanalysis*, *12*, 468–482.
Ferro, A. (1999). The bi-personal field. In *Experiences in child analysis*. London and New York: Routledge.
Freud, S. (1900). The interpretation of dreams. *S. E., 4–5*.
Freud, S. (1905). Three essays in the theory of sexuality. *S. E., 7*.
Freud, S. (1908). Creative writers and day-dreaming. *S. E., 9*.
Freud, S. (1912–1913) Totem and taboo: Some points of agreement between the mental lives of savages and neurotics. *S. E., 13*.
Freud, S. (1914). Remembering repeating and working through. *S. E., 12*.
Freud, S. (1915). The unconscious. *S. E., 14*.
Freud, S. (1916) On transience. *S. E. 14*.
Freud, S. (1916–1917). Introductory lectures of psychoanalysis. *S. E., 16 & 17*.
Freud, S. (1920). Beyond the pleasure principle. *S. E., 18*.
Freud, S. (1924). The economic problem of masochism. *S. E., 19*.
Freud, S. (1937). Constructions in analysis. *S. E., 23*.
Green, A. (1969). *Un oeil en trop. Le complexe d'Oedipe dans la tragédie*. Paris: Minuit/ Series "Critique".
Green, A. (2005). Key ideas for a contemporary psychoanalysis. In *Misrecognition and recognition of the unconscious*. London and New York: Routledge.

Grier, F. (2023). Illusion, musicality, and evanescence. *International Journal of Psychoanalysis*, *104*(6), 986–1005.

Hughes, A. (2004). Talking makes things happen. A contribution to the understanding of patients' use of speech in the clinical situation. In E. Hargreaves & V. Varcherker (Eds.), *Pursuit of psychic change. The Betty Joseph workshop*. New York: Brunner-Routledge.

Jakobson, R., & Pomorska, K. (1983). *Dialogues*. Cambridge, MA: The MIT Press.

Klein, M. (1975). *On the theory of anxiety and guilt, envy and gratitude and other works, 1946–1963*. London: Vintage. (Original work published 1948)

Laplanche, J., & Pontalis, J. B. (1973). *The language of psychoanalysis*. New York: W.W. Norton.

Loewald, H. W. (1975). Psychoanalysis as an art and the fantasy character of the psychoanalytic situation. *Journal of the American Psychoanalytic Association*, *23*, 277–299.

Mahon, J. E. (2004). Playing and working through: A neglected analogy. *Psychoanalytic Quarterly*, *73*, 379–413.

Manolopoulos, S. (2003) The sense of transience in transferential and transitional phenomena. *Israel Psychoanalytic Journal*, *1*(2), 225–245.

McDougal, J. (1985). *Theatres of the mind*. New York: Basic Books.

McDougal, J. (1989). *Theatres of the body. A psychoanalytic approach to psychosomatic illness*. New York and London: W.W. Norton.

McLeish, K. (2001). Aristotle's Poetics. In L. Theodoridou (Trans.), *Greek*. Athens: Enalios Publications. (Original work published 1998)

Meltzer, D. (1978). *The Kleinian development, part II, Richard week by week*. Perthshire: Clunie Press.

Merleau-Ponty, M. (1964). *Signs* (R. McClearly, Trans.). Evanston, IL: Northwestern University Press. (Original work published 1960)

Miller, P. (2019). Working through the body-ego in the analytic process. *EPF Bulletin*, *73*, 134–141.

Money-Kyrle, R. (2015). *Man's picture of his world and three papers*. London: Harris Meltzer Trust.

Nehamas, A. (1992). Pity and fear in the rhetoric and the poetics. In A. O. Rorty (Ed.), *Essays on Aristotle's Poetics*. Princeton, NJ: Princeton University Press.

Nuetzel, J. E. (1999). Psychoanalysis as a dramatic art. *Annual of Psychoanalysis*, *26*, 295–313.

Ogden, H. T. (1999). The music of what happens in poetry and psychoanalysis. *International Journal of Psychoanalysis*, *80*, 974–994.

Ogden, H. T. (2004). The analytic third. *Psychoanalytic Quarterly*, *73*(1), 167–195.

Parsons, M. (2000). *The dove that returns, the dove that vanishes*. London and New York: Routledge.

Parsons, M. (2007). Raiding the inarticulate: The internal analytic setting and listening beyond countertransference. *International Journal of Psychoanalysis*, *88*(6), 1441–1456.

Pedder, R. J. (1977). The role of space and location in psychotherapy, play and theatre. *International Review of Psycho-Analysis*, *4*, 215–223.

Pontalis, J. B. (1974). Freud in Paris. *International Journal of Psychoanalysis*, *55*, 455–458.

Rolland, J.-C. (2005). The magic of the image. *Greek. Ek Ton Isteron*, *13*, 7–23.

Rustin, M., & Rustin, M. (2002). *Mirror to nature: Drama, psychoanalysis and society*. London: Karnac Books.

Sykoutris, I. (1991). Comments on Aristotle's Poetics. In *Greek*. Athens: Estia. (Original work published 1937)

Taiana, C. (2022). What does poetry offer psychoanalysis? *Canadian Journal of Psychoanalysis*, *30*(1), 61–76.

Taplin, O. (1988). The ancient Greek tragedy in scenic presentation. In V. Assimomytis (Trans.), *Greek*. Athens: Papadima Publications.

Vygotsky, L. (1934). *Thought and language* (A. Kozulin, Ed.). Cambridge, MA: MIT Press.
Winnicott, D. W. (1965). *The maturational processes and the facilitating environment*. London: Karnac. (Original work published 1990)
Winnicott, D. W. (1971). *Playing and reality*. London: Tavistock.
Winnicott, D. W. (1988). *Human nature*. London: Free Association Press.
Zajko, V., & O' Gorman, E. (2013). *Classical myth and psychoanalysis*. Oxford: Oxford University Press.
Zimmermann, B. (1991). Greek tragedy. In T. Marier (Trans.), *An introduction*. Valtimore and London: The John Hopkins University Press. (Original work published 1986)

Chapter 2

Euripides' Hippolytus
Drives unleashed[1,2]

In 428 BC, Euripides taught *Hippolytus Crowned*. The title is taken from the scene where the statue of Artemis is crowned by the pious youth. A year before, the poet had taught *Hippolytus Veiled,* in which Phaedra herself confessed her love to the hero, who, upon hearing this, covered his face with his hands in shame. The Athenians rejected the first version since they were not prepared to tolerate on stage the sexual excitation of "fire worse than fire" (Barrett, 1964, pp. 11–15).

In this masterpiece, the 'rag-stitcher' poet suddenly breaks the flow of the action with everyday familiar scenes. He, thus, provokes the surprise of the sense of uncanny. We can think that the 'familiar' things introduce parental sexuality and cause a breach in the fantasy of the narcissistic union.

This tragedy presents existential agonies, extreme passions, elusive appearances, self-destructive actions, denial of adult sexuality, and belief in childhood innocence. It is a play of the impossible links that lead to an impasse. It is about speech, silence, knowledge, and ignorance (Hurmuziadis, 1991; Kovacs, 1995; Halleran, 1995). It involves the arrogance that maintains the fantasy of omniscience, the stupidity, and the attacks on the links of meaning (Bion, 1958/1967, 1962/1967, 1962/1977; Segal, 1986).

The fantasy of participating in the primal scene and identifying painfully with either of the two parents enriches the growing child's psychic bisexuality and love of knowing. It is also linked to the adolescents' breakdown (Laufer & Laufer, 1984). The maturing aggressive/sexual body demands to be integrated and mobilises the "familiar things".

Hippolytus Crowned presents the adolescent's struggle to reach his innate capacity for self-teaching, his primary creativity (79–80). A consideration of the transformation of the myth into tragedy and a comparison of the two versions of this tragedy invites us to examine learning from experience as a creative attempt to face the unconsciousness' negativity (castration and separation anxiety, and fear of death) through the symbolisation processes. Euripides presents Hippolytus as a remote and untouched youth. In his painful death, he acquires a human body where his emotions, fantasies, and drives find a home.

This play illustrates the psyche-making turn of the drives upon the self and into the opposite. Freud's (1915) study of the vicissitudes of the drives helps us reflect on how the ego becomes the subject of its experiences and fantasies. Similarly, in Euripides' plays, we can think of the peripeteias – unanticipated twists of action and unexpected reversals – as processes of subjectivisation.

There are tremendous changes in action in typical scenes of passionate discourse, self-sacrifice, and recognition (De Romilly, 1995). With the sudden overturns of the plot, the poet tells us that we do not really know. The moment we think we know, a change occurs. The poet of the unexpected presents on stage the failure of an environment mother who did not protect the growing child from coincidences. This child, later in life, reuses the material of these early failures and stages new unexpected overturns.

In translating Hippolytus' myth, the poet makes a tragic plot – an interpretation – that creates a realisation of an emotional experience, which we (the audience) share with the persons of the drama. Tragedy, like psychoanalysis, is an experience which enables us to unlearn what we know and learn something new about ourselves and human life.

This experience is formed by movements between regressions and integrations, libidinal and traumatic lines of development, repressions, and splittings, and the narcissism of life and death. These movements meet in successive transcriptions at junctures that are contemporary and universally valid. The tragic plot is analogous to an analytic construction that invents a convincing story. We, the spectators, live the experience, wait, and only afterwards do we reflect and think about the meaning of it.

In nodal moments, certain persons of the drama – the bearers of an emotional experience – meet. Being subject to the consequences of an appropriation from forces (sexual and destructive drives) that are beyond them, they become subjectivised. On the stage of the tragedy, the myths are transformed into an unfolding life process that occurs in real-time. The mythic heroes become bearers of individual and shared unconscious fantasies that through interpretation become lived experiences. They become 'humans', subjects to sexuality, historicity, and mortality, to consistent and true ideas that transfer the ferocity of the unconscious instead of empty words.

Euripides is in contact with primitive areas of the psyche where splitting processes and attacks on linking prevail. The most primitive attack is the one against the primal scene. His plots are characterised by distraction, where it is difficult to pay attention and concentrate. His plots lack cohesion; they are fragmented. Then, as a 'ragsticher', he tries to link the unconnected fragments of experience.

Euripides struggles to transform the traumatic perception of raw perceptual traces (somatic roots of emotions, memories in feelings, beta-elements) into the tragic recognition of meaning (Freud, 1896; Klein, 1955; Bion, 1962/1977). However, he shows that the stage as a containing frame cannot be taken for granted. The symbolisation processes fail, and the meaning that envelops the plot cannot be taken for granted. Euripides' plots are led to an impasse. Thus, he introduces the innovation of a 'deus ex machina'. Blume (1978/1993) thinks that the deus ex machina offers solutions to the impasses in the plot. Visual effects of such an *epiphany* – like acting out and dreams within dreams – constitute an attempt of the ego to restage the trauma, to draw from the illusions of primitive magical thinking and to create a revelation, a scene, a context greater than the analysis of the unconscious fantasy (Anzieu, 1989). They create a simulation of the entirety that envelops the fragmented (split-off) traumatic elements. The magical deus ex machina brings an end to the plot, but the impasse (the splitting) is not solved. However, some new links of meaning are created in our, the spectators', mind. Some experiences of trauma are created anew, in real-time, with the aim of obtaining a name, a cause, and a meaning.

The poet introduces uncanny episodes which contain preverbal, unrepresented experiences that need to be acted out, given meaning, and put into a story. The unfamiliar 'familiar things' become elusively present in public and also absent through the mechanism of negation so that they become acceptable to our conscious (Freud, 1925). Euripides also introduces highly sophisticated philosophical arguments on stage, in self-contained episodes, that constrain the play in order to be integrated into the plot. He struggles to link the secondary thought processes to their primary sources. He approaches dangerously close to the limits of human life, and he challenges "the thing in itself" to reveal itself. He takes the extreme negative position against (radically disproving) his own argument in order to gather bits of authentic findings of reality. He creates a torrent of terror in order to keep in the forefront the fears that the object and the self may not survive (Ferenczi, 1933/1955).

The plot

Theseus is the King of Athens. Hippolytus is Theseus' illegitimate son with the Amazon Hippolyta. Phaedra, the princess from Crete, is the King's lawful wife. The drama takes place in Troezen, before the palace of Pittheus, Hippolytus' grandfather, who raises him as his successor. The Amazon Hippolyta, Hippolytus' mother, and Aethra, his grandmother, are absent from his drama. Theseus, together with Phaedra, has taken refuge in Troezen. He was exiled from Athens in order to expiate himself from the murder of his cousins and would-be usurpers of power. He brings to his native town an oedipal model (differences of sexes and generations). He demands of Hippolytus that he be born in a story that is not yet his.

In her prologue, Aphrodite discloses the story: "Hippolytus, . . . says that I am the worst of deities. He shuns the bed of love" (12–14). For his Hubris, he will be punished this day, and the virtuous Phaedra will be destroyed. When Phaedra first saw Hippolytus in Athens, she fell in love with him, and her heart was seized with a dreadful longing. Now that she is physically close to him, she is overcome with passion. She is tortured.

When the arrogant Hippolytus enters the scene with his peers, huntsmen honouring Artemis in hymns, Aphrodite ironically finishes her prologue by saying: "Clearly he does not know that the gates of the Underworld stand open for him" (55–57). Hippolytus approaches Artemis' altar and lays down a garland made of wildflowers from a virgin meadow in springtime, and "reverence tends it with streams of river water, for those to pluck who owe nothing to teaching" (78). He feels he is one with his patroness (85–86). He ignores the others.

The Chorus of the women of Troezen contrasts Hippolytus' innocence with the passions of female sexuality. They speak of the Queen's unspeakable sorrow.

> She lies afflicted, they say, on a bed of sickness and keeps indoors, with fine-spun clothes shading her blonde head . . . wishing because of some secret grief to ground her life's craft in the unhappy journey's end of death.
>
> (133–140)

Grief is then associated with the desire to learn (141–175).

Then, Phaedra's tragedy begins. In contrast to Hippolytus, who has declared total war against the drives, Phaedra surrenders herself to them. She is overcome by her passion. Her Nurse bears the weight of her sickness. She speaks of an area beyond ordinary ambivalence. Mortals consume "whatever this is that shines on earth, because of inexperience of another life and non-revelation of the things beneath the earth" (194–197).

Phaedra wishes to find freedom in nature, representing the pre-ambivalent unspoiled mother. She feels ashamed and asks to be covered with the veil (243–245). She prefers "to die without awareness" (250). The Nurse reminds her of her children. Should she die, their riches will be taken by the Amazon-born "master" of her house – false but passing for true (305–308). Hippolytus is an illegitimate, not a true, son of Theseus.

"It will be your downfall if you learn", she warns the Nurse, and comes into contact with her own primitive inheritance, her mother Pasiphae and her sister Ariadne (337–343). She finally reveals her passion. The primitive emotional experiences can only be lived and suffered. They should not be put prematurely in the abstract words. It is a catastrophe not to be able to transmit your preverbal experiences through projective identification to a containing object (Bion, 1958/1967). An early trauma happens when the mother refuses to enter the state of primary maternal preoccupation and fails to respond with adequate actions to the infant's ego needs, as Winnicott says. Thus, the child prematurely develops ego functions and intellectual capacities. Thus, the child may lose contact with the psychosomatic sources of primary creativity, the wildflowers from a virgin meadow in springtime, and become an omniscient "wise baby", who owes nothing to teaching (78). With his religious inspiration and devotion to Orpheus, his ideal ego, Hippolytus poignantly exploits his primary narcissism; thus he defends himself against his fear of loss of reality, in Winnicott's terms. He longs to access his primary processes in the springs of the psyche that are governed by musicality.

Cypris, the seductress, is "the one who sows and gives desire, from which all of us who live upon the earth are born" (447–450). The Nurse promises Phaedra a magic cure with herbs and charms (479). Will the herbs purify her from her passion, or will they make him love her? Phaedra is at an impasse. She is trapped in her own splitting. She knows, and she does not know. However, she asks the Nurse not to speak to Theseus' son. The Nurse will do exactly the opposite. She realises the double pain, the love, and the despair: "mortals should not mix the cup of their affection to one another too strong and it should not sink to their very marrow" (254–255).

Here, despair is caused by the inability of the subject to link the object of the drives (object mother) with the object of the ego needs (environment mother) to create a depressive position (Winnicott, 1963/1900). The fear is that the maternal object, the holding environment, "the house", will not survive.

Phaedra states: "there are two kinds of shame: one is good (it prevents everyday offences) and the other one is a burden for the household!" (386–387). The pride that is associated with the drive of Life results in self-respect. The pride that is associated with the drive of Thanatos results in arrogance (Bion, 1958/1967).

The Chorus pleads with love not to strike in an excessive, beyond meaning manner, like thunder, and recounts the story of Iole, roused by Aphrodite and thrown into the arms of Heracles all fire and passion "in a bloody wedding!". However, the silence has been broken. Suddenly, we hear a shouting from within the palace. Hippolytus, in horror, rejects the Nurse's proposition. He threatens to speak out since it was his tongue that swore to keep silent and not his heart (612). He condemns women as the source of all evil and wishes the seed for children could be ready-bought by them from Zeus' temples in exchange for gold, iron, or copper. Phaedra is eavesdropping. "Wherever will I escape this torture?" (673). She is trapped in her splitting. She does not listen to the Chorus' advice to accept what has happened. She rises from the couch. Now, she will turn her passivity into activity. She will act alone. She never meets Hippolytus on stage. She now imagines him suffering as a consequence of his actions (730–731). He will suffer, like she does.

Phaedra's tragedy ends with the inevitable association of the ship in which Theseus returned from Crete after slaying the Minotaur. Now, his own son, Hippolytus, the object of her love, will be destroyed. When Phaedra and the Nurse enter the palace, the Chorus consoles us with peaceful sounds and recalls the "white-winged Cretan ship" which brought Phaedra, a foreigner arriving in glorious Athens followed by bad omens in a ship destined for double loss (752–759). The Nurse appears and announces Phaedra's hanging.

Then, Theseus returns home from visiting an oracle, wearing plaited leaves on his head. He has to face the bitter sight. He grieves to find Phaedra dead. He cries in despair when he finds Phaedra wearing in her hand a tablet on which she had written her accusation that Hippolytus had raped her. "Ah, why am I wreathed with these plaited leaves on my head, since my visit to the oracle brought me misfortune?" When he discovers the writing tablet, he cries out: "an unbearable and unthinkable horror" (874–875). The tablet screams of abominations. He asks his divine father, Poseidon, who had granted him three fatal curses, to destroy his son before the day is over.

Hippolytus appears before Theseus. The King, in hatred against his son, invokes the enemies he has murdered. Hippolytus holds true to his oath of silence. He seeks a witness and makes a desperate attempt to tell the truth without telling it. He says that such an act would be unthinkable to him. The Chorus is also silent. His father condemns him to exile and a slow death (1053–1054).

In the face of an unthinkable scene, when he feels absolutely alone, Hippolytus takes the fundamental step to self-observation. "I wish that I could stand opposite and look at myself, so that I could cry over how badly I suffer" (1077–1079). So that he sees himself as he is.

Then, the Chorus of the hunters and the women of Troezen beseeches Hippolytus to bid farewell to the fantasy of his childhood innocence. The messenger arrives at the palace and recounts how Hippolytus, on his way to exile, speeds on the road next to the Saronic Gulf, but the familiar route suddenly becomes terrifying. Poseidon stirs up an earthquake. Out of a divine wave reaching the sky and covering the earth rises a "bull, a savage monster" (1214). The horses bolt and pay no heed to their master, to the reins, and overturn the chariot (1224–1226). Hippolytus loses control, gets caught up in the loops of the reins, and is fatally beaten against the ground. Then, the earth opens and swallows the horses and the bull.

We can think that Hipoolytus' unbending character traits are overthrown and cannot function as bolts that secure his splittings. His ego is overwhelmed by the waves of traumatic affects. Another perspective, however, now opens. The plot is reversed. The Chorus pays homage to Aphrodite, who rules "the unbending mind" of both gods and mortals (126). Artemis then appears as a deus ex machina and reveals the truth to Theseus. He did not give his son the time he needed but cursed him as he would an enemy. What saves him as a father is that he did not know (1317–1324).

Theseus, filled with pain, receives his son's dismembered "body of wounds" that is supported by his companions. Artemis does not sully her glance with tears at the sight of blood and the sound of a mortal's death rattle (1396, 1437): human sexuality. She distances herself. She then raises Hippolytus to a cult hero (1425–1426). Hippolytus observes the ease with which Artemis takes leave of their long friendship. He is finally enlightened (1415). He wishes mortals could curse the gods. In an incredibly moving death scene, father and son make up as if asking for peace. The dying Hippolytus pleads with his father to lay the veils quickly upon his face (1458).

The primordial one and the primal scene. Mythic and historic reality

In the first version of the tragedy, a perverse anal parody of genitality triumphs (Chasseguet-Smirgel, 1984). In the second version, adult sexuality and the differences between the sexes and generations are also denied, but what is prominent is the early loss of the maternal object, the narcissistic trauma, and the representational wounds that need to be libidinised and restored.

The arrogant youth declares total war against the drives. He scorns traditional order and seeks familiarity with the divine. His purity glorifies Artemis. He denounces a goddess who is worshipped at night (106). He is ignorant of the mania of the maternal womb. He wishes for a male parthenogenesis without the need for women (616–629). He believes that humans come from the primordial one (narcissism). Still, the gates to the other (sexual/death) life are open, as an inescapable downfall.

Phaedra's primordial pain is silent. She wants to know what lies 'beyond' the primal scene, what lies beyond ordinary ambivalence. Her 'true-false' dilemma is related to the passion generated before the object that is out of her control. The object is the source of life. However, when its reality is not born psychically, it reproduces the greedy, endless, and ungrateful claim of the cruel pre-oedipal maternal superego.

The adolescent boy is born autonomous when he is 'exiled' from his mother's body, which he ruthlessly attacks. Will the exile become an alien land – his parents' sexuality – which he inescapably undertakes? Will he internalise his omnipotence, bisexuality, and drives? The ascetic adolescent neutralises his impulses and undermines his superego – which links him with the tradition of the previous generations and the community – in order to retain his fragile narcissism intact. When Phaedra's letter is read, Hippolytus' tragedy begins. Phaedra was moved by something beyond his control. However, the roles of father and son are reversed. From within the abyss of non-understanding rises the desire of one for another. Hippolytus returns on stage; his body is wounded. Artemis does not sully her glance with the human sexuality of the mortal body (1396, 1437). The impossible link (arrogant attack on emotion) is transformed into a boundary of prohibition through the sexualisation of trauma. With her interdiction, Artemis designates an area where the law of the father will be put into effect. Beyond meaning, there is no longer silence, the unspoken disinvestment, but rather the unrepresented experiences that are played on stage.

The adolescent boy's mother allows him to turn to his father to be homosexually loved, to be passively penetrated by his father's penis. This enables the adolescent boy to identify with his masculinity. The hero's tomb of worship suggests the anal localisation, the sexualisation of the traumatic breach, which establishes a boundary between external and internal reality; it introduces historic time and the passing on of cultural customs.

When the primary masochism is insufficient, then an external punishment is needed to supplement the missing internal fusion of the drives (Freud, 1924; Aisenstein, 2019). What kind of a helmsman was Hippolytus? His name indicates rebellious adolescent freedom but also the loss of mastery, his powerlessness in the face of the object's influence. It reminds us of the insufficient fusion of the drives that leads to a weak core of primary masochism. According to Kitto (1971), a temperament without counterbalances is insecure (pp. 1420–1422).

Hippolytus denies reality. He is a triumphant hunter who avoids the oedipal relationship. How will he begin living in the world of objects? How will he understand "these things" that overturn his balance? In the face of the sexual object, Hippolytus faces, by definition, the impossible because he must already be inside it to make a manic restoration. In his strange talk with Artemis, Hippolytus uses the verb "$συνειμι$?" ("I am one with you") to indicate his fantasy of a narcissitic union.

In order to preserve this union, he has to deny some of his human sides (Vernant, 1985). The characters of this tragedy remain true to their titanic nature. How will the otherness of an object be introduced? A transition from myth to history is needed.

Aphrodite, in the begining, simply and with no hesitation, sets the seal of divine 'injustice'. She establishes the framework of the play, which is expressed as a definite statement. In this context, the archaic begins to unravel in a cyclical time of repetition. We immediately sense the absence of the Amazon Hippolyta, Hippolytus' mother. We are transported to the silence of the 'dead mother' who disinvests the child. Was the Amazon killed at Theseus' side while fighting others of her race who had returned from the barbarian north? Had Theseus himself murdered her? The dead mother returns to life in the child's fantasy that the father has killed her in a violent, sadomasochistic primal scene (Green, 1983/1986).

Hippolytus' myth is Peloponnesian in origin. It is archaic, dating back to the Bronze Age, and spread to Athens in the 6th century BC. Troezen is suited for this plot. It is close to the primeval and lies far from Athens. It is the native city of Theseus' mother, Aethra, who, apart from sleeping with Aegeus, had also made love with Poseidon. The god of the sea granted Theseus three wishes. He used the last one to kill Hippolytus and bring to awareness the primal scene, the passage of time, the issue of succession, and the passing of cultural inheritance through the parental superego. Through the parental unconscious fantasy, a transmission of sexuality occurs in the child (Laplanche, 1992a, 1992b).

The archaic bull changes from an immutable image that evacuates frustration to a symbolic representation which traverses the boundaries of space and time and creates a meaning-making experience. This is the curse, the psychic life, the history, the politics, the world of objects. There is no way to escape human life; it can only be repeated in an effort to either integrate it and be responsible for it or evacuate it. The bull, a condensation, a mute possibility expressed in the indicative, strikes a blow to infantile omnipotence. This is the mutative moment of psychic registering of sexuality in Hippolytus' tragedy.

Theseus becomes human because, without distancing the present from the past, internal from external reality, he becomes transgressed, overcome with passion, curses his son, and thus makes him a participant in human sexuality. Not knowing the truth, he considers his son to be his enemy and so becomes his son's enemy, uncertain and vulnerable. The condensation of the bull that he killed in the labyrinth is now present and is restaged in the context of a present relationship. Here and now, the persons of the drama and the spectators are acted upon (tolerate and suffer) their emotions, stage and share an emotional experience, and learn from it. In this context, 'Hippolytus' is related to Sophocles' 'Trachiniae'. It is about the spread of the "disease" of sexuality, as noted by Easterling (1982) in relation to Euripides' reference to Iole (p. 546).

Theseus killed his father, realising his oedipal fate, by neglecting to change the black sails. Hippolytus and Phaedra do not realise their oedipal desires. Of course, conquering the body of knowledge demands a real transference, not an illegitimate son and an adoptive mother. It demands the ferocity of the drives. However, the play brings the elements of primitive emotional experiences together, and this has a tragic effect.

The psychic, the public, the written, and the theatrical space

The oedipal catastrophe, the arrogance, the ignorance, the stupidity, and the compulsive need to know happen on stage in this play. All these elements are manifestations of a very early maternal failure. This is the failure of the infant's fears of death to be communicated, taken in, and responded to adequately by a living, maternal reverie (Bion, 1958/1967, 1962/1967, 1962/1977). The maternal reverie results in the infant linking together the elements of primitive emotional experience. The double turn of the drive upon the self and onto the opposite gathers together the dispersed 'things' into a subjective experience.

The theme of arranging (integrating) dispersed elements through recognition is inherent to the myth. We can juxtapose here Hippolytus' name that signifies the lack of power, with Plutarch mentioning that Theseus' name means "having been placed" but also "acknowledged": When Aethra gave birth to a son, he was at once named Theseus, as some say, because the tokens for his recognition had been 'placed' in hiding; yet others say that it was afterwards (après coup) at Athens when Aegeus 'acknowledged' him as his son (Perrin, 1914).

As a line of defence against the unthinkable (trauma of the primal scene), Hippolytus' tragedy suggests the splitting: silence, covering of the face, veils of denial, prohibition of contact, the concealment of the secret, the closed doors of the palace, the walls of the prison, the walls of the labyrinth. Denial is finally transformed into negation in connection with the acceptance of parental sexuality (Freud, 1925; Vergopoulos, 1986). The acquisition of knowledge is illustrated in the references to the eyes, which throw light on the dark area beyond. Empedocles defined the eye as a lantern: Aphrodite gave birth to the round eye, fire confined in delicate cloths through which it is let out (Padel, 1992).

In his myth, Theseus descended into Hades. Hades makes us think of the void, the terrifying Gorgo, and extreme otherness, which charms and averts our glance (Vernant & Vidal-Naquet, 1972). In another version of the myth, Theseus does not descend into Hades but is confined in prison, the prison of self-knowledge, paying his life debt of making links of meaning between the inner and outer world. It is interesting that, in the Biblical myth, Joseph learnt to interpret dreams in prison. In his work on 'The uncanny', Freud (1919) uses the example of Joseph from the Bible. "Pharaoh called Joseph, he to whom secrets are revealed (heimlich councillor)" (Freud, 1919, p. 235).

In contrast, in this tragedy, Theseus did not take the time to think. Similarly, Hippolytus was speeding with his chariot along the sea with destructive results. They both feared passivity. They could not be patient and take a passive, receptive, feminine position.

Related to the recognition of otherness is the fact noted by the commentators that in the third scene, unexpectedly, male participles are used (1105, 1107, 1121) next to female ones (1111, 1118), although the action of a double Chorus cannot be assumed.

The propositions of distance, difference, and absence are inherent from the beginning of the plot. We can observe a mutation with the introduction of a distance – put by the function of the eye that observes – between the thing and its symbol.

At the beginning of the play, Theseus is at Delphi as an official observer. He is a theoros. This word has the same etymological root as theatre. Pausanias mentions that in the Acropolis of Athens, Phaedra founded the temple of Aphrodite in honour of Hippolytus. From there, she gazed towards Troezen, on the other side of the Saronic Gulf, for a sight of Hippolytus. In Troezen, there was the temple of 'watching' (*Spying, Katascopias, Κατασκοπίας*) Aphrodite from which Phaedra could look into the stadium next door and watch an unsuspecting Hippolytus train (Barrett, 1964).

An environment mother who cannot 'watch over', differentiate, and contain her infant's and her own passions may become an object mother prematurely. The universal power of Aphrodite, to whom Artemis is complementary, carries the omnipotent desires with which we must come to an understanding. This tragic realisation reminds us of Euripides' Bacchae, where the violence of the drives is linked to the processes of identification (Potamianou, 1984). In the end, it is painfully accepted that people learn to recognise (integrate) the power of drives (the extreme otherness) and their inescapable consequences. This is the most tragic realisation of otherness.

The capacity to become a tragic subject is connected to human fate (moira), our demon, our 'infantile' self. Parents fear their children's primitive emotional experiences and fantasies. Freud (1912–1913) thought that human fate is to suffer and accept the psychic responsibility of the archaic totemic crime. Winnicott (1960) thought that we need to transform our traumas (personal and those of previous generations) into present experiences that we struggle to endure, share with others, and assume their responsibility. Thus, our creativity is connected to overcoming the fear of passivity.

What connects the two symmetrical parts of Hippolytus' tragedy is the writing tablet left behind by Phaedra. Here, writing is considered a message (container/contained function) that represents the female body and the traumatic public disclosure of the sexual parental couple. The fantasised parental intercourse does not allow the child to enter the womb again and be one with the mother. Instead of seeking refuge in a narcissistic union, Hippolytus turns to himself to reflect.

Lesky (1987) points out the moment when Hippolytus is sentenced by his father and makes the curious statement that he would like to stand opposite himself in order to cry for his unhappiness (1077–1079). He would like to look at how he is made to look (feel) like. At precisely this moment of ultimate surrender, he turns to himself, willing to undergo self-observation and self-knowledge.

This tragedy is classic because it offers itself for a new reading. It resists saturation, first, because it represents the unruliness of the mnemonic traces and, second because it acts for the reader as the day residues. It culminates in the moment when Phaedra's letter is read.

Freud (1917, p. 418) discovered how the manifest dream content is formed through the regression of word-to-thing-representation involving considerations of representability. He added, however: "Only where the word-presentations occurring in the day's residues are recent and current residues of perceptions, and not the expression of thoughts, are they themselves treated like thing-presentations and subjected to the influence of condensation and displacement". We can think that this is how Hippolytus used the words that Phaedra wrote in her letter: as thing-representations, introducing the primal scene and breaching the fantasy of narcissistic union.

The 'written' and the 'theatrical' space represent a common (between the persons of the drama and its readers/spectators) space of shared fantasy, in which the traumatic elements are transformed and recognised as messages of communication. In ancient Greek, anagnosis means bith, reading, and recognition, which is the most mutative moment in tragedy.

The symmetry and complementarity of the plot maintain the asymmetry and non-complementarity of the relationship between the drive and the object. In the beginning, Aphrodite's epiphany is followed by the hymn to Artemis. At the end, the hymn to Aphrodite is followed by Artemis' epiphany. The implantation of sexuality is followed by the narcissistic turn to oneself, much like an 'object mother' is sustained by an 'environment mother' in Winnocott's words.

According to C. Segal (1991/1996), Phaedra's murderous plan is not just words, as oral communication is. It is a memory, a present, and a future. The primal scene and death give birth to the subject (Arvanitakis, 2019). The elements that comprise writing, just like Hippolytus' chariot mechanisms, run the risk of becoming 'a thing-in-itself', elements of technology that are striped of meaning and, thus, are no longer nodes of integration and communication. I will return to the theme of technology in the final chapter of the book.

Repetition and sexuality

We feel a tragic responsibility in the face of adolescent development. We must not waste it out of cowardice. We hope the adolescent himself will become responsible for the traumas and conflicts of his development. Adolescents need to confront the violence of their drives. They need their mother's hate, Winnicott says. They do not need a sentimental mother. Their mother's refusal to receive their projective identifications creates the monster of a Minotaur and the beta-screen of the walls of the labyrinth (Bion, 1962/1977). Thus, these adolescents may break with reality, lose the thread of their thinking and lose their way back to their hearth, to their self. The flow of the life of ascetic (narcissistic, borderline) adolescents is interrupted by the 'familiar things' of the primal scene that introduces parental sexuality.

Constantly seeking the mythical origin of things, mortals traumatically realise that the world traces its beginning to the differences of the sexes and the generations and the passage of time (mortality), all the while believing in – but simultaneously also doubting – the gods that give them ideas (enigmatic messages that they need to translate). Before the end of the tragedy, the persons of the tragedy begin to communicate through ironic, symbolic messages that transform reality.

Euripides' *Hippolytus Crowned* is about the tragic awakening of the sense of self inside jaws and teeth that tear apart and wheels that are being set into motion when the familiar things of repetition are overturned by the unfamiliar ones of sexuality and destructiveness through object intervention (Freud, 1919). The fantasies that the uncanny activates interpret the experiences that are created and staged in the present. Thus, they create a new chronicle of transference (a tragic plot), overturning repetition cycles and introducing the narrative tense of a painful process of changes.

Normally, the ego attempts to confront the wild awakening, the traumatic experience of recognising the negativity of the unconscious, with symbolisations. In order for this to succeed, another subject must listen attentively and subjectively undertake the multiple meanings of the message in its own associations. Otherwise, the unconscious part of the communication will remain a dead letter.

Words connect to the unconscious thing, not as relationships between signifiers and signified but sensorily. Words sense and perceive the unconscious things and represent them (Rolland, 1998). Words make these connections because a part of them is inside the meaning of representations, and a part of them stems from somatic sensory-motor and perceptual roots. When splittings sever the ties of words to their somatic roots, they render them deaf, dumb, and incapable of perceiving the unconscious things.

Freud (1939) studied preverbal trauma, where recognition of the infant's experiences from the primary object did not occur. This resulted in the development of early defences against links with objects. The ego is to henceforth avoid, in any manner and at any cost (perpetually splitting), and for every relationship, the impressions of that experience that pose the threat of re-traumatisation. These character defences repeat the threat and perpetuate themselves.

Hippolytus' name refers us to untied reins, to the defences of non-integration. It is an organisation that is based on splittings. The links of fusion between the libidinal and destructive impulses are loose. The object investments are weak. Thus, the individual lives in an impasse with impossible links. When the reins are loose, they are at risk of being untied. This means that the horses may be freed, and the rider will lose his control over his chariot. We can think that if the drives are not adequately bound and contained in infancy, they may later become unleashed and bring devastation to the psyche and society. Hippolytus is an ascetic adolescent who has declared a total war against his drives. Phaedra, his other self, has completely surrendered herself to the drives. Suddenly, the violent monster of passions rises from the depth of the unconscious, overthrows the chariot, the reins are broken, and the horses run wild.

The drives are now unleashed and devastate the adolescent, his family, and his city. When Phaedra reveals her passion to Hippolytus through the Nurse, he is overwhelmed. This is not possible! Theseus also becomes overwhelming to his son. He does not take time to think and know (to transform) reality. We can think that what is not possible in the end becomes what is forbidden through the enactment of the primal scene fantasy, which contains the death of the narcissistic adolescent and the birth of a new subject. The omnipotence is sacrificed for the sake of recognition of otherness and the reality of the object.

Tom was a college student who studied to become a Navy officer, like his father, in an effort to obtain an identity and become able to control his drive, which he feared would become wild and drive him crazy. Tom lived with his alcoholic mother. His father had remarried another woman and lived with her and Tom's younger brother. Tom had to stay at home, awake all night, in absolute terror, beside his mother, who was out of control, saying all kinds of horrible things against his father. Tom was terrified that his own drives would be unleashed and really damage his objects. He had to freeze this traumatic situation in order to control it. He could not speak and tell anyone what was happening. He had to remain silent, like Hippolytus. He was afraid that he would reveal secrets that would cause the dissolution of his family and the destruction of any order, even if that order was a tyranny of collusion between his two parents. Tom feared that he would be punished by his father if his mother complained that Tom did not take care of her. He finally developed a somatic symptom. He kept silent, but he tried to speak through his soma. Suddenly, in public, his body would violently contract and take a stance as if he were ready to fight an enemy who attacked him. When he was in public, he imagined that he met his father, and engaged in a mortal confrontation with him. The working through of this insight and his mourning work for the loss of his childhood parents allowed him to remember something he had forgotten. He recalled that when he was four years old, and his mother was in the hospital to give birth to his younger brother, Tom was found by his father in the morning in the parental bedroom, in front of his mother's mirror, crying, alone. His father asked him why he, a big boy, was crying. He replied: 'What is it to you? I only want to see myself as I am'. The way he looked at himself was the way he felt, the way he was.

Hippolytus' tragedy helps us think of the transformation and integration of drives, omnipotence, and psychic bisexuality as outcomes of mourning work (Priel, 1999). Phaedra's letter – which introduces the 'lie' of her love – is delivered to Theseus, who in turn gives the order for Hippolytus' death – the couple functions, albeit destructively.

Hippolytus shuns love and Aphrodite. He remains in the outskirts, hunting in the woods with his companions, worshiping Artemis. He lives on the border of polis, on the outskirts of the oedipal situation. He is forced to fall into the cogwheels of sexuality. He is thrown there by the deadly encounter with the deceit of Phaedra's love. In the letter that she wrote, she falsely accused him of raping her. She accused him of lies, the same way that he 'accused' (not believing) her of not being truthful when she said that her love was genuine and tormenting. She gave the order for the passion of love to be transferred to him. His father hastily gave him a deadly curse. Through Poseidon, he caused the awakening and violence of the sexuality of the bull that runs through the generations, going back to Pasiphae.

Hippolytus' tragedy begins when Phaedra's letter is read. The future opens. What will happen to him? Will the mother's letter/provocation of incest and the father's curse/threat of castration (transmitting the bull of the previous generations) become enigmatic messages that transmit sexuality? Will they be de-metaphorised and become concrete elements of a death commandment against the life process? The primal scene's sexuality commandment is that the adolescents be differentiated. The object of the drive's mother is supported by the environment mother who holds the adolescent's processes of symbolisation and her/his primitive anxieties. The mother who contains the child's and her own primitive passions is the one who can differentiate self and object. Then, the parental sexual relationship can pronounce a commandment of a 'death sentence'. This is the 'death' of the narcissistic union between the child and mother.

Notes

1 The direct line quotes are taken from Kovacs, D. (1995). Euripides: Children of Heracles, Hippolytus, Andromache, Hecuba. In *Loeb classical library*. Cambridge, MA: Harvard University Press.
2 This chapter is based on a paper that was read at the Fourth Delphi International Psychoanalytic Symposium on "Oedipus Complex and Adult Sexuality", 23–28 July, 1996. Another version of that presentation, was published as S. Manolopoulos (1999). Euripides' hippolytus: 'The familiar things'. *Psychoanalytic Studies*, *1*(2):177–189.

References

Aisenstein, M. (2019). *Désir-Douleur-Pensée: Masochism Originaire et Theorie Pychanalytique*. Paris: Ithaque.
Anzieu, D. (1989). *The skin ego* (C. Turner, Trans.). New Haven, CT: Yale University Press.
Arvanitakis, K. (2019). A psychoanalytic perspective of tragedy, theatre and death. In *Tadeusz kantor and the ontology of the self*. London and New York: Routledge.
Barrett, W. S. (1964). *Euripides' hippolytus*. Oxford: Clarendon Press.
Bion, W. R. (1967). On arrogance. In *Second thoughts. Selected papers on psychoanalysis*. New York: Jason Aronson. (Original work published 1958)
Bion, W. R. (1967). A theory of thinking. In *Second thoughts. Selected papers on psychoanalysis*. New York: Jason Aronson. (Original work published 1962)
Bion, W. R. (1977). Learning from experience. In *Seven servants*. New York: Jason Aronson. (Original work published 1962)
Blume, H. D. (1993). Einführung in das antike Theaterwesen. Darmstadt: Wissenschaftliche Buchgesellschaft. In M. Iatrou (Trans.), *Greek*. Athens: MIET. (Original work published 1978)
Chasseguet-Smirgel, J. (1984). *Creativity and perversion*. New York: Norton.
De Romilly, J. (1995). *Tragédies grecques au fil des ans*. Paris: Société d'Édition Les Belles Lettres.
Easterling, P. E. (1982). *Sophocles' trachiniae*. Cambridge: Cambridge University Press.
Ferenczi, S. (1955). The confusion of tongues between adults and the child. The language of tenderness and of passion. In E. Mosbacher et al. (Trans.), *Final contributions to the problems and methods of psychoanalysis*. London: Maresfield Reprints. (Original work published 1933)

Freud, S. (1896). Further remarks on the neuropsychoses of defence. *S. E., 3.*
Freud, S. (1912–1913) Totem and Taboo: Some points of agreement between the mental lives of savages and neurotics. *S. E., 13.*
Freud, S. (1915). Instincts and their vicissitudes. *S. E., 14.*
Freud, S. (1917). A metapsychological supplement to the theory of dreams. *S. E., 14.*
Freud, S. (1919). The uncanny. *S. E., 17.*
Freud, S. (1924). The economic problem of masochism. *S. E., 19.*
Freud, S. (1925). Negation. *S. E., 19.*
Freud, S. (1939). Moses and monotheism. *S. E., 23.*
Green, A. (1986). The dead mother. In *On private madness*. New York: International University Press. (Original work published 1983)
Halleran, R. M. (1995). *Euripides' hippolytus*. Warminster: Aris and Philips.
Hurmuziadis, N. (1991). Terms and transformations in ancient Greek tragedy. In *Greek*. Athens: Gnosis Publications.
Kitto, H. D. F. (1971). *Greek tragedy*. London: Associated Book Publishers.
Klein, M. (1955). The psycho-analytic play technique: Its history and significance. In M. Klein, P. Heinemann, & R. E. Money-Kyrle (Eds.), *New directions in psycho-analysis*. London: Maresfield Library.
Kovacs, D. (1995). Euripides: Children of Heracles, Hippolytus, Andromache, Hecuba. In *Loeb classical library*. Cambridge, MA: Harvard University Press.
Laplanche, J. (1992a). Seduction, translation, drives. In J. Fletcher, M. Stanton (Eds.), & M. Stanton (Trans.), *A dossier*. London: Psychoanalytic Forum, Institute of Contemporary Arts.
Laplanche, J. (1992b). Interpretation between determinism and hermeneutics: A restatement of the problem. *International Journal of Psychoanalysis, 73*, 429–445.
Laufer, M., & Laufer, E. (1984). Adolescence and developmental breakdown. In *A psychoanalytic view*. New Haven, CT and London: Yale University Press.
Lesky, A. (1987). *Die Tragische Dichtung der Hellenen*. Göttingen: Vandenhoeck Ruprecht.
Manolopoulos, S. (1999). Euripides' hippolytus: The familiar things. *Psychoanalytic Studies, 1*(2), 177–189.
Padel, R. (1992). In and out of the mind. In *Greek images of the tragic self*. Princeton, NJ: Princeton University Press.
Perrin, B. (1914). Plutarch: Lives. In *Theseus and Romulus, Lycurgus and Numa, Solon and Publicola*. London: Loeb Classical Library.
Potamianou, A. (1984). *Les enfants de la folie, Violence dans les identification*. Toulouse: Privat.
Priel, B. (1999). Bakhtin and Winnicott: On dialogue, self, and cure. *Psychoanalytic Dialogue, 9*, 487–503.
Rolland, J. C. (1998). Some psychical implications of the difference between analytic and scientific communication. *EPF Bulletin, 51*, 26–35.
Segal, C. (1996). L'homme grec, spectateur et auditeur. In J. P. Vernant, V. Tsikopoulos (Eds.), & C. Tasakos (Trans.), *Greek. The Greek man*. Athens: Ellinika Grammata Publications. (Original work published 1991)
Segal, H. (1986). The work of hanna segal. *A kleinian approach to clinical practice*. London: Free Association Books.
Vergopoulos, T. (1986). Le problématique du déni ou les enfants qui refusent de marier leurs parents. *Revue Française de Psychanalyse, 4*, 1183–1211.
Vernant, J. P. (1985). *Mythe et pensée en Grèce ancienne*. Paris: Éditions La Decouverte.
Vernant, J. P., & Vidal-Naquet, P. (1972). Mythe et pensée en Grèce ancienne. Paris: Éditions La Decouverte.
Winnicott, D. W. (1960). The theory of the parent-infant relationship. *International Journal of Psychoanalysis, 41*, 585–595.
Winnicott, D. W. (1990). The development of the capacity for concern. In *The maturational processes and the facilitating environment*. London: Karnac. (Original work published 1963)

Chapter 3

Euripides' Medea
The barbaric reality[1,2]

I wish to introduce Euripides's Medea as a metaphor for the psyche's attempt to express and symbolise preverbal, unrepresented experiences and wounds visited upon it before there was any word for trauma. I suggest that Medea, the wild foreigner whose murderous magic is unleashed when her environment betrays her, could be thought of psychoanalytically as the uncharted realms of primitive traumatised existence, yearning to find a way to represent itself on the stage of language and reality. Euripides can help us understand this deep realm of the psyche, with which psychoanalysis also grapples; he presents the realisation of an object that traumatically fails to contain preverbal elements and transform them.

Introduction

Euripides, the 'rag-stitcher', collected whatever scraps of experience he found and wove them into tragic plots. He gave his mythical heroes and gods the appearance of ordinary people. Thus, his Medea takes leave of her myth and becomes disturbingly accessible.

Medea is tragic because it presents on stage the elements of trauma that lie beyond language and meaning and that resist embarking on the painful processes required for transformation (mourning, symbolisation, internalisation). The psychoanalytic study of Medea's tragedy enriches our understanding of how we gain access to primitive, 'untamable', traces of unrepresented experiences. A constant process of psychic construction is realised and resisted in oscillating movements between repetition and fantasy, regression and integration. Through the function of repetition, preverbal memory traces are transferred into the present as images on the stage of consciousness and in the presence of others to complete their transformation. These regressive movements reach hallucinatory realisations of perceptions from which we construct fantasies to interpret the experiences we repeat and create on the stage of everyday life (Bion, 1962/1977, 1965/1984; Freud, 1919a, 1919b, 1920, 1937; Green, 2012).

Delcourt (2004) gives us the following description of the tragedy. Euripides presented *Medea* in 431 BC in the sacred theatre of Dionysus in Athens. The granddaughter of the Sun, overcome by erotic passion for Jason, helps him steal the Golden Fleece. For his sake, she betrays her father and her homeland and murders her brother. She later brings about the death of the aged Pelias by tricking his daughters into cutting him into pieces and boiling them in water in order to rejuvenate him supposedly.

Euripides had narrated this story 20 years earlier. What is new this time around is the danger of consorting with a sorceress, a murderess, because of which there is no home to return to. In Corinth, where Medea and Jason – now a married couple with two children – have fled, the daughter of King Creon is captivated by the handsome Jason, who abandons Medea. Determined to remarry this woman, he waits for his wife to leave the city. Now, the foreign barbarian woman Medea finds her place in the Greek world threatened. She convinces the king to allow her one last day in the city before she departs.

Suddenly, out of nowhere, she is visited by Aegeus, King of Athens, who returns to Athens puzzled because he does not understand the oracular prophecy about his childlessness. Medea promises to help him have children, and in return, he promises to give her refuge if she can escape Corinth and go to Athens.

Now, Medea's plan for revenge against Jason for his betrayal takes its final shape. She decides to leave Jason childless. She sends his young bride a dress soaked in poison that burns the young woman alive, along with the king of Corinth, who runs to save his daughter. As soon as Medea is certain that Jason has lost everything, she kills their children – her own and Jason's – with her own hands and flees to Athens.

The myth of Medea has existed since the 8th century BC. In the 5th century BC, it appeared in the poetry of both Pindar and Euripides. Medea's name is linked etymologically to thinking, providing, and ruling, but it also shares a common root with Medusa. As her myth evolved, the maiden-helper who can contrive, invent, and become the dangerous woman who can destroy and take revenge. Medea was presented as provoking terror and envy because she was a barbarian and wise; she was different, and she had knowledge; she was a woman – a woman to be feared like an evil spell. Medea came from a barbaric country (Colchis) to a Greek polis, the civilisation of which can be taken as a metaphor for the organisation of the ego-superego-id structure, founded in the oedipal plot through the painful processes of loss, mourning, and internalisation.

On the other hand, the sudden appearance of Aegeus introduces the primal scene that connects the savagery of this barbarian woman with the birth of Theseus, the founder and reformer of the polis of Athens and its 'first father', source of the superego, which, of course, has its roots in the id and its primitive traces.

Medea's tragedy takes us back to what is foreign within each of us. She calls upon us to confront the unthinkable. The drama of *Medea* can be used as a metaphor that carries us back to the wild, primal depths of a country full of riches. A sorceress who can conquer the forces of nature, Medea brings us unrepresented elements from the wells of memory. What is beyond language? How do we deal with unthinkable elements that invade the space of meanings?

The tragic plot

The play begins with the nurse's image from the past, that of the black rocks: "Would that the Argo had never winged its way to the land of Colchis through the dark-blue Symplegades" (1). Now, everything is hostile, and those most loved will suffer. "For Jason, abandoning his own children" (15).[3] Medea struggles with pain, "wasting away in tears all the time" (25). Time itself becomes petrified: "She is as deaf to the advice of her friends as a stone or a wave of the sea" (28); she refuses to listen. Medea's heart has become black and like a stone: *"The poor woman has learned at misfortune's hand what a good thing it is not to be cut off from one's native land"* (34).

The torment has no end. The day will not go by. A sense of threat hangs over it, real yet not credible. "She will soon kindle with even greater passion the cloud of lament now rising from its source" (107). The women of the chorus ask Medea to come out; grief is a public affair. The play begins with the recognition of her traumatic losses. She must communicate these losses to herself and others, clearly, as they actually are.

In response to the chorus's request, Medea emerges on stage, stunned by her pain: *"Oh, what a wretch am I, how miserable in my sorrows! Ah ah, how I wish I could die!"* (96); *"O accursed children of a hateful mother, may you perish with your father and the whole house collapse in ruin!"* (112). *"Ah, ah! may I find my rest in death and leave behind my hateful life!"* (147). She wants to vanish from the face of the earth; she wants to eliminate the world from her eyes. The chorus replies: *"Do you hear the bitter lament sung by this woman of sorrow? What is this desire you feel for the bed of death, the bed we should not approach, foolish woman?"* (149).

The chorus observes how sweet the tears that accompany the sweet music of a lament are. It speaks with the rhythm of the body, the melody of the speaking voice, the sound sources of representations now in danger of being swept up in wild emotion. In the rustlings of nature, the chorus listens for the memories that come back and gives us the courage to go on. Death is easy. Life must be endured. Human beings are but fleeting shadows. The rustlings of nature, like the sorceress' gathering of herbs, roots, leaves, and flowers, remind us of the fleeting shadows, the impressions that a child heard or saw before acquiring speech. Euripides' chorus does not participate in the plot; rather, it sings a commentary that uses words to mitigate the savagery of passion. For example, the chorus sings about Aphrodite drinking from the sweet river Kifissos and filling it with a temperate breeze, her breath as fragrant as the roses that bind her hair (822–828). The songs transform into images the emotions aroused when our bodies vibrate, touched by the object's poetic speech (Danon-Boileau, 2007).

We can think of the chorus in Medea as narrating the movements of repetition, fantasy, and subjective appropriation of preverbal elements ingrained in myth. These are the fragments of historical truth that we collect and (re)construct through words in everyday life (Freud, 1937). We construct a fantasy with which we 'interpret' the repetitions of preverbal experiences; we situate them on the stage of language and reality (linked to sexual differences). We construct a subject to experience them and a place – a meaning for them in personal history.

Euripides describes with traumatically perceptive clarity the nature of Medea, who, like language, has her roots in the body. Thus, she is able to work magic and to show by way of the tragedy's deus ex machina that we must believe her. Language works magic, and Medea can work her own magic in the pronunciation of words that cast a spell on someone: that is, their sensory, kinetic, and perceptual roots are linked to meanings and objects. By virtue of this double origin of words, we can regress into a dream until we arrive at a sensory vividness of hallucinatory embodiment and enactment that persuades us of its reality. For Euripides, the deus ex machina performed this regressive hallucinatory function.

Thus, the poet regresses, leading us back to preverbal levels, where everything is ambiguous, prophetic, ecstatic, and terrifying, where an infant feels the anxiety of annihilation. Medea returns to her origins, to her bodily roots, to the original and authentic terror of existence. Through primitive sensory, kinetic, emotional, and perceptual images, she abolishes the logic of secondary processes, daring to confront the depths where words 'sense' unconscious things and represent them (Rolland, 2007). Medea's words perceive, touch, and wound; they 'speak' by linking meanings to primitive images and objects. Since the links have been traumatically lost, her words desperately attempt to make them present again.

Medea speaks with preverbal honesty, fury, and violence about vows that have not been kept: "finding herself thus cast aside, calls loudly on his oaths, invokes the mighty assurance of his sworn right hand, and calls the gods to witness the unjust return she is getting from Jason" (21–24), invoking Themis, the goddess of prayer, and Zeus, the treasurer of vows (169).

Medea bellows like the sea. She opposes, she laments, she attacks, she explains in passionate words, but words are untrustworthy: they can betray, be substituted, and lie. Thus, Medea gives voice to Euripides' mistrust of words:

> I realise I have far different views from the majority of mortals/To my mind, the plausible speaker who is a scoundrel incurs the greatest punishment . . . So, it is with you. Do not, therefore, give me your specious arguments and oratory, for one word will lay you out (579–587). . . . This subject, however, I now leave behind. Ah me, I groan at what a deed I must do next.
>
> (790)

However, she herself uses forceful rhetoric to persuade Creon not to exile her at once; she gains a day, a day without end. She lies (through her use of rhetoric) in order to make reality bearable. As a human being, she does not resist falseness. She fears the moment that the reality is imminent (Bion, 1965/1984).

Medea feels the pain of reality when the stopped clock of melancholy turns to action in the real-time of the tragedy. It is now that she risks her actual involvement, the experiencing of her true self in action. Medea does not leaven her hatred with "frothy charm": "*In every way the situation is bad*", but "*he has permitted me to stay for this day*"; this will be the last day. Now since I possess many ways of killing them (Jason and his lover), I do not know which I should try first *(Jason and his lover)*. "Shall I set the bridal chamber on fire or thrust a sharp sword through their vitals . . . Best to proceed by the direct route, in which I am the most skilled, and kill them with poison" (364–385).

The chorus sings: "*Backward to their sources flow the streams of holy rivers, and the order of all things is reversed*" (411). The rivers flowing up present a rupture of the flow, like a void separating the waters of river and sea. Euripides uses his poetry to create a rupture in the natural flow, forming a void.

Then, all of a sudden, Aegeus appears just in time, out of nowhere, "*as a harbour for my plans*" (768). In the safe harbor of Athens, Medea can tie an oedipal knot. Her invitation to Athens signifies the might of the city that welcomes her without fear. It signifies, moreover, the might that the city will acquire through internalisation of the primitive powers of the archaic mother.

Medea promises Aegeus to help him father children, and at once, the solution becomes clear to her: she decides to leave Jason childless. Aegeus, an oedipal father, appears suddenly and divides Medea's tragedy in two. He introduces a non-understanding, a capacity not to know, an opening, an affirming-negating invitation for Medea to flee toward life. The encounter between Aegeus and Medea results in a moment of recognition. Suddenly, Medea feels convinced, as if she has realised what she has always known but never thought.

Euripides was a master of staging and creating impasses in which reality is imminent, repetitions endless, and the outcome to be feared. At the conclusion of his tragedy, he achieves a resolution to the impasse through the device of a deus ex machina: a dragon-drawn chariot, sent by her grandfather, the sun god, lifts Medea aloft and takes her far away to Athens, which is open to receiving foreigners.

In Greek tragedies, and above all in those of Euripides, the deus ex machina – a fantastic resolution of a complicated situation – is an unexpected plot device that keeps the story moving. It involves the sudden intervention of a new event: normally, the appearance of a god who descends onto the stage or is lifted up high by a crane, surprising the audience. In Medea, it is the heroine herself who is lifted to a faraway place. We can also think of the unexpected appearance of Aegeus in the middle of the play as a divine intervention that alters the course of the plot, much as the deus ex machina does.

The Gods bring about the unexpected. Kovacs (1994/2001, p. 280) sees the unexpected appearance of Aegeus in connection with divine intervention (764, 802, 1231, 1260): The commonest form of punishment for not keeping one's oath is the "root-and-branch destruction with loss of all progeny". The discovery of reality, of the difference of the object realised inside the fantasy of a primal scene, is unexpected. Medea must set the stage to confront her own terrifying primal scene, pursuing it to its ghastly conclusion.

Medea murdering her own children is an attack against the proof of the reality of her sexual link with Jason. By her act of revenge, she symmetrically gets even and restores balance. "*Let no one think me weak, contemptible, untroublesome*" (805). The chorus comments:

> we too possess a muse, who consorts with us to bring us wisdom: not with all of us, for it is some small clan, one woman among many, that you will find with a share in the Muse. I say that those mortals who are utterly without experience of children and have never borne them have the advantage in good fortune over those who have.
>
> (1085–1094)

Medea sends with her children the poisoned garments to burn Jason's bride and her father, Creon, who will be united with his daughter in death. Medea faces the psychotic terror of melancholy: the murder of the object, discovered in its hateful otherness.

While she emerges as independent, Medea must preserve contact with primitive parts as the last bodily links with her lost object. As she prepares her children for their death, it is of their wedding she speaks – identifying in bodily images their part in a lineage that continues. She links the children's bodies with the sounds of words. At the same time, she asks herself to forget that she loves them, to forget that she gave life to them: "*Instead, for this brief day forget them*" (1250).

The children are on stage before Medea appears. They are in danger, and so the nurse "covers", "hides" them: "Go quickly into the house" (100). They reappear when Medea sends them to deliver her poisoned gifts.

Twenty-five lines later, the children return from their murderous errand, and Medea bids them farewell in a harrowing monologue (1020), speaking of their sweet smiles, their round laughing eyes, hands, lips, sweet embrace, soft milk-white skin, fragrant breath, as if she were lulling them to sleep. These children will die soon, and only then do we hear their voices, a scream . . . a few lines of weak, protesting cries (De Romilly, 1986).

In the end, Medea becomes something analogous to a force of nature. This can be thought of as a transformation from knowing to becoming. She will become the "thing" she is to know – the "thing" from which words and meanings originate (Bion, 1965/1984). We can also think of language as a force of nature: it separates us from illusion, overthrowing myths but also uniting us with bodily sources of the words and the object.

When the deus ex machina carries Medea away, Jason tries with words to reach her, with all the hatred and desperate violence he now feels. But in the fiery chariot of the sun, no one can touch Medea. The orbit of the sun turns to day. The dawn now celebrates the passing of time. For a moment, Medea passes through the hallucinatory enactment (the deus ex machina); then, a new day begins, and an inexplicable redemption is accomplished.

Medea ends with the chorus, exhausted by the frightful drama, saying: "many are the things the gods accomplish against our expectation. What men expect is not brought to pass, but a god finds a way to achieve the unexpected. Such is the outcome of this story" (1415). There has been an outcome. The 'poetic' work of the psyche can make links: it works! It confirms that the elements of past experience have left traces; they do have a place in one's functions. The traces of the past have not been destroyed. The psyche functions, trying to situate in meanings the lost (but not erased) fragments (Loraux, 2006).

Tragedy opens an uncanny void, here bridged by a 'construction' – an invitation to Athens, a place for Medea to nurse her desire to live. A fixed sequence of repetition has been abstracted, and in its place, Euripides offers a new chain of meanings, restoring Medea's 'genetic' code of identity. Her magic will be placed in the service of life, of being conceived and born.

Euripides narrates the achievement of internalisation of new possibilities, i.e.: (1) reversal of the natural flow and a return to the original sources of meaning, to the roots of words in the body, (2) the recovery of the primary ambiguity of words, (3) the psychic constructions that create links of meanings, and (4) the parental couple's union, giving birth to a flesh-and-blood child.

As a poet, Euripides is himself a prophet – since he creates symbols that open a path to the future – and the enchantress Medea, as priestess of Hecate, is able to read prophetic oracles. The words of a poet and an oracle may be vague, yet they speak to deep areas of the psyche. They come from the area of preverbal ambiguity in which the paradoxical coexistence of internal and external, sensations and meanings, is accepted.

Euripides offers poetics as redemption. We are given a new chance: the unrepresented elements can be put into words linked to an object and relegated to the past to serve as a background to psychic life.

A slave opens the play with an image of the journey, the adventure of life that begins with the traumatic caesura of birth, by the passage through dangerous black rocks, a loss of mythical union, an act of origin that one may wish never to have occurred. The slave talks about freedom in thinking and autonomy in deciding to internalise or to kill (to reject) the birth and life of children, representing elements of psychic growth.

Discussion

Medea betrayed her fatherland and killed her brother, her father's heir; since then, she has been exiled; she seeks a home to which to return. She came from the world's eastern edge, the dangerous land where the sun rises from the underworld. She has betrayed Colchis for the love of a man because she believed his words; for his part, he has betrayed her by breaking his oath.

She came from a land where every stranger was killed, and she came as a stranger into a new story (an oedipal plot) that is not yet hers. The illusion of being in love is ruptured by reality, that is, the traumatic discovery of the difference of the object, introduced via the awareness of the sexual parental couple. Medea was forced to internalise this oedipal story and to become a link in the chain of its telling. The discovery that the object of desire is a whole object, different, and always escaping the subject's illusions is by itself felt as a deception. For the primitive psyche, it lies beyond meaning.

De Romilly (1986) observed that Euripides is narrating a living story, one beginning with impossible contradictions. This innovator of myths goes on to shock the Athenians – dispelling prevailing notions, the panoply of false pretexts. In myth, he seeks only exceptional moments when the casing of the psyche is forcibly ripped open to reveal its insides. Euripides tears apart the myths surrounding words that are woven into links of meaning. For him, language is fictitious; it betrays the authenticity of experience. But he understands its frightening power to inflame, to wound, to destroy.

Euripides's poetic treatment of myths, from which he extracts a profoundly tragic plot, recalls how, in psychoanalysis, interpretations and constructions loosen the knots of meanings surrounding the historical truth of the original psychic inscriptions. Analytic work, too, extracts at unexpected, uncanny moments (often in the form of hallucinatory productions of sensory images) the events in which the infant-parent drive and affect exchanges, object relationships, object representations, and words begin to be conceived and internalised (Freud, 1919a).

Euripides's commentators note that he (the 'stage philosopher') was influenced by Anaxagoras and Socrates, but also by the Sophists, teachers of rhetoric who used language in a clever way to win arguments. He utilised his plays to talk about what he had learned about science, perception, language, knowledge, thought, and truth. And he was fascinated by the use of sophisticated rhetorical speeches.

For Euripides, words either say things as they are or, through an intense dialectic, they utter 'lies' that make the truth felt, or they may signify nothing. Words differentiate us from our primary object. In Orestes, Electra reminds us of her ancestor Tantalus's original sin: he was able to speak and thus offended the gods. Words maintain their roots in the passions of the soul – desire and sadness at the loss of the primary object with every step toward representation.

Loraux (2006) pointed out that, in tragedy, the sounds of words express the primitive elements of psychic life. Medea is ruled by her passions: her desire, her rage, and her endless grief. The theatre of Dionysus was located beside the agora, where Athenian political life was conducted. In the theatre, elements of passionate grief (banned from public life) could be openly expressed. Loraux linked the words aei (without interruption) and aiai (inarticulate cries of mourning).

The melancholic murder

We find many versions of the ending to the myth of Medea. In one, her children are dedicated to the temple of Hera; in another, the angry Corinthians violate the asylum of the temple and kill the children to take revenge for Medea's having killed their king and his daughter. In yet another, Medea kills her children by accident.

Euripides's originality lies in the portrayal of Medea herself as killing the children intentionally and assuming personal responsibility for her act. We can think that, in killing her children, Medea kills a part of herself, believing that this is how it must be.

Is this her only means of revenge – identifying her children with her helpless child self (revived by Jason's betrayal) and assuming the role of murderess? Is this how she 'saves' the children (narcissistic extensions of herself) from a threatening world in which she cannot imagine them existing without her? Does she kill the children's bodies as projections of their father? Is it for Jason, and all men, that she takes up the role of primordial sorceress to absolve them of their own guilty wish to kill their siblings in the primal scene? Or is she assuming everyone's guilt for their attack on the containing mother?

We are asked to accept what we cannot understand, what is beyond meaning. Can Medea's melancholic murder be thought of as a way of returning the children to her womb? Possible interpretations of a repetition that makes such a preverbal terror psychically present are endless. However, we can say that, with the murder, Medea reverses the natural flow of the river of time. With the fantasy of merger, conflict and traumas cease, and she is ready to start again from the beginning.

The deus ex machina brings an outcome; then, the primitive experiences can be performed anew. Poetry promises to restore the wounded integrity of the self. Thus, Euripides is expressing the poetic reversal of the flow of time and the longing to return to a fusion with the primary mother.

Through words, Euripides takes us to the children's murder. In Medea's monologue, we hear, on the one hand, unbearable pain, which may be thought of as a metaphor for the pain caused by the poet's descent into the Hades of the unconscious, activating primitive elements and emotions that have not yet become affects. We are faced with the danger of a rejection of the links, but we also listen to a mother's transformative speech. Medea's words retain the links with the body.

However, Medea's 'psychotic' functioning also uses words that have lost contact with their bodily roots and with the object (Freud, 1915). We hear Medea 'killing' the children, not metaphorically in order to let them sleep, but literally, putting them back to sleep inside her womb. At the same time, we hear her singing to them – invoking their smiles, their laughing eyes, their hands, lips, soft milk-white skin, and fragrant breath. Her threat alternates with her profound concern for their psychic growth.

The poet, regressing to the depths of magical, prophetic ambiguity, where things are also their opposites, touches upon the terror where existence itself is at risk. Every step in psychic growth signals the death of the union with the primary mother, but it is also accompanied by the opposite movement: the sacrifice of the children's lives so that they can be offered as energy to the sun god in order to rise again, so that human and divine worlds may become one.

Like the poet, Medea defies public discourse, the language of the establishment. Poetry, like Medea, speaks a foreign language, the language of a foreign land, the unconscious. We learn a foreign language when we acquire our mother tongue. We learn language through our contact with the sensations of our invested body through the intervention of the object. We learn words when we make the transition from primary identification to secondary identification as the result of cathecting the (otherness of the) object.

The theatre of threat

Delcourt (2004) remarks on the many layers of irony that Medea's barbaric ancestry reveals. In Medea, the poet fashions a woman indomitable – wild, unbridled, passionate, fiercely in love – who loses her reason when she is betrayed. What makes her terrifying is that she is in command of the secrets of nature and is determined to use them.

Euripides sees Eros as passion, as an all-powerful force of nature that threatens to destroy, but also as a secret source of creativity that humanises our bodies. The princess of the sun is tormented because she feels mortal. She feels herself to be part of an oedipal situation, that is, a scene in which differences between sexes and between generations force humans to live a terrestrial life inside time, language, reality, and object relationships as subjects of their destructive and erotic fantasies. For the sake of Eros, Medea became human. But Eros launched her on a torment-filled journey toward mourning the loss of omnipotence, the internalisation of drives, and the need to assume responsibility for them.

The origins of Eros are barbaric. André (2011) explains that the anxiety concerning our female nature demonstrates the primacy of the other. Mother's position is asymmetrical, and her passions violently intrude in the infant's world. She installs herself as something 'foreign' within us.

Medea can be thought of as a metaphor for the activation of a threat when unrepresented elements are introduced into an oedipal plot. The loss of omnipotence is felt as life-threatening. Destructive attacks are unleashed. There must be no process, no links that make meaning, which is evidence that the life of couples goes on. She wants not to feel, not to live, not to exist in history; she wants Jason's marriage with the king's daughter not to take place; she wants there to be no succession to the throne, no birth of children – the primal scene – or, even more terrifying, for its traces to be entirely erased.

Mastronarde (2002) writes that a passionate woman, miraculously insane, represents a threat to overwhelm our capacity to contain a wild nature through words. The sorcery of Medea – who is a relative of the witches Circe and Pasifae – is bound to the earth, to the body of the mother and its senses.

In Euripides's tragedies, the realism of the amphitheatre arises on stage. It is as if documentary details try to convince us of the truth of traumatic reality since metaphorical links (the result of mourning work) are not yet adequate to make meaning from it. In familiar situations, everyday people at times try to avoid something to gain time; they fear reliving the pain of loss, becoming entrapped in impossible stalemates. We hear explanations and responses, in fact, and we hear unbearable pain split off. Jason and Creon offer Medea solutions so that she need not experience inexorable grief and infernal hatred. However, an everyday dialogue reveals in the end that Zeus has been on stage all along.

Excessive reality is barbarous when an experience does not allow construction of meaning to be completed and an outcome to be realised. The poet combats the gravest threat of all: the paralysis of action, the impasse of the plot, and the death of the process. The lack of outcome is an experience on the order of the psychotic, in which the links between words, objects, and their bodily roots have been attacked. The ultimate danger is a repetition with no past, an ever-present fear of breakdown (Winnicott, 1974).

The play's plot reminds us of those forced to comply with peremptory demands that they were unable to question in thought or speech. They have endured heavy burdens that they were unable to represent. The key with which to gain entry to their preverbal experiences lies at the somatic pole of their emotions (McDougall, 1989). We can say that, in such cases, the drives are felt as threats because they give meaning to the object. Then the withdrawal of investments, the death of love for life, is an extreme defence.

I used the somatic pole (sensorimotor elements) of emotions to gain contact with a traumatised adolescent girl who came to therapy because she had to spend hours arranging the folds of her dress obsessively in a way that only she knew. The folds of her dress took the meaning of the folds of her body (erotogenic zones) and their innermost folds of her existence that were shivering because of primitive agonies due to early trauma that had been regressively activated. The meaning we gave to the folds of her dress contained the unfolding of the story of her transference experiences. Out of the external boundaries of space and time, the transference created the matrix of the frame, where the psychic transformations occur (Manolopoulos, 2023).

Primitive elements on stage

Ultimately, we might arrive at the belief that, for the sake of Divine Eros, Medea became human as a metaphor for the hallucinatory embodiment of primitive elements of preverbal experiences that are revived in a new context of psychic construction. Her actions stand for the primitive elements that are left over (split off) as the actual residue of the unrepresented. No form of processing can exhaust them. They constitute the contents of primary repression or of primitive, unelaborated, split-off material (Levine, Reed, & Scarfone, 2013). In Medea, the primitive elements of memory (poisons cooked up in the cauldrons of witchcraft, unworn clothes soaked in poison, jewels dipped in the stuff of pregenital oral and anal remnants) maintain continuity of self despite the threat. These leftover elements are repeated in action; they also contribute to fantasy formation through their integration and interpretation in subjective history.

Medea's monologue (1020–1080) is astonishing for its extreme oscillation between the tenderness she feels toward her children and her cruel use of them for purposes of revenge and protection of her self-esteem (Simon, 1988). Her monologue is an agon played out not between two protagonists but between two split parts of herself (Freud, 1940). The repetition of the pain of her trauma is depicted in various scenes. For example, as she prepares to murder her children, they smile at her, and she cries: "Why do you smile at me this last smile of yours?" (1040).

Medea would gladly have taken a stand in battle three times rather than give birth even once; her pain is insufferable. She emerges from her myth: she is born into her tragedy, creating her history as a clearly defined person, a compelling figure to both herself and others. She cannot do otherwise: here she is, here she stands, insistent, taking up space and asking for time. Her birth as an individual, her arrival in the world, and her very freedom are gained through a loss of mythical omnipotence each time a new meaning is formed.

Euripides's plots pose a question: How does one proceed to the next stage, to changing and yet remaining the same, while maintaining one's core identity intact? What happens to the remains of what existed before? Fenichel (1934) examined the fate of pregenital elements, for the oral, anal, and phallic elements – poisons, feces, dragon's teeth, (Golden) Fleece – all need a space to be remembered (linking and holding), in contrast to threats of dismemberment (fragmentation and evacuation).

We need to place primitive preverbal elements in a context (Medea in Athens). Tragedy is a method of ordering mythical material for presentation, just as transference is the psychic method that grants us access to primitive elements.

A tragic plot brings the mythical material up to date. The tragic poet inserts actuality (in contrast to potentiality) into the mythical material in order to transform it into tragedy. He inserts action having an end embodied in it (Ramfos, 1992–1993). Similarly, transference inserts the plot missing from primitive material; it inserts action (repetition) and its interpretation (fantasy), which is a function of the ego processing material from the id.

Green (2012, p. 1246) refers to the primitive traces Freud (1900) called untamable. We should not confine remembering to the function of unconscious representations. A significant portion of the psyche operates with "unrepresented forms of remembering . . . similar to hallucinatory structures of psychosis" that are primitive traces of the id. How do we acquire access to these pre-representational layers of memory? Dream study shows that the regression we undergo in sleep allows us to "go back as far as possible towards the hallucinatory perceptual pole, thereby attaining a surprising degree of sensory vividness". Euripides achieves such sensory vividness with the hallucinatory appearance of the deus ex machina – which, like constructions and delusion, reconnects sensations both with words and with the object.

The poet's thematic expressions

Euripides's plots are notable for their uncertain outcomes. He returns us to the ambiguity of the embodied roots of words. He asks us to tolerate uncertainty about our own identity. What is at stake is the construction of new meaning. In a moment of hallucinatory realisation, the deus ex machina appears suddenly, makes a pronouncement, 'picks up the pieces', and announces a plan for the future. It breaks out as a magical and credible phenomenon. It appears in unexpected moments of surprise in which dim experiences are revived in a process whereby the sense of self is revealed.

During his journey back to the psyche's embodied roots, Euripides faces the revival of trauma that has erased the link to a return 'home' (mnemonic traces). He provokes a torrent of terror in order to retain the situation of despair in sharp focus – the impossible situation without an outcome. Finally, he creates the deus ex machina, a hallucinatory realisation that constructs links and offers solutions to the plot's impasses.

The issue is not whether Medea herself killed her children. The matter of the tragedy is one that every Athenian will 'decide' deep within his own psyche. It is the Athenians who will interpret and decide if all this makes sense, and it is they who will become the subjects of all this. They will take responsibility. They will decide whether children will be born, whether they will live out their time, and whether they will discover the history of their birth. They will decide about change and the new and strange things that children signify.

It is possible that Euripides was mindful of the war traumas that Athenians had to work through between 479 and 404 BC. Tragic poetry, like psychoanalysis, attempts to prevent catastrophe from gaining the upper hand. Tragedy equates the work of the poet with both paternal and maternal functions; tragedy is the creative work of linking that brings 'children' into the world – new assertions that astonish.

The function of tragedy

Tragic poetry was born when myths encountered words. We can also say that affects are born when emotions meet the words through an object. From lamentation, we pass into the poetry of lament, beneficent representations, and beauty in a world full of terror and fear (De Romilly, 1986). In poetry, the sound images of words convey meaning. Incoherent cries, tears, and laughter make up the dark rudiments – it is these that are expressed in poetry, said Loewald (1978), following Valéry.

In our psychic constructions, we find at the heart of meaning the historical truth of these primitive truths, truths a child heard or saw before acquiring speech (Freud, 1937). Psychic constructions use poetic links in a way similar to that in which prophetic and magical language uses early, foreign, and incomprehensible words.

Medea is the priestess of Hecate, who grants her magical powers and eloquence. In the end, the magical notion that the word and the thing form a unity renders words capable of practicing magic, of opening doors into the unknown, of changing the meaning, the place, the time, and the shape of things.

The representing of a word recurs with its regression back to where it came from originally: the sensory image and the iconic presentation of the thing (Freud, 1900, 1919b; Rolland, 2007). The gift, the spells, and the poisons show how the development of sexuality (fantasy) interprets and transforms the reality that repetition presents. They also indicate the threat against the container (the Golden Fleece; skin covered in ointment, invulnerable to dragon fire; the burning bridal dress) and against words, which risk losing their capacity for containment.

Spectators in the tragedy track down the bodily components, the emotions, from which they construct tragic affects as they listen, for example, to Medea's monologue, and they follow the pathway of the hands, the skin, the eyes, the nose, which link to the sound components of words. It is a miracle of restitution, the restoration of the capacity to make links, forming a representational web. Art is sought out for its power to heal narcissistic injury through the work of mourning.

From the agony of annihilation to the re-organisation of defences

Euripides was fascinated by extreme experiences. However, he allows us to make our own contribution, as an audience, to the intrigue played out on stage. Even in the most extreme moments of regression to hatred and despair, the agony of annihilation, and in the radical withdrawal of the drives from objects and the collapse of meaning, in the confusion and mist of undifferentiated shapelessness, discrete tragic affects will emerge out of primitive images and emotions through words.

Tragedy begins when the inevitable failures of the environment's holding functions create situations of crash of omnipotence and bring to the present our infantile agony of annihilation. However, this situation creates a new chance for a new re-organisation of our defences. It is a chance for the re-organisation of the frames of our transitional space. It is a new experience from which we will learn something new. We have a choice: to feel our feelings and create a learning experience.

This is indeed a miracle of restoration. What is being restored is not an actual original event but the capacity to make emotional links with one's origins – to have a true sense of self, to feel alive, to create, live, and think about one's experiences, to be in contact with one's soma, to desire and feel related to others. Aristotle (1984, 1991), in the 4th century BC in his Poetics and his Rhetoric gives meaning to Homer's (2003) verse (8th-century BC-a, book 23, line 108; 8th-century BC-b, book 4, line 183): *"thus he spoke, and stirred in them all a desire to mourn"*. Homer (1998, 2003) speaks of the importance of creating affects and being able to feel them.

Commentators on the poetics of tragedy give significance to the emergence in the audience of the capability of differentiating tragic affects from the mixture of transitional forms of primitive images and emotions (Benjamin, 1925/1998; Steiner, 1963/1988). From the murky waters where the transitional forms of psychic elements coexist, the discerning compassion of the spectator's soul emerges.

Euripides's Medea tells us how precarious the poetic work of psychic constructions is. Medea's tragedy can be thought of as a metaphor for preverbal traumatic elements that can neither come to an end nor be repressed. Rather, they need to be given a new life, a new chance for recognition in a transference situation within an oedipal context; they need to be placed in the vast realm of unrepresented states where they can be accessed through psychic constructions, gradually forming the potential past of the subject.

Notes

1 The original version was published as Manolopoulos, S. (2015). Medea by Euripides: Psychic constructions for preverbal experiences and traumas. *The Psychoanalytic Quarterly*, *84*(2), 441–461. I have made a few minor changes to the original text.
2 The direct line quotes are taken from Kovacs, D. (1994). *Euripides: Cyclops, Alcestis, Medea*. Cambridge, MA: Harvard University Press, 2001.
3 Parenthetical numerals following quotations from Medea refer to line numbers; see Kovacs (1994). Translations from the ancient Greek were revised and supplemented by Irene Noel Baker.

References

André, J. (2011). From femininity to the primitive forms of psychic life. *EPF Bulletin*, *63*, 215–232.
Aristotle. (1984). *Rhetoric. The complete works of Aristotle* (Vols. 2, J. Barnesm, Ed.). Princeton, NJ: Princeton University Press.
Aristotle. (1991). *Poetics. Introduction, text and interpretation by I. Sykoutris, 1937* (S. Menardos, Trans.). Athens: Estia.
Benjamin, W. (1998). *The origins of German tragic drama* (J. Osborne, Trans.). New York: Verso. (Original work published 1925)
Bion, W. R. (1977). Learning from experience. In *Seven servants*. New York: Jason Aronson. (Original work published 1962)
Bion, W. R. (1984). *Transformations*. London: Karnac. (Original work published 1965)
Danon-Boileau, L. (2007). La force du langage. *Revue Française Psychanalyse*, *71*, 1341–1409.
Delcourt, M. (2004). *La Vie d'Euripide*. Bruxelles, Belgium: Editions Labor.
De Romilly, J. (1986). *La Modernité d'Euripides*. Paris: Presses Universitaires de France.
Fenichel, O. (1934). Outline of clinical psychoanalysis–concluded. *Psychoanalytic Quarterly*, *3*, 223–302.
Freud, S. (1900). The interpretation of dreams. *S. E.*, *4–5*.
Freud, S. (1915). The unconscious. *S. E.*, *14*.
Freud, S. (1919a). The uncanny. *S. E.*, *17*.
Freud, S. (1919b). A child is being beaten. *S. E.*, *17*.
Freud, S. (1920). Beyond the pleasure principle. *S. E.*, *18*.
Freud, S. (1937). Constructions in analysis. *S. E.*, *23*.
Freud, S. (1940). Splitting of the ego in the process of defence, *S. E.*, *23*.
Green, A. (2012). On construction in Freud's work. *International Journal of Psychoanalysis*, *93*, 1238–1248.
Homer. (1998). *The iliad* (B. Knox, Ed., & R. Fagels, Trans.). New York: Penguin Classics.
Homer. (2003). *The odyssey* (H. Rieu, Ed., & E. V. Rieu, Trans.). London: Penguin Classics.
Kovacs, D. (2001). *Euripides: Cyclops, Alcestis, Medea*. Cambridge, MA: Harvard University Press. (Original work published 1994)
Levine, H. B., Reed, G. S., & Scarfone, D. (2013). *Unrepresented states and construction of meaning: Clinical and theoretical contributions*. London: Karnac.

Loewald, H. W. (1978). Primary process, secondary process, and language. In J. H. Smith (Ed.), *Psychoanalysis and language*. New Haven, CT and London: Yale University Press.

Loraux, N. (2006). *The mourning voice: An essay on Greek tragedy* (E. T. Rawlings, Trans.). Ithaca, NY and London: Cornell University Press.

Manolopoulos, S. (2015). Euripides; Medea. Psychic constructions for preverbal experiences and traumas. *The Psychoanalytic Quarterly*, *84*(2): 441–461.

Manolopoulos, S. (2023). Transference. The matrix of the frame. *Psychoanalytic Quarterly* *92*(4):687–712.

Mastronarde, J. D. (2002). *Euripides: Medea*. Cambridge: Cambridge University Press.

McDougall, J. (1989). *Theatres of the body a psychoanalytic approach to psychosomatic illness*. London: Free Association Press.

Ramfos, S. (1992–1993). Mimesis against form: Explanation in Aristotle's Poetics. Volumes A, B. In *In Greek*. Athens: Armos Publications.

Rolland, J. C. (2007). Lavoisier's law applies to mental matter. In A. Green (Ed.), *Resonance of suffering: Countertransference in non-neurotic structures*. London: International Psychoanalytic Library.

Simon, B. (1988). *Tragic drama and the family: Psychoanalytical studies from aeschylus to beckett*. New Haven, CT and London: Yale University Press.

Steiner, G. (1998). Introduction. In W. Benjamin (Ed.), *The origins of German tragic drama*. London and New York: Verso. (Original work published 1963)

Winnicott, D. W. (1974). Fear of breakdown. *International Review of Psychoanalysis*, *1*, 103–107.

Chapter 4

Euripides' Orestes
The contamination of the city

Euripides taught *Orestes* in 408 BC. At the time, the citizens of Athens were fearful that they no longer had a future. Their war has devastated their motherland. In times of war, the bonds connecting the private and public spheres are traumatically severed. Reality becomes incomprehensible and menacing. The fear of not having a future is equivalent to annihilation anxiety. The city is sick from the woes of war. In Attica, the Spartans had long before conquered Decelea, following Alcibiades' treacherous advice, and are now sieging Athens.

Euripides stages the ailment of his city. In Argos, the heroes of the play are besieged. They live in fear of the impending reality, the horrible end. After the matricide and the violent final eviction of his mother, Orestes is sleeping, sick and withdrawn. The people of Argos are gathered in the agora, furious with the murderer Orestes and his sister Electra.

Orestes had not left his home to go out with the others in the common world. He was exiled by his mother, and then he returned and took revenge. He changed, but he did not find a hospitable home (self) to return to.

A year earlier, in 409 BC, Alcibiades' victory in Cyzicus and the destruction of the Spartan fleet had brought hope from the East. Sophocles had moved the Athenians in 409 BC with Philoctetes, the owner of Heracles' invincible bow needed for Troy to be conquered. In *Philoctetes*, a sick hero is wrapped in pain and abandoned on a desert island that he stubbornly occupies. In 408, Euripides turns towards the young who do not want to take responsibility for their city.

Orestes stays at home, sick, lonely, and asleep. He has a sister, Electra, and a friend, Pylades, on his side. Electra is caring for him, crying. Orestes murdered their mother, Clytemnestra, and her lover, Aegisthus. Electra bemoans the curse she has inherited from her ancestors, the Atreids. She is in anguish. Will the people of Argos condemn Orestes and herself to death? She longs for Menelaus – her father's brother – to return from Troy. She longs for a strong brother. Menelaus arrives at Argos with Helen. Helen learns the bad news from Electra and shows compassion for Orestes, attributing all the evils to Apollo. The gods had caused the Trojan War, she says.

Helen is afraid to bring offerings to her sister Clytemnestra's grave. She is afraid the citizens of Argos who had family members killed in Troy will be hostile towards her. She asks Electra to go in her stead. Electra refuses and suggests that Helen's daughter Hermione, who, during the war, lived in the palace as Clytemnestra's protégé, should go. Hermione takes the choes. Electra, along with the women of the chorus who are of the same age as her, laments for the calamities that have befallen Orestes and herself.

Orestes hears the lamentations and wakes up. He tells his sister that six days after killing his mother, he cannot withstand the relentless persecution by the Erinyes (Furies). Electra tells him not to be afraid because Menelaus, who cares about him, has returned from the war.

Menelaus enters and does not recognise Orestes, whose rage and grief have changed him so radically. He does not make a commitment to help Orestes by taking up for him with the citizens of Argos. He wants to calmly calculate the situation before deciding. Orestes' grandfather – Helen and Clytemnestra's father – appears on stage, attacks Orestes with some strong words, and threatens Menelaus not to take up for Orestes or he, too, will lose his position in Argos.

There is an assembly, but Orestes has nobody close to him to recognize acknowledge and, represent him in the agora. It is difficult for him to be together with others, to be persuasive and reach a favourable consensus. He does not have an external object, another self, to undertake his drives, fears, emotions, and fantasies in his/her reverie and elaborate them before they are returned to him and make him their responsible subject (Freud, 1915/1917; Bion, 1962/1967; Winnicott, 1965/1990).

Orestes claims that he killed his mother to avenge his father and that it was Apollo who led him to matricide. Menelaus does not interfere; he does not take sides, and he does not undertake Orestes' destructiveness as another self to help him own it himself. However, Pylades appears and supports him. He persuades him to go with him to the assembly, to influence it, and to achieve a favourable decision.

Electra is left behind, discussing the two men leaving with the chorus. The messenger brings the news. Orestes and Electra have been sentenced to death by the assembly. Electra mourns and assures Orestes of her love. Orestes, Electra, and Pylades plan to take revenge on Menelaus for his indifference by killing Helen and holding Hermione hostage. Hermione arrives, learns about the sentence from Electra, and wants to help but is lured into the palace where her captors await. One of Helen's slaves exits the palace and announces that when Orestes and Pylades attacked Helen, she suddenly vanished. It is then that Menelaus arrives, sees Orestes on the roof, holding Hermione captive, and calls the people of Argos against the young man.

Orestes threatens to set the palace on fire to kill Hermione, and, in this way, destroys the parental couple. Perhaps he projects his fears of his own violence, which erupts when he is about to form a bond and be a couple with an object. Orestes prepares to set the palace on fire when Apollo appears as the deus ex machina and offers a solution to the impasse. He declares that Helen has ascended to the stars, Orestes will go to Areopagus to be exculpated, he will marry Hermione, and Pylades will marry Electra. Reconciliation is achieved. What kind of reconciliation is this?

From the private to the public house

Adolescents struggle to conquer their sense of self, to become subjects of their experiences and the fantasies that interpret them. They struggle to organise two positions. The first is the concept of the past, the space of their subjective history, where they can place the things that they experience and process psychically. The second one is the concept of 'public', the ability to co-construct with others a space that they will use for public exchanges of private thoughts and feelings. They struggle with the conflict between loyalty to family bonds and social-political bonds.

The development of these two positions is a result of maturation processes and a facilitating environment provided by their parents and their social group (of friends) that allows them to go out in the world and bring home the tragic sense of mortality of time that passes. It allows them to conquer their 'home' where they can co-exist with others.

In adolescence, playing and acting are privileged forms of expression, connecting the infantile part of the self to the need to communicate publicly. In playing and acting, somatic events are connected to sexuality and destructiveness and comprise life experiences with meaningful plots (fantasy).

There are somatic, psychic, and political events located within a plot with a sequence of senses, movements, perceptions, images, representations, and emotional links. They become experiences that can be shared. They are located in a process, a series of changes, that has a beginning, a middle, and an end. This means that a subject can think about them. However, there are events whose connections to one another have been severed. They are incoherent, irrelevant, unrelated. They do not make sense.

I do not refer to unconscious processes, where connections are not evident but still exist in latent associations. I mean that a negative anti-process is in progress, where the self cannot be located in time and space because it falls through 'holes' of time and space that are created through primitive splittings, disavowals, narcissistic and autistic retreats.

I refer to anti-dialectical defences of splitting that attack the emotional links that connect the pre-psychic and psychic elements, self and objects, words and erogenous zones of the body, internal and external reality, past and present. Without such links, a psyche and a society cannot produce meaning with subjective and common sense.

The emotions freeze. Then, the self does not keep a psychic distance from the objects and does not allow for a latent period so that it can return at a later time to give meaning to the experiences. The self does not use the findings of fantasies and emotions as lenses through which it can distinguish and locate the objects in time and space so that it can lose them, mourn them, and symbolise them. Object losses that cannot be mourned resist being rendered public. They cannot be publicly shared. They do not sound sincere to – or persuade – the self and others.

There are early and traumatic events that do not exist, for we, as subjects, are not there to experience them because we split our emotions. Our emotions guarantee that we feel alive, real, and present. When emotions are unbearable, and their pain is extreme, we split them. Splitting of affects eradicates the subject. Apart from splitting, we are also relieved from being a subject with the employment of experiences and fantasies of fusion of self and object that cause depersonalisation. Many of the adolescent's rough contacts with external reality (accidents, provoked reactions of others, self-injuries) are meant to give them a sense of existing and being real.

If an adolescent repeats unrepresented experiences and employs primitive splitting, her/his psyche-soma is invaded by excitations, sudden silences, and part objects. This adolescent cannot create a personal history or a public life from the presentations of his private experiences, which he expresses and discharges but never discloses. She/he does not take a place in the world. She/he always checks out but never leaves.[1]

We encounter the inability to use the public space in Euripides' *Orestes*, in Shakespeare's *Richard II*, and in Chekhov's *The Cherry Orchard*. These characters are noble yet weak; they evade reality and live their life as if it were a blissful journey. They feel like a spoiled child without discipline, consistency, and maturity. They hate the truth and only want to hear good news. Then, a crucial moment comes when they discover reality. They experience betrayal from those around them and feel all alone, left without support. Finally, they painfully separate from their primary illusion as they take a hard road of suffering towards self-knowledge.

These characters are unable to get involved in an oedipal condition and live inside reality and time. They lose their home, and yet they do not react. They interpret the public space based on their personal assumptions. They fight their battle on the brink between abstract public affairs and personal things.

Euripides, Shakespeare, and Chekhov create situations that are incredibly familiar to us. At the same time, we are confronted with a torn tissue of meanings that allows us to see the deeper experiences of psychic life right before our eyes. Our attempt to 'heal' the traumatically severed links consists of the creation of transference experiences. These are 'revelation' events through which we reach the sense of tragic; we undertake the responsibility of our fate and turn it into destiny.

The social fabric has already been ruptured

In Euripides' *Orestes*, the social fabric has been torn and cannot be repaired. It cannot hold people, especially young ones called to carry the torch of tradition and push history forward. Helen cannot visit her sister's grave to bring offerings. She is afraid that if she makes a public appearance, she will be ridiculed by the mob. Later, it is Orestes and Electra that are threatened to be stoned.

Orestes wants to speak publicly, but he is a shadow of his former self. He cannot articulate a persuasive, drastic speech in front of the people. In this instance, there is a split between an erotic mother (Helen) and an insufficient environment mother (a broken social fabric) that cannot hold Orestes. Specifically, the conflict between private and family bonds and the public sphere is rendered tragic. We have Orestes with his psychic and family ties on the one hand and the mob in the agora that will determine his and Electra's fate on the other.

Caring for ourselves is up to us. But if we make our private thoughts public, we bring ourselves into conflict with family ties. When Britton (1994) studied publication anxiety, he conducted an in-depth investigation of the conflict between publication, communication, and affiliation. Humans are political animals. They fear that they may be ostracised from their social group. They feel alienated, like having fallen off the world, if their social ties are broken.

Euripides helps us contemplate the differences between the people and the mob. The mob behaves like a perverted parent who confuses the child's language of tenderness with the language of passion (Ferenczi, 1933/1955). It threatens that our legitimate illusion of narcissistic union will be destroyed, and at the same time, offers protection from its threats – as long as silence is imposed. We identify with our attackers, assuming the guilt that they themselves cannot feel. We split ourselves. One part terrorises, and the other cannot speak.

Orestes cannot speak because he does not feel safe that his true self has the right to not communicate; that it is protected from being exposed (Winnicott, 1965/1990). Orestes' speech could be dramatic but is ineffective. It lacks the polyphony of the signs that connect thought and words with their somatic roots, which render the meaning-producing relationships adequate. It lacks this polyphony because Orestes is not sufficiently differentiated. His speech cannot be an effective declaration. It is not poetic. It is not drastic. It is not the end result of an inner process of loss, mourning, and symbolisation. It sounds like a lie. It cannot become public. It is not an assembly where people and their experiences come together to make a persuasive story.

Menelaus also represents the failure of a perverted superego. When the functions of the superego – which accompanies us with its advice, restrains us with its moral guidelines and prohibitions, and guides us with its instructions – fall apart, we feel that we are not real, we are not authentic, we are usurpers of the positions we occupy. We feel that we have no right to speak. We feel that we have deceived everybody; we are impostors, and this will be revealed very soon. Like Orestes, we fall ill, we reach an impasse. We constantly doubt we become inactive, we leave by not moving, and we waste time. We do not use objects; we misuse them or waste them. We take revenge in order not to change. We remain victims. We have no adequate internal object to confirm our investments. We cannot open our mouths to speak for ourselves and say the words in public in order to be with others and persuade them. We are the ailment of our polis.

Today, we often feel that we do not have an adequate public sphere to envelop us. We do not have a guide. We feel at a loss. We are not politically correct. A mob has decided that we have spoken in an unacceptable manner, and we are ostracised. The mob in the agora of Argos does not function as a paternal superego that guides and accompanies the struggle of the individual's superego to be integrated. It functions as a primitive, cruel early maternal superego.

We hope that the Athenian supreme court (Areopagus) will function as a mature oedipal paternal superego. Again, we know that the roots of the benign paternal law always lie in the preoedipal primitive forces of violence. Euripides, like Klein, Bion, and Winnicott, tell Freud that we cannot take early maternal care for granted and begin the story from the Oedipus complex. We have to take into account the failures of early maternal care to hold and contain the infant's fears of death.

Early traumatic ruptures of the development cause confusion between the superego, the ego's ideal, and the ideal ego. The superego and the ego's ideal contain the dimension of differentiation of time and space. Conversely, the ideal ego abolishes time and space. It eradicates moral motives. The subject's narcissism is then based on the object that now assumes enormous dimensions. The ideal ego invades the ego.

In *Orestes*, Menelaus is not able to assume the role of the father as an object of admiration, keeps the distance as another self, an external subject, and is available to the child for primary identification. He refused to understand him and communicate with him in an effective manner. He refused to assume the role ascribed to him by the adolescent. He, thus, rendered himself an omnipotent object with no qualifications and no abilities. He became a "slave to Necessity" (715–716).

Orestes approaches the limits of absolute destruction. He is then overwhelmed by the fear that a non-represented unspoken trauma of annihilation will be revived. And he identifies with the annihilation. He turns it into his purpose, which, of course, is under his control. This is the morality of nihilism. He identifies with the source of the fear of eviction and becomes the harbinger of destruction.

If the object loses its functional value, the ego's function is undermined. They are both invested with negative narcissism that is connected with destructiveness. If the child has experienced periods where the parents failed in an extreme way to hold the ego's needs, then the primary identification channels overflow with emotions of traumatic tension.

If it is not possible for the excitations to be represented, then the object-mother is used to provide an environment. The object-mother is perverted in order to cover (patch up) the deficits of the environment mother who failed to secure stable, reliable care. Through projective identification, an exciting relationship emerges between the child and the object-mother that creates a reassuring illusion. The adolescent focuses his/her attention and diverts ours towards an external perception (in a perverse, fetishistic manner) in order to escape contact with the reality of the object's otherness.

Orestes attempts to resolve the oedipal conflict in a manic way. He revives the trauma. The external destructiveness increases the internal one, which in turn increases the fear of attacks. Orestes, in a manic delirium, identifies with the attacker, threatens to kill Helen and her daughter Hermione, and then sets the palace on fire. On the one hand, we hear the omnipotent part of the self that wants to undertake the functions of the object and place itself entirely at its service. On the other hand, we listen to the real, vulnerable part of the self that wants to be understood. Orestes is deprived of help. At the same time, he rejects any possibility of consolation. He is overwhelmed by a profound anguish. He does not have a place to put himself in, a position on which to stand. He appropriates the parental role.

Without narcissistic support, adolescents split their emotions; they cannot create an emotional experience in which they could be present as subjects. They evict themselves and are deprived of a somato-psychic aliveness, of proof that they exist and they are real. An example is that of an adolescent 'healing' his depressive mother. A depressed mother is isolated from her social group. The decision about her life is made in the 'agora' while she awaits the verdict, confined in an endless mournful cycle of nostalgic, painful investment in a lost object. If a sufficient social space does not exist, the supportive framework of positive narcissism is absent. There are no mirrors to reflect the investments of the subject. No narcissistic support can be given to the adolescent by the mother's lost objects who have no voice to speak for themselves (who are deprived of public representation). The adolescent identifies with the disinvesting mother.

Orestes represents the peaceless mortal conflict between Electra and her mother. Aegisthus wants to kill her. Clytemnestra marries her off to a simple farmer. To avoid being killed, Electra 'depressively' accepts having her house stolen from her and living with a husband of humble descent. In essence, she remains without a marital bed. This is what her name, Electra, literally means.

In psychotherapy, a girl in the latency stage was struggling to postpone the inevitable separation from the primary object and mourning. She believed that her father would wait for her and marry her. She unconsciously perceived that her father did not tell her that this was impossible, not because of any practical reasons but because there is a natural prohibition against incest. This never ends in the life of this girl. It is brought up in life again and again when the opportunities allow it.

The oedipal situation is a structure that inherently contains its own resolution, which is one's ability to have a purpose, a course, and a destination, rather than being a possibility that is never realised, thus perpetuating the narcissistic disappointments that constitute the basis of the psychopathology of people who cannot commit themselves.

Critchley (2019, pp. 322–325) explains: Instead of a catharsis of rationality, neat narratives, and a happy ending, Euripides exposes the absolute acting of tragedy towards something mad, uncontrollable, and ethically shocking. At the end of the play, Orestes, Pylades, and Electra sit on the rooftop of the palace, arguing fiercely with Menelaus and his troops, who are ordered to kill them. Orestes threatens Hermione (Helen's daughter) with his sword. The three of them hold lit torches, ready to burn down the palace. It is an ugly moment. An impasse. Suddenly, Apollo, a deus ex machina, appears and gives his prophetic instructions. Orestes will marry Hermione. Pylades will marry Electra, and he will be happy. Orestes, after a year of exile, will return to Argos as a king. In the meantime, Helen will be transformed into a goddess who shines in the night sky like a star that will guide the mariners. The apparent solution of the deus ex machina solves nothing in reality. It is a hallucination. It leads the experience of the outcome to completion. The deus ex machina shows the inherent irrationality of the wish for organic integrity, a clear solution, and a settled outcome. It is a false solution, a false reconciliation. It is cheating, a fulfilment in reality of the hallucinated wish.

However, the deus ex machina can be thought of as the first science fiction example of time travelling. Euripides asks us to imagine the present from the point of view of somebody that comes from the future: What would happen if . . . ? First you imagine, you believe in an illusion, you allow the reality to bring disillusion, and then you construct a symbol that brings the future.

The somatic excitations should cross the border and be represented in the psyche. This is an ego need. It requires that the ego relate to another ego in search of means that will contribute to the psychic elaboration of un-represented traces. It is thus that an experience is completed, fulfilled, and rendered meaningful. It is no longer a ghost eradicating all that is real. It is symbolised.

In cases of early narcissistic traumas, the person turns into a fanatical, devoted saviour-warrior, a determined avenger who knows that the end is not a new beginning but rather a nihilistic obliteration of objects. The individual identifies with the machine and lives a mechanistic life so that time does not pass. He wastes time, and then time wastes him, as Shakespeare's Richard II said.

Oedipus lives in time. At Colonus, he heard the omen from the gods that the time of his death had arrived. He brought Theseus as the only witness of the place of his death. No one else should know. Only the ruler of the city and his heirs are burdened by the duty of knowing. It is their destiny. At the end of his life, he reaches the end of his tragic story with a revelation.

There is no end to our thought, we continue to transform reality. In order to do this, we must respect the existence of the unknown, the unformed. This means that we can never achieve knowledge. We will always question whether what we think corresponds to something perceivable in reality. Our relationship to reality is based on trial and error. We do not know the limits in advance. We learn them from experience. This is what Orestes did. We also need good fortune. This uncertainty constitutes the limit of our omnipotence. This is the essence of democracy. We think, and this is the manner in which we do so, and we make any decisions based on this thinking.

Note

1 Paraphrasing the Eagle's rock hit of 1976, "Hotel California".

References

Bion, W. R. (1967). A theory of thinking. In *Second thoughts. Selected papers on psychoanalysis*. New York: Jason Aronson. (Original work published 1962)

Britton, R. (1994). Publication anxiety: Conflict between communication and affiliation. *International Journal of Psychoanalysis*, 75, 1213–1224.

Critchley, S. (2019). *Tragedy, the Ancient Greeks and US*. London: Profile Books.

Ferenczi, S. (1955). The Confusion of tongues between adults and the child. The language of tenderness and of passion. In E. Mosbacher et al. (Trans.), *Final contributions to the problems and methods of psychoanalysis*. London: Maresfield Reprints. (Original work published 1933)

Freud, S. (1917). Mourning and melancholia. *S. E., 14*. (Original work published 1915)

Winnicott, D. W. (1990). *The maturational processes and the facilitating environment*. London: Karnac. (Original work published 1965)

Chapter 5

Euripides' suppliant women
Mourning and femininity[1]

The ideas of psychoanalysis and those of Euripides' *Suppliant Women* (or *The Suppliants*) meet in a tragic reading of politics. This reading enables us to link the foundations of the subject and our social institutions to the helplessness of the infant and the integration of split-off psychic elements. Through Euripides' tragedy, we can think of the many faces of Hubris in public life today. We can think about our fractured societies that 'heal' themselves through populism, autarchy, cruelty, fakery, and the culture of lying.

A psychoanalytic assessment of the key political themes of the play can be made by considering the phenomenon of Hubris in public life indirectly through its transformations in tragic poetry. In tragedy, we can find a mirror in which to reflect. In the eyes of the poet, we see how we feel inside, who we are, and our psychic and social realities.

Euripides' painful diagnosis is that politics is a struggle to understand and integrate split-off, 'supernatural' forces and unknown limits that lie beyond the order of politics, words, and reason. These forces come from the past, and psychoanalysis calls them unconscious. Politics is a struggle to give our society a sense of the tragic.

Euripides' *Suppliant Women* is interpreted by scholars as representing the struggle of the Athenians to implement laws replacing mythical and religious beliefs and maintain a moderate democracy based on acknowledging individual and group responsibility for actions and beliefs.

We can think that the tragic poet proposes himself as the modern prophet needed for the politics of the democratic polis. The laws of the polis are linked to – but do not replace – mythical and religious beliefs. The modern democratic polis is based on the rule of law, thinking, and change.

Following Euripides' text, we can think that in our societies, we need a transitional space of politics where contradictions are tolerated and can co-exist without being split off or glossed over, covered up, with individual (character) and group (institutional) compromises (sacrifices of autonomy and authenticity). We need to take sides, confront each other, and find creative ways to deal with conflicts.

Euripides presents politics in a moderate society as the struggle to recognise and deal with the irreducible splittings that are inherent in human life. On the one hand,

DOI: 10.4324/9781032712864-6

we need to compromise and create equality, reciprocity, mutual benefit, and harmony of peace. On the other hand, we need to tolerate – not obliterate – contradictions and differences, which are necessary preconditions that generate conflicts.

The human world and its mental life are variegated, motley (Freud, 1930). While politicians often become entertainers who gloss over differences, poets present a painfully accurate diagnosis of human life and its politics. *The Suppliants* present the unconscious conflicts involved in forming and maintaining a democratic polis. The foundations of the polis are linked to the integration of split-off elements (mourning and femininity). The aims of scholars who study the play correspond to psychoanalysis' work towards understanding the psychic and social reality of politics.

In *The Suppliant Women*, politics in a democratic polis is the struggle of humans to establish the rule of law and integrate – not replace – primitive forces. This struggle takes a dramatic course in a crisis when the polis is in transition and in need of re-inventing its identity. Drama allows a stage where these past unassimilated traces of self and object (our ghosts) can be played out so that we recognise them. Through the tragic plot, they come out of their half-existence and exist, being placed out there in a specific place and time. Putting our 'ghosts' into words, actions, and feelings puts them to rest. We can then live with the living and keep the dead in memory.

Politics in a democratic polis is the art that manages the tensions inherent in social institutions while at the same time opening them up to unknown new areas. Politics is a struggle to hold unbridgeable contradictions, that is, split-off, impossible links leading to impasses, and to transform them into paradoxes that we can tolerate in transitional spaces.

Through ancient drama, Athens interprets the myths with words and actions, transforming them into a tragic plot. Athens, also through this drama, enters into the myths of other cities. The myth of Theseus crosses over to the myth of the seven generals who were killed in Thebes. Eleusis becomes their burial ground (Storey, 2008). *The Suppliants* converge with the myth of the battle to the death of Oedipus' children.

The plot

The Suppliants is one of Euripides' two political plays (the other being *The Children of Heracles*). It is a political play in the sense that it uses the problems of human fellowship as its artistic material. In this sense, it is ecumenical (Zunt, 1955).

Burian (1985, p. 129) argues convincingly: "This play, more than any other in the canon, cries out for political interpretation, and it has received many". Some interpretations tried to isolate politics *in* the play. Burian suggests that "It is the politics *of* the play that demands attention, the politics encoded in the structure of its discourse . . . its political codes". What Euripides perceives in his world influences his choices of expression. However, his choices are made for internal reasons. "In the last analysis, we take Euripides seriously as a political thinker only if we take him seriously as a dramatist".

I agree with those who believe that *Supplliant Women* is a profound and moving but neglected masterpiece. The play does not just give us material for interpretation. It constitutes a political 'working through' of conflicts and traumas. Euripides makes a moving comment on his polis' struggles, woes, and greatness.

He wrote *The Suppliants* around 424 BC, seven years after the beginning of the Peloponnesian War. That year, the Athenians were negotiating with the Thebans over collecting their dead from the recent battle of Delium, in which Euripides' friend, Socrates, had also fought as a simple soldier.

In *Suppliant Women*, the seven generals from Argos who had marched against Thebes were defeated and killed before its gates. They had fought on the side of Polynices against his brother, Eteocles. Both brothers were killed in battle, fulfilling the curse of their father, Oedipus. Creon, the new King of Thebes, forbade the burial of the seven generals.

Their elderly mothers, together with Adrastus, King of Argos, came from Argos to Eleusis to find Aethra, who had gone there to prostrate herself at the sanctuary of Demeter and Kore. They went to beg her to intervene and ask her son, Theseus, King of Athens, to persuade Creon to hand over their deceased sons to them to bury.

Theseus appears afterwards on stage, having been invited by his mother. Initially, he refuses to help Adrastus because he has sent his own army into destruction without circumspection. Ultimately, Theseus' mother convinces him to take action. If the seven generals had committed a crime, their deaths would have been severe and adequate punishment. It is not necessary for them to also be deprived of a burial.

Theseus turns around. He allows himself to be influenced by his mother's reasoning, and he changes his mind. He then begins his campaign by speaking and democratically convincing the citizens of Athens. He also prepares an army so as to recover the dead by force if the Thebans are not persuaded to give them up peacefully.

Euripides' tragedy is an early statement of what democracy means. Real, living people meet in person at the agora and debate the truth. It is not about having the logic of words and reason on one side and the logic of passions on the other. What the people share in their meetings in the assembly is the passion for thinking together (Aisenstein, 2019).

The herald appointed by Thebes arrives and presents their arrogant demands with the audacity of a terrorist. He inserts the logic of the inevitable that leads to war. Theseus protests the superiority of democracy. In Athens, the ruler, the assembly, and the meetings with ambassadors of foreign cities are all simply political tools. They are not sources of authoritarian power. Athens defends the rule of law. If Creon does not agree to negotiate and peacefully hand over the dead, Athens will go to war.

The Athenians, with Theseus as their leader, fought and won. They brought the seven dead generals back to Eleusis, burned them on a pyre, and delivered their ashes to their sons. Only for one, Capaneus – the sacred of the seven because he was struck down by Zeus' lightning bolt on top of the walls of Thebes – Theseus prepared a separate pyre.

It is then that Evadne, Capaneus' wife, appears out of nowhere, mad from the anguish of her loss. Despite her father Iphis' pleas, Evadne, maniacal due to her unbearable grief, commits suicide by throwing herself into her husband's funeral pyre. We can think that she is pushed by an intense desire to reunite with her husband in an eternal marriage that destroys reality.

In the end, another woman, the goddess Athena, appears to teach Athenians a lesson on politics. She advises Theseus to demand a sworn, practical political exchange from Adrastus and the Argives as payback for what he has done for them.

> Athena tells him ... that another kind of logos is needed ... an oath to be broken at incalculable peril. For the *memory (mnēmēn)* on which Theseus relies, Athena substitutes the concrete *token (mnēmeia)* of a bronze tripod ... to be "set up in Delphi as an unchanging witness of what happened there".
>
> (Burian, 1985, p. 153)

We can imagine that the symbols (bronze tripod, etc.) are vessels of historical time. They have their roots in infant development. The original inscription of a trace of an experience is also an embodiment of the time of the experience. The experiences are originally inscribed in forms that are unknown to us.

When, later in life, an original experience is created anew, its embodied time is enacted. We can think that something similar happens in a society with the management of symbols on which the oaths are inscribed.

The tragic position

Ancient tragedy stages the shattering of omnipotence (Hubris). Omnipotence is based on impossible links that lead to impasses. The impasses are maintained by splitting processes. A tragic plot consists of the transformations of internal impossible links in external reality. The impasses become paradoxes of the tragedy and the politics.

The tragic plot holds in time the processes of being and becoming the subject that thinks. Before anything else happens, humans need to attain the 'tragic position', the status of being a separate entity. Adequate maternal care holds in time the ego needs of the infant that gradually emerge as a separate subject, thinking and living inside time and reality. After the separation from the primary union, humans struggle to recover from the shock of the loss of omnipotence through the use of transitional objects and phenomena.

The tragic position is the fundamental drama humans go through when they suffer the loss of omnipotence and emerge from the primary union as thinking subjects. Through words and actions, they intervene in the external reality. Through playing, children select a sample of psychic life and play it out in the external reality (Winnicott, 1971). They struggle to internalise their drives of love and hate, their omnipotence, and bisexuality. They reach ambivalence, abandon their arrogance, tolerate the unknown, and create their interiority.

Euripides' *Suppliants* presents a complex political vision of a complicated world where people struggle to withstand reality and construct its multiple meanings with words and actions, which connect them to other speaking subjects in the public domain. People have beliefs and ideals towards which they strive. Their struggles are never conclusive because human lives follow unexpected turns brought about by irrational forces. Humans get together to create and find reality.

Politics is an answer to the question of how much reality the citizens and their city can bear. How much meaning and truth can they struggle with? How much shock can the bridge sustain when action is taken to cross the borders and transgress the lines of the unknown?

When an individual or a society moves towards a new integration, a paranoiac fear of attack from outside is raised (Winnicott, 1988). Theseus is suspicious and defends against integrating Adrastus' supplication as a threat to the coherence of his city. Aethra offers a different kind of defence to the coherence of the polis. She offers the mourning work, which allows us to renounce our infantile omnipotence and bind the drives (Salonen, 2018; Aisenstein, 2019).

The city needs men with political responsibility. It is held together by those who preserve the human and divine laws. The dramatic relevance of Aethra's argument lies in her linking political considerations with religious, ethical, and personal arguments that call for action. This deep feminine intelligence contains the seed of the tragic, that is, the emergence of a subject from a primary union.

The subject is not the centre of initiative; it is subjected to 'mysterious' forces that come from an unknown past and demand from us to bear and undertake personally their responsibility. The emerging subject retains a basic element from the original mother/infant union. This is the feminine capacity of being receptive and passive towards an experience to which one becomes a subject. Aethra proposes that the coherence of the social fabric depends on internalising our omnipotence, drives, and psychic bisexuality. However, in reality, these processes always remain incomplete. Our debts to society will never be settled.

In breaking away from the primary union, humans emerge as tragic subjects who undertake the responsibility of giving meaning and integrating – and learning from – the experiences they create and share with other selves on the stage of everyday life. Euripides realises, as psychoanalysis does, that humans hate restrictions imposed by the meaning-giving and integration processes and seek the primitive pleasure afforded them by the annihilating attack on any line of difference and order of the object and the thinking processes.

Aisenstein (2019) remarked: "Functioning should not be confused with thinking". Thoughts require a subject who thinks of them and an internal object that confirms the investment in them, as Green (1991/2001) has observed. In his work on Negation, Freud (1925) described the original 'no' of the child that separates inside from outside and becomes the origin of the subject. By contrast, the splitting of the ego is a rift that never heals (Freud, 1940). A conformist false self is built on this non-dialectical rift of recognition and simultaneous denial of reality.

In *Suppliant Women,* humans yoke the necessity to represent, differentiate and integrate (internalise, subjectivise) their drives, omnipotence, and bisexuality, as these are expressed in the passions of mourning and femininity, which lie beyond any order of words or reason.

A tragic plot begins to unravel when the subjects dare go down the painful path of mourning work that leads to internalising this necessity in their psychic and public lives. They become tragic subjects. The plot of *The Suppliants* is tragic; it shows the struggle of humans to emerge as thinking subjects, to mourn their lost omnipotence, to create their transitional space of playing, and to constitute an oedipal situation.

Burian (1985, p. 155) concludes:

> Those who have tried to understand the play as patriotic drama, and equally those who have seen in it a thoroughgoing satirical or ironic intent, seem to expect it to preach its truth. It withholds that comfort, insisting that even admirable aspirations and achievements are beset by uncertainty and subject to distortion by passion and the passage of time. Its complex structure corresponds to a complex vision. The Suppliant Women . . . is nevertheless political to the very core, a tragedy of men and women doomed not to heroic isolation, but to an imperfect society, for better or worse.

Politics is the struggle of humans to integrate irreducible, split-off elements that are linked to the work of mourning and are expressed in mythical, religious, and poetic acts. An important achievement of the work of mourning is that the subject emerges and is able to think, fuse the drives, separate, and link internal with external reality. Politics enables humans to negotiate alliances of community, sustain participation in a common culture, construct and find a shared reality, and allow an open-ended process of transformations to continue.

Myths play an important role in politics. They contain grains of untransformed reality, which makes them immortal. These elements of unelaborated violent reality give the weight of historical truth and convincing reality to the inscription of modern written laws and the foundation of institutions. Humans assign (give the right to express) their violence to the city. Believing in and identifying with their myths (heroes) makes citizens feel that they themselves, as well as their city, are immortal.

The work of mourning

The staging of *Suppliant Women* is the burial of the dead of war, the symbolisation of the reality of loss, the painful work of mourning, and the separation between the dead and the living. Where do those who died in war go? Are they placed where they belong, in the past, as our living memories? Or do they become haunting eternal undead ghosts appearing in incomprehensible displays of private and public enactments in demonic repetition compulsions?

The bedrock of reality is a metaphor – the rock is often used in *The Suppliants* – for the unmourned traumatic losses. The time of separation, the time that passes linearly, is a painful loss that humans have to bear (1112, 1113). We have two options. The work of mourning that gives us the future, the succession of time, and the next generation, which guarantees our sense of immortality. In contrast, the compulsion to repeat gives us eternity; the traumas are compulsively repeated and never completely mourned.

Euripides presents a reality that is by definition traumatic and becomes unbearable when we live as prisoners of a regime of real oppression, or in a prison of the compulsion to repeat, or captives of the lost object that we have narcissistically identified with and let its shadow fall upon the ego. In such cases, we sacrifice our subjectivity, literally offering ourselves to fill the gaps of society, to become shields and bridges, to heal the splits. Euripides, in *The Suppliants*, begins with the arrogance that abolishes all limits and promises the extreme pleasure of absolute freedom from all restrictions.

The tragedy begins with a holy place, Eleusis, and an inevitable separation. Then it introduces the encounter with a new object, Theseus, that raises anticipation for the future, mobilises memories from the past, and starts an unknown, unpredictable course of events, a process, confirming once again that history continues; there is always a next step, a potential change.

The Suppliants ends with the prediction of another war and another catastrophe. The children of the seven generals, the hope of the mothers of those who were killed, will continue the war in the name of their fathers. The tragedy speaks of our inability to ponder our own death (479–483).[2] When the time comes to decide to go to war, we always think that the others will die, not us. Some wars are just. But Hubris is part of human life. The Athenians defend the rule of law. Yet they recognise that the opposite force exists in the world, the Hubris of Thebes, of anti-Athens (Zeitlin, 1986). They recognise and converse with the Hubris of Thebes with the intervention of a transitional space, Eleusis. Argos is the other anti-Athens, also a source of identification in this drama: an ambiguous city, a potential ally or enemy, reckless, incomplete, on the verge of collapsing, but also capable of being restored.

What does remain? The struggle (550). This is what Euripides offers Athenians as a solution. They should continue to struggle for the survival of their object and the self. This is what politics means: to struggle.

Ancient tragedy puts in our minds the unthinkable of which we are deeply aware. We are compelled to internalise it, notwithstanding the fear involved. Then, "we can understand the gripping power of Oedipus Rex, in spite of all the objections that reason raises against the presupposition of fate" (Freud, 1897/1954, p. 223).

Oedipus struggles to know why the plague has visited Thebes; he wants to know who is responsible, and he wants to know himself. Not everybody attains the capability of separation, mourning, the Oedipal complex, and the sense of reality. The play does not end until the sons of the dead assume the guilt as responsible subjects of their fathers' deaths. No father can die until he finds someone to kill him and take his place. No one can die until a body is retrieved and identified. No father's remains can be buried until the subject guilty of his death comes forward to assume responsibility.

A father who is killed becomes God, as well as a totemic animal victim, triumphant in the end. He then becomes God and a king, whose authority is defined by voluntary obedience and freedom, by commitment instead of submission that corresponds to perpetual guilt and rebellion by the sons (Freud, 1912–1913, p. 151).

Green (1980/1985) notes: The meeting with Oedipus made Theseus forsake divinity and choose to live on the earth. By assuming man's fate, Theseus became an exemplar of what he was struggling to become the subject of. He chose to live within time.

The myths of the Suppliants and Oedipus show an evolution towards the foundation of the realm of politics. Forced by the epidemic that erupted in Thebes, Oedipus began to search for the cause, only to turn inside himself in order to discover and internalise his fantasies of omnipotence, his bisexuality, and his drives; in the end, he became a subject accountable for them, a truly tragic, political, subject.

Beyond the political order lies an untamed land populated with early unsymbolised experiences that are organised with deep splits, the archaic logic of which the poets help us think. Out of the horror of the abyss, humans create the horrible Sphinx as a permanent habitat of the splits of psychic and social life. The Sphinx, a prehistoric monster, is our gateway to anxieties of extinction in a black hole. We can think that this black hole is transformed into a secret place of Oedipus' ascension, on which the power of the leaders of Athens is founded. Oedipus' time had come, but he had no place to die. He went to Colonus, Athens.

In Athens, Oedipus was granted asylum by Theseus. Athens had the fortitude to integrate horrifying strangers. Theseus accompanied Oedipus to the secret place of his ascension. Only Theseus knew this place, and he was only allowed to reveal it to his own successor. Each new leader of Athens knew the secret place. From this knowledge, he derived his power and undertook, on behalf of the people, the immortality project of each generation. Political order is based on the oedipal situation.

The feminine core

A feminine intelligence lies at the foundation of the polis. Politics is the struggle of humans to integrate irreducible, split-off elements of the feminine core of existence that are expressed in mythical, religious, and poetic acts. Much of Euripides' use of argumentation depicts the human effort to buffer the acute paranoid fear of attack from outside when integration takes place. Paranoia is inherent in an organisation. It is a disturbance of the linking between psychic and social reality that simplifies complex things. There is a parallel between the neo-reality of the paranoiac and the early relationship between a daughter and her mother (Green, 1972).

A middle-aged woman would wake up at 4 am to clean the kitchen floor from spilled food and leftovers, evidence that her two teenage sons had returned home late. She was again excluded from the oedipal primal scene. She feared that violent passions and internal conflicts would awaken and destroy the order of her world. She compulsively tried to put things in order, to say a "no" with her body, and also to discharge her tension with her muscular effort. Her aggression was also an anal expression of her movement to separate from her mother. She then recalled a family custom they had when she was little. Her parents were separated. She visited her mother's house on holidays. Her periodic return to the maternal home allowed me to remind her of the myth of Demeter and her daughter Persephone. She said that in the evening, the day before she was due to travel to return to her father's home, where she lived, she, her mother, and her grandmother silently cleaned the house meticulously because if it were spotless, she would return to the maternal home. This was a ritual of silent mourning for three generations of women. It was very different from her cleaning up the kitchen at 4 am, which aimed at attacking her thinking and exhausting her bodily self. It entailed the assumption of the passive feminine position. The maternal silent mourning, together with the maternal reverie, was the work of the vigilant mother of a newborn baby, whose nursery is frequented by unmourned ghosts of the family. It is a work that contains and binds the devastating drives. It places the feminine in the core of the self.[3]

Central to *The Suppliants'* tragedy is the Demeter-Kore (mother-daughter) drama. Both had Eleusis as their stage. Evadne's suicide is presented as a sacrifice of the individual for the common good and as an act of freedom. She opens the way for Athena to take her place and give Athenians the truth about politics and for the Epigonoi (the children of the seven slain generals) to undertake future actions of revenge.

Euripides brings the lamenting mothers to the agora. Aethra tells us that we can take the complex and painful reality of motherhood as a model for our social wellbeing. The lamenting mothers seek to represent and internalise the loss of their children. This can only be done through the painful work of mourning (Freud, 1915/1917).

In sharp contrast, at the end of the tragedy, Evadne performs a 'marriage with death'. She throws herself into the pyre in order to be united with her husband for eternity, to accompany him on the deathbed of loneliness. Evadne renounces her bond with her father, Iphis, and her sons; she destroys the reality of time and surrenders to the flames so as not to be separated from her husband.

Moreover, the self-sacrifice of Evadne opens a window to the Eleusinian Mysteries, where the initiated secure eternal life. Iphis reminds us: "*Femininity is a riddle*" (1064). Freud (1937) discovered that both men and women found it very hard to accept their femininity.

The Eleusinian Mysteries also represent the sacred union of the infant with the primary mother, the access to the feminine element of being, and the unknown underworld of early exchanges of humans with the primary mother.

These early exchanges take place in an extreme asymmetry between a helpless infant facing the reality of death and the mother. With her adequate responses, the mother helps the child literally survive and inscribe these early experiences in traces of memory. These early links of unity between an infant and its mother are sacred in all societies. They are the foundations of all societies. The functions of linking, forming unities, transforming meanings, and integrating wholes maintain their sacred nature throughout life in the internal reality of individuals and in the social-external reality.

Similarly, there is something holy and sacred in the bond between comrades in arms. In Euripides' tragedies, women are sacrificed, Iphigeneia, Evadne, and Polyxena, in order to remind us of the altruism that we see in battle. In battle, you defend the life of your comrade, who has entrusted his own life to your hands and depends on you for survival, as the infant depends on its mother. The ethical responsibility for the fellow human being begins in infancy (Freud, 1895).

The Suppliant Women seek, in Eleusis, the wisdom of the feminine element of being, the capacity to tolerate passivity and accept the inevitability of reality, to transform reality and form alliances with confidence, without fear of surrendering to others. The play concludes with Athena inviting the Athenians to create meeting places with allies, transitional spaces, and to focus on politics as an art that links internal and external events into mutual information and signification.

Humans fight and destroy, but in the end, their survival depends on their capacity to think, recognise reality and form alliances. Their politics is incomplete, but there is always Kairos (appropriate measure, favourable time, time).

Two deities, representing irreconcilable aspects of the world, preside over the play. One is Demeter, the goddess of fertility, marriage, and the cycle of life, death, and rebirth; the other is Athena, the goddess of wisdom, political discourse, and military action.

> The two framing deities, present only at the beginning and the end of the play, set as foreground the world of human activity and individual tragedy against a wider background; the context of genetic and universal forces (or divine beings personifying those universals.
>
> (Scully, 1995, pp. 4–5)

Demeter, the holder of the Eleusinian land, symbolises earth (the mother). Athena is not born by a woman and has nothing to do with feminine matters, such as mother-daughter loss, mourning, or melancholy. However, both goddesses, Demeter (with grief and rage) and Athena (with political and military action), meet on the never-ending demand for blood vengeance.

Demeter represents the 'supernatural' forces of femininity, fertility, and primary identification. She represents what Winnicott calls the 'being'. Athena represents the 'doing', which Winnicott (1971, pp. 72–85) assigns to instinctual drives. She was born of her father's intelligence. Athena is the necessary complement to Demeter, who bears the pacific spirit. However, 'being' and 'doing' are intertwined.

The sanctuary of Eleusis and the agora of Athens, Demeter, and Athena, are two aspects of the polis. Demeter links us with mourning and femininity; her mystery is Panhellenic and offers a 'communal experience' of light and hope, bridging the gap between death and immortality. Athena, the goddess of Athens, offers boundaries of institutions and frames of separations that are the foundations of civilisation. Zeus, the father of the gods, is always somewhere, working in mysterious ways on the psychic and social scene.

Politics lie in a space of struggle between these two irreconcilable goddesses, two aspects of the identity of the polis. They lie in the transitional space between illusion and disillusion, between primary identifications and object ties, and between the pleasure and reality principles. The tension between pleasure and reality principles is never quite settled.

Also, the conflict between male and female elements is inherent in the foundations of the polis. The constant negotiation in *The Suppliants* does not aim at resolving the conflict between paternal and maternal identifications that constitute psychic bisexuality. It aims to maintain the tension between them, from which creative solutions are generated.

We can associate the Eleusinian Mysteries with the horror we feel when we are suddenly confronted with an uncanny experience (Freud, 1919). Eleusis is the place in which death and birth alternate. Here, Euripides casts birth, marriage, death, and war together, which suddenly bring forth the unfamiliar, what is outside the hearth of the house, outside the subject, and the safety of the city's stable frames.

The word of the law has its roots in magic, which bears the curse and is transformed into a religious oath and prayer (wish), social convention, and, ultimately, written law. In a basic substratum of primary aloneness and intimacy, a primordial matrix of intersubjectivity, undifferentiated traces of the self and the object are inscribed. These symbiotic elements are deposited initially into the mother (our first legislator), then the family, and they are, finally, laid down in the settings of our institutions.

In these frames, we 'deposit' our immortality. These frames are constantly disturbed, our individual and social narcissistic integrity is overturned, and the undifferentiated traces of experience are liberated, available for new meaning and integration. Then, new forms of sociality and galaxies of subjectivity emerge but never get resolved (Bleger, 1967/2013; Bion, 1962/1977; Winnicott, 1974, 1988).

The order of politics

Humans struggle to integrate split-off forces and limits that lie beyond the order of politics, words, and reason. This struggle takes a dramatic course in a crisis when the polis is in transition and in need of re-inventing its identity. The tragic poet is the modern prophet needed for the politics of the democratic polis. Euripides' theatrical, poetic metaphors encompass the prehistoric and pre-political mythical and religious acts, which lie beyond meaning and reason. They are used to inscribe oaths and laws of community alliances that are integral in politics.

In Euripides' tragedy, Theseus becomes a tragic hero who personally undertakes the necessity to undergo a process that would change him during its course so as to enable himself to recognise the links of pity and friendship. He becomes the tragic subject of the city he founded. His mythic origin is a model of bravery that we identify with and take courage from to stand up to dictators of cruelty, fanaticism, racism, misogynism, and the culture of lying. In politics, the only thing that is impossible is omnipotence. Politics in a democratic polis transforms the impossible impasses into a transitional space of paradoxes. It is the art of setting limits.

The Epigonoi will take revenge for the sake of their fathers. Seferis (1995), a modern Greek poet, continues in his poem 'Mycenae' Aeschylus's and Euripides' tragic reading of history, following *"the path . . . / from punishment to the next murder"*. In the foundations of democracy lies the source of the constant threat against its edifice, the destructive drives (Freud, 1930). Euripides hates war but accepts that the pleasure of destruction is inherent in human lives. Greece is crazy about war.

Suppliant Women shows that people feel justified to go to war to bring back the dead of a previous war in order to bury them finally. These are ghosts from previous generations that can never be completely mourned.

A boy was raised in a village in modern Greece by a mother who had lost her father when she was 18 months old. Her father was killed in Minor Asia in 1921 in the war of the Greeks against the Turks. The custom in that village was to burn all photographs of the deceased in a ritual that helped them mourn. His little daughter could not participate in this ritual. She grew up and transmitted to her boy her unfulfilled desire to see her father, even in a picture, so that she could know how he was. She had no evidence that he ever existed. She had no body to bury, to mourn. This unresolved maternal mourning put a bias on the development of her son. In his adult life, he read books on the history of wars, saw war films, and intensely followed any news about wars. In a session after the Israel-Hamas war started, he said: In 1922, the Greek army was destroyed fighting in Minor Asia to rescue people from genocide in Pontus and rescue the Megali Idea (Great Idea) of making Greece great again. Greece did not exist for centuries. It was only an idea in peoples' minds. In 1922, the Greeks fought in order to bring back the dead bodies of all those who sacrificed their lives in previous wars of independence. All wars are made to bring back the war dead to bury. How many wars are needed for the people of Israel to bring back home the 6,000,000 ghosts, the Jews that were murdered in concentration camps, to bury? How will these missing people become our ancestors?

Theseus learns from experience and turns around. He is committed, alive, and fully present. He takes care of the dead himself (758–768). In contrast, Adrastus, full of pain, declares how much he would like to die along with them. Theseus was summoned by his mother to come (to be born) to Eleusis as a liberating leader to free her from the bondage of the supplication of the deceased generals' mothers. Eleusis has the same etymological root as 'arrival' (eleusis) and 'freedom' (eleutheria).

When a baby is born, and subsequently, in every step of its development, the mother is liberated. The baby's nursery is frequented by ghosts (unmourned, undead, traumatically lost objects from the past) (Fraiberg, Adelson, & Shapiro,

2002). The mother's mourning work is required so that these ghosts do not haunt the baby's development with narcissistic interferences.

Euripides believes that life continues in cycles. Is there really a more appropriate setting for the tragedy of *The Suppliants* than Eleusis, the sanctuary of Demeter and Kore, with the cycles of death and rebirth?

Kore, in contrast to Euridice, was able to return from Hades and joins her mother and grandmother in order to make Earth blossom again. We can think that she was able to return because she had a good object that she was able to separate from, to lose and mourn it in order to become a couple with a man who, like her father, enabled her to keep her links with her primary object. Euridice could not be put at a distance to be part of a visual scene and be seen. She was in an adhesive identification contiguity with the object (Ogden, 1989). Distance, separation, meant to vanish. Kore was able to separate in order to form a link and be part of a couple. The primal scene was staged, and time began. She lived inside time. One epoch succeeds the other.

In the transitional space of politics, contradictions can co-exist. They need not be split off nor be glossed over with character compromise formations. The aim of politics is to put an end to the work of unresolved mourning, to not allow it to continue as an endless pain. When the experiences that we create are put into words, they acquire meaning; they are internalised. We accept responsibility for them. The Suppliants mourn, imploring Theseus with words (284). Theseus proposes discourse as a component of public life. He invites his mother, Aethra, to speak to him, the leader of Athens, her son (112): "*Nothing reaches completion except through narration*".

Aethra will not stay silent; she will help (like Athena) her son to think with words. Silence is imposed by fear (300). Adrastus is appointed by Theseus to publicly say a few words for each of the fallen generals. *The Suppliants* begin with the deceased's right to die, to be buried, and to be accompanied to death. The lost objects have the right to be mourned and this involves putting their feelings into words.

Euripides' *Suppliant Women* say that nothing ends until it is put into words. However, there is a preverbal psychic work. The mothers of newborns do two kinds of psychic work for their infants. On the one hand, they dream of their baby's fears and return them to it, metabolised. On the other hand, they do a silent work of mourning; they put the ghosts to rest.

With each step of representation and internalisation of the unassimilated traces of experience, new connections are created, which increase the capacity of the network of exchanges (internal and external). With the work of mourning the fog of depression, the defence that covers pain is lifted, and the sense of reality becomes clear. This is how a clear focus on the exchanges that will benefit everyone – both people and cities – is achieved.

Agreements are made on the basis of clear, sincere exchanges. There are no ghosts without fog. We then listen to clear voices transmitting meanings. These agreements are unstable yet free because the value of communication that practical rewards have varies from context to context. Words are a symbolic compensation that is required by humans in order to accept a loss. The exchanges through words are essential in the politics of a moderate democracy. The play ends with negotiations through language. With words, we tame reality, we transform it. Our words sound sincere when they are the result of true mourning work.

Arvanitakis (1998) relied on Euripides's *Bacchae* and Aristotle's interpretation in order to examine the defining moment of the tragic, the pathos of fragmentation, as its Dionysian origin points out. There is a mutative movement from the myth of an original unity to the logos of differentiation, which represents a formative violent act in the service of the drives of Eros. Logos aims to construct a meaning that integrates contradictions and gives coherence to the plot.

The chorus represents the assembly of the people who converse and research a case concerning the city. The hypothesis of every research is concluded when the members of a plot meet in the same assembly, the same place, the same space. This gathering happens in both internal (remembering) and social reality (the democratic process of civic participation).

The protected city of the Athenians is a place of the work of the rule of law, institutions, predefined rewards, freedom of speech, poetry, history, democracy, tragedy, creation of ideas and philosophy, and doubt.

This, however, is not real life. Real life is where unrepresented trauma, Hubris, war, destructiveness, authoritarianism, and discrimination co-exist. Real life is where humans are separated violently from their loved objects and are being flooded with stimulation that surpasses their ability to restore the continuity of existence and cohesion. In real life, the agony of extinction, the dissolution of the bonds between individuals and the city, prevails. Ultimately, the laws of civilisation do not stop wars. Thucydides (1915) in his *History of The Peloponnesian War* is a realist like Euripides.[4]

An Ur-text of political theory

Euripides reshapes the myth of the Suppliants into a tragic plot of the human struggles to recognise and deal with deep irreducible splits inherent in individuals and their polis. Politics is a tragic process of internalisation that transforms women and men into citizens and the space of their life into a city.

The tragic poet becomes a prophet and sees beyond. He reads politics as a continuous struggle to: (1) integrate split-off 'supernatural' (unconscious) elements of human nature that lie beyond the order of politics, words, and reason, (2) form alliances of community, sustain participation in a shared reality of a common culture, and (3) work through each experience so that the order of politics is reconstructed.

Politics is a transitional phenomenon of culture (like art and religion). Politics uses not only words and reason but also mythical and religious acts, which are integrated into theatrical poetic metaphors. These acts give the weight of historical truth and convincing reality to the inscription and implementation of written laws and the construction and function of institutions.

The tragic is a psychic quality, a basic dimension of existence, a position of psychic and social development. The tragic position encompasses a separation from the primary union, an emergence of the self, the shock of the loss of omnipotence, the development of transitional objects and phenomena, the acceptance of ambivalence, the beginning of symbolisation and internalisation processes, and the recognition of reality.

The capacity to become a tragic subject is linked with the courage to act and then to suffer and assume intrapsychic responsibility for one's traumatic experiences, to make them personal. It is linked with the capacity to be the thinker that can think – to be a subject of – his thoughts (Aisenstein, 2019). It is the capacity to be a suppliant, that is, to arrive at, to make one's way, to plead for the response of the object, which returns the investments in it.

Humans yoke themselves to integrate their drives, omnipotence, and bisexuality. In *The Suppliants*, these necessities are manifest in the inevitability of the work of mourning and in femininity, which are interwoven in internal and external reality and lie at the foundations of human (psychic and public) life.

The moderate democratic polis is based on the rule of law. The rule of law is based on written words, reason, and also on the historical truths of untranslated experiences that lie beyond meaning and are expressed in religion and poetry. Democratic public life is an open-ended process. The polis is constantly in transition, in crisis, and in need to reflect critically on its current state and re-invent its identity.

The development of democracy continues in cycles of unintegration-integration-disintegration processes like individual development. Friendship and pity sustain the cohesion of the polis. The subject forgives, lets the lost object die, and moves on to live among the living and inside time, ultimately becoming able to die when the time comes. In order to let the object die, the subject needs a substitute object.

An essential paranoia linked to the feminine core of existence lies at the foundations of the polis (Green, 1972). With every movement towards integration, a paranoiac fear of attack from outside and dissolution of the polis' organisation crops up. A polis introduces the transitional phenomena of politics to help cure this acute paranoia. It is an open-ended, always incomplete work in progress.

Politics is the struggle to innovate institutions so that they are defined by permeable boundaries, which constitute a zone of exchange. This is an area of a third transitional reality, maintained with negations and functional transient splitting between internal and external reality. An institution consists of a capacity, a stable web of links of relationships, a room where new experiences can be stored and reality can be found and constructed.

The polis consists of transitional meeting places (the agora, the theatre, sanctuaries of religious rites, school classes, and feasts), where people gather to find reality to give meaning and integrity to their polis. There, people function with positive capabilities (they know and act with certainty and clear differences) and negative capabilities (they tolerate the uncertainties of ambiguities and turn them into paradoxes).

The transitional space of the 'theatrical stage' of politics links and separates the opposites, the differences. In such a 'playground', everyday traumas and conflicts are transferred, expressed, interpreted by unconscious fantasies and myths (collective fantasies), and put into words. When the experiences we create and share are put into words, they acquire meaning; they are internalised. We accept responsibility for them. We become their tragic subjects.

Notes

1 This chapter is based on my book *'Psychoanalysis and Euripides' Suppliant Women. A Tragic Reading of Politics'* published by Routledge/Focus in 2022. The direct line quotes are taken from Euripides. (1938). The complete Greek drama. In W. J. Oates, E. O'Neill Jr. (Eds.), & R. Potter (Trans.) *Two volumes. 1. Iphigenia in Tauris.* New York: Random House.
2 Freud (1914) said the same thing: Although we accept the deaths of others, we cannot think of our own death. Only the death of those close to us (who are part of our self) can rupture the denial that protects our sense of self.
3 I am indebted to Simo Salonen for reading in my book on Euripides' *Suppliant Women* "a new level of psychoanalytic understanding of the role of the feminine in the constitution of the primal matrix of the human existence, i. e. the mother's silent work of mourning containing and binding the devastating drive elements from escalating freely in her child's inner world. In extending over three generations of women, this constellation creates the first inner front line of defence against an individual succumbing to despair and to a society in chaos. Could Sophocles' Theban Plays reflect the second front line, on the more structured level of psychic organisation?"
4 Thucydides' history (Book 1, 1,8) proves that every polis that thinks itself more powerful will always fight to dominate any other that is weaker. The strong do what they can, and the weak suffer what they must. What is right is an issue only between those who are equal.

References

Aisenstein, M. (2019). *Désir-Douleur-Pensée: Masochism Originaire et Theorie Pychanalytique*. Paris: Ithaque.
Arvanitakis, K. (1998). Some thoughts on the essence of the tragic. *International Journal of Psycho-Analysis*, 79(5), 955–964.
Bion, R. W. (1977). Learning from experience. In *Seven servants*. New York: Jason Aronson. (Original work published 1962)
Bleger, J. (2013). *Symbiosis and ambiguity: A psychoanalytic study*. London and New York: Routledge. (Original work published 1967)
Burian, P. (1985). Logos and pathos: The politics of the suppliant women. In P. Burian (Ed.), *Directions in Euripidean criticism. A collection of essays*. Durham, NC: Duke University Press.
Euripides. (1938). The complete Greek drama. In W. J. Oates Jr, E. O'Neill Jr (Eds.), & E. P. Coleridge (Trans.), *Two volumes 1 the suppliants*. New York: Random House.
Fraiberg, S., Adelson, E., & Shapiro, V. (2002). *Ghosts in the nursery: A psychoanalytic approach to the problems of impaired infant–mother relationships*. London and New York: Routledge.

Freud, S. (1895). Project for a scientific psychology. *S. E., 1.*
Freud, S. (1912–1913). Totem and taboo: Some points of agreement between the mental lives of Savages and Neurotics. *S. E., 13.*
Freud, S. (1914). Thoughts in times of war and death. *S. E., 14.*
Freud, S. (1917). Mourning and melancholia. *S. E., 14.* (Original work published 1915)
Freud, S. (1919). The Uncanny. *S. E., 17.*
Freud, S. (1925). Negation. *S. E., 19.*
Freud, S. (1930). Civilisation and its discontents. *S. E.,* 21.
Freud, S. (1937). Analysis terminable and interminable. *S. E., 23.*
Freud, S. (1940). Splitting of the ego in the process of defence. *S. E., 23.*
Freud, S. (1954). Letter to Wilhelm Fliess of 15th October 1897 letter 71. In E. Moscbacher & J. Strachey (Trans.), *The origins of psychoanalysis: Letters to Wilhelm Fliess, drafts and notes, 1887–1902.* Lindon: Imago. (Original work published 1897)
Green, A. (1972). Aggression, femininity, paranoia and reality. *International Journal of Psycho-Analysis*, 53, 205–211.
Green, A. (1985). Thésée et Oedipe. Une iterprétation psychanalytique de la Théséide. In M. Fragopoulos (Trans.), *Psychanalyse et culture greque. Confluents psychanalytique.* Paris: Les Belles Letters; Athens: Rappa Publications. (Original work published 1980)
Green, A. (2001). *Life narcissism, death narcissism* (A. Weller, Trans.). London: Free Association Books. (Original work published 1991)
Manolopoulos, S. (2022). Psychoanalysis and Euripides' suppliant women. *A tragic reading of politics.* London and New York: Routledge/Focus.
Ogden, T. (1989). On the concept of an autistic-contiguous position. *International Journal of Psychoanalysis*, 70, 127.
Salonen, S. (2018). Meta psychological perspectives on psychic survival. In *Integration of traumatic helplessness in psychoanalysis.* London and New York: Routledge.
Scully, S. (1995). Introduction. In R. Warren & S. Scully (Trans.), *Euripides' suppliant women.* Oxford: Oxford University Press.
Seferis, G. (1995). II Mycenae, October 1935. In E. Keeley & P. Sherrard (Trans.), *George seferis complete poems.* London: Carcanet Classics.
Storey, C. I. (2008). *Euripides: Suppliant women.* London: Duckworth.
Thucydides. (1915). *The Peloponnesian War.* London: J. M. Dent, New York: E. P. Dutton.
Winnicott, D. W. (1971). *Playing and reality* (pp. 72–85). London: Tavistock.
Winnicott, D. W. (1974). Fear of breakdown. *International Review of Psycho-Analysis, 1,* 103–107.
Winnicott, D. W. (1988). *Human nature.* London: Free Association Books.
Zeitlin, F. (1986). Thebes: Theatre of self and society. In P. Euben (Ed.), *Greek tragedy and political theory.* Berkeley and Los Angeles, CA: University of California Press.
Zunt, G. (1955). *The political plays of euripides.* Manchester: Manchester University Press.

Chapter 6

Euripides' Alcestis
Narcissism and anti-narcissism[1]

Euripides' *Alcestis* was performed for the first time in 438 BC, seven years before the beginning of the Peloponnesian War. That year, the poet won the second-place award with the tetralogy of *The Cretan Women, Alcmaeon in Psophis, Telephus*, and *Alcestis*. Euripides was 43 years old at the time. This is his earliest surviving play. His first endeavor in theatre was in 445 BC. He was given a chorus to teach a play 22 times. He only won a few prizes. He would always shock audiences with his realistic and extreme plays.

The most tragic of poets, who constantly doubts and overthrows certainties, introduces us to the unthinkable. He presents to us our most primitive experiences. Euripides' tragedies use everyday realities as expressive means. It is as if, suddenly, the boundary that separates the stage from the audience is removed. Then, too much reality invades violently, traumatically psychic and public space. Our world becomes fragmented. Our survival is threatened.

None of the music of words, the prosody of the voice, and the rhythm of the chorus taught by Euripides in 438 BC survives today. What is it that turns us into the audience of a production of Alcestis today?

I postulate that there are three ecumenical tragic movements that permeate the drama, rendering us its audience: First is the question of inescapable Necessity: How death (a law of nature) becomes integrated as a personal experience. Second is the question of what constitutes reality: How the work of mourning lifts the fog of depression that covers reality. And third and most tragic is the question of anti-narcissism: Why is it that by loving the object, the subject must die?

The plot

Zeus struck Asclepius down with a lightning bolt, reducing him to ashes because, as a physician, he did not confine himself to healing. He had started raising the dead, thus committing Hubris, as human nature is by Necessity mortal. Apollo avenged the death of his son, Asclepius, by slaying the Cyclopes that were constructing Zeus' lightning bolts. Zeus was enraged and wanted to throw Apollo, his son, into the furthest reaches of Hades, Tartarus. He was persuaded by Leto, Apollo's mother, to convert the sentence. Zeus condemned Apollo to serve the new king of

DOI: 10.4324/9781032712864-7

Pherae, Admetus, as a slave for a period of nine years. The conversion of a severe sentence to something lighter is an element of the myth. Prefacing the drama, Apollo informs us that in the years that he had been herding Admetus' cattle, he had developed feelings of friendship towards the young king of Pherae of Thessaly. He made sure that his palace would prosper. He aided Admetus in marrying Alcestis by harnessing a lion and a wild boar to his chariot, as Pelias, the king of Iolcus and Alcestis' father, had challenged him in order to agree to the marriage. The Hubris of denying our mortal nature enters our minds again. Our associations bring to mind Pelias' two older daughters – not Alcestis, however – who had been deceived by Medea into tearing their father to pieces and boiling him in a pot so that he would be reborn as a young man.

Apollo helped Admetus evade his destiny, which would have him die at a young age. He made the Moirai (Fates) drunk and convinced them to spare the young king's life, provided that someone else agreed to take his place in death. The question of inescapable Necessity (our death) is posed from the very beginning. Admetus' parents did not agree to die in his place despite being old and having lived their lives. The person who agreed to die was Alcestis, his prudent and devoted wife.

Today is the day. The queen is about to die. Apollo is now ready to leave the palace. The cruel incarnation of Death appears, determined to take Alcestis with him to the Underworld. Apollo leaves in order to avoid the miasma of the imminent death. Before leaving the stage, he foretells the ending of the tragedy, namely the defeat of cruel death by life. The chorus, consisting of the City's Elders, appears, floating in uncertainty, anxiously enquiring whether the queen is still alive or already dead. Death is a certainty, but it has not yet occurred. Afterwards, the maidservant exits the palace and announces to the anxiously awaiting chorus that the queen no longer holds any hope. She wept before her bridal bed, she yearningly embraced her children, she made sacrifices on all the altars of the gods, and she bid farewell to the people of her house.

Alcestis then comes on stage. She comes to bid farewell to the outside world. She is followed by her husband, her children, and the slaves. Admetus is crushed and implores her not to leave him. Alcestis, through a deep lament, makes her husband promise that he will not remarry but will instead remain single for their children's sake; he will not give them a stepmother. Admetus promises and then Alcestis lets herself die. Her youngest son bursts into a lament. Admetus declares that Thessaly is in public mourning, which will be repeated every year. Suddenly, Heracles appears as a bouffon, bragging on his way to his next labour. Admetus conceals from him the fact that his wife has died. It is forbidden to turn away a stranger that comes to your household. And Admetus is known to be very hospitable.

The funerary procession begins. Up to this point, silence prevails regarding all the contradictions. It is then that Pheres, Admetus' father, appears bearing gifts to accompany the deceased queen. A powerful, chilling, inappropriate agon between the two men breaks out. The son turns away the father who refused to die for him. The father reveals the cowardness and egotism of his son, who has allowed his wife to die in his place. In the meantime, Heracles enjoys the hospitality, eating and drinking inside the palace chambers, unaware of what is going on. He drunkenly philosophises about the meaning of life. He is dumbfounded when he is informed by an indignant servant that the deceased is Admetus' wife and not some distant relative. He is ashamed of himself. He instantly decides to fight Death and bring the queen back. He succeeds and brings her back to the king, covered in a veil – a silent stranger – to test the oath of eternal fidelity he had given his dying wife.

Euripides drew the plot from the story of Alcestis and Admetus, which was popular in Ancient Greece. Many traditional songs of the time recounted her myth. It is a tale common for many peoples today (Lesky, 1925, cited by Iacov, 2012). Alcestis and Admetus were also Chthonian deities who were worshiped in Thessaly and in the Peloponnese. In a version of the myth, Persephone herself brought Alcestis back to life.

The inescapable necessity

The question of inescapable Necessity is posed from the very beginning. It comprises a central underlying tragic theme. Gods and men obey Necessity, the law of nature. The chorus sings (966): "*nor is there any cure for it*". What is highlighted in the play is the necessity of death. How can one integrate this law of nature into one's self? How can one make death personal?

Without its mother's holding, the helpless infant will literally die. The Fates are already present at a baby's birth. One of them, Atropos, determines the time at which our thread of life will be cut short. Therefore, the aim of the mother's holding is to keep the thread intact so that life can go on.

Some scholars think that if there is something tragic in this play, it is the characters of the dramatic persons that make them inescapably express certain behaviours, that correspond to existing ideas inside social conventions (institutions) (Topouzis, 1993). For Heraclitus, "a man's character is his fate". The ethos of humans is their demon. The characters' repetition is both compulsive and daemonic (Freud, 1919, 1920). Humans form their character and social institutions on the model of their infantile experience of maternal care and its inevitable failures.

Euripides stages the extreme realism of failures of maternal care. We can find such failures in split-off traces inside the character traits, as well as in the rules and regulations of social institutions that organise society. The character traits secure splittings like vises. They create compromises, stop time, immobilise conflicts, and lock the transitional space. Characters encounter, in institutions, the certainties they need so as to be validated and perpetuated. The character (for example, the devoted wife) creates deadly impasses in collusion with an institution (marriage).

Up until Pheres' and Admetus' father and son chilling agon, all contradictions hide behind collusions of characters and institutions that give a pretence of cohesion: The man that egotistically requests the sacrifice and the man that feels desperation for being so alone. The mother that abandons her children and the mother that sacrifices herself for her husband. The mother who asks her husband not to remarry and give a stepmother to her children, and a woman who wishes to punish the 'untamed' (as is the meaning of his name) Admetus by never letting him be married, by depriving him of his sexuality.

What Admetus is saying echoes as improper; he uses an incorrect tone. It seems as if he has walked in from a comedy, while Alcestis belongs in a tragedy. Everybody is playing their 'pieces', which are unconnected to one another and are forcing the plot to include them in the story. It is as if everybody is acting in their own play. According to some scholars, Alcestis' decision is the only tragic choice in the entire drama (Kott, 1971/1976).

What was Alcestis' choice? Plato sees in Alcestis the courage that is inspired by love. The courage to face physical death? In contrast to Plato, psychoanalysts and tragic poets think that our courage consists of the choice to feel our emotions. To recognise our feelings, to not split them off, to be real and present, to live the experience. To experience the conflict of love and hate and to connect the two, all the while enduring the ambivalence and mourning the idealised object.

Admetus and Alcestis are the rulers of the land. They guarantee the unity and immortality of the city. They are institutions, the keepers of the gates. They are the founding parents of a cult, Chthonian deities, and the bearers of dark incorporations. They remind us how dangerous it can be to be intimate with a stranger, to be receptive-passive to – internalise – new experiences that grow inside you without you knowing what they will become.

I think that Alcestis' drama is played on two levels: First, the impasse and ambiguity of a demonic repetition. Second, the paradox and transitional phenomena of the tragic. Euripides leads us from daemonic repetition compulsion to the necessity of making a choice, from the need to gloss over contradictions with compromises and to split them off, to the struggle to accept the paradox of them coexisting inside the transitional space (Winnicott, 1971).

Alcestis is an odd drama. It shows how variegated the human world is (Freud, 1930). Topouzis (1993) writes: It is neither a satirical drama nor a tragedy. It is a comic tragedy. It is an ambiguous play (Kott, 1971/1976). The chorus is anxiously enquiring whether the queen is alive or dead (105): *"And yet this is the fated day . . ."* When the maidservant comes on stage, she ambiguously states (141): *"You might call her both living and dead"*. The poet offers us a clear picture of the ambiguous state of being of Alcestis. She first has to see herself as she is. When she comes to the gate to bid farewell to the world, Alcestis says (244–246): *"O sungod, light of day, eddies of whirling clouds in the sky!"* Life is like the light of day, beautiful because it is transient. Admetus is even more ambiguous than Alcestis is. For Apollo, he is a "godly man", for his parents, he was "respectful", and for his friend Heracles, he was "too hospitable". Apollo's stay at the palace and the hospitality towards Heracles are two similar aspects of Admetus' character (Iacov, 2012, pp. 94–96).

Admetus promises his wife he will not remarry; he will not give their children a stepmother. He will forever be beside her, the same way that he will be beside her in the Underworld when he himself dies (347–350):

An image of you shaped by the hand of skilled craftsmen shall be laid out in my bed. I shall fall into its arms, and as I embrace it and call your name I shall imagine, though I have her not, that I hold my dear wife in my arms.

Her statue will have embodied the movements of time of Alcestis' life experiences that made it. As a piece of art, like a dream, it can be a substitute for her.

The manic desire to live coexists with the pain of mourning (Winnicott, 1935/1996). When Heracles is feasting inside the palace chambers, people in other chambers are mourning Alcestis' death. Utilising the device of the ignorant guest, Euripides renders hospitality a prerequisite for Alcestis' salvation. Hospitality of what? The mourners dare open themselves and offer hospitality to – represent and internalise – the lost object, who returns as a stranger. The chorus has a good premonition (597–605): The hospitality towards Heracles, in spite of Admetus' mourning, will have a happy ending (Iacov, 2012, pp. 15, 59). *Alcestis* can also be read as an ode to hospitality. We can speculate that Heracles' feasting represents the feasting that follows death, where we symbolically feast on the deceased, thus internalising him.

We mourn the deceased by celebrating his life. Madness is a victory of the Life drive. In contrast, psychosis is the triumph of Thanatos (Green, 1980/1986). Segal (1990) states: Concrete symbolisation is conspicuously at the root of pathological mourning. If the dead person is felt as a concrete dead body, then normal mourning is not possible. It is only if the dead person can be felt as symbolically represented in the mind that internal reparation can be done. Admetus asks Alcestis to visit him in his dreams, as a symbolic representation, not as an unmentalised ghost.

What is reality?

The Alcestis that returns from death is an enigmatic, silent stranger. She is veiled. Is she real? What is reality? This question is the second fundamental tragic underlying current. Our psychic life depends on truth, just like our body depends on food. Our survival, however, depends on our capacity to protect ourselves from the truth that can be devastating if we take it in a raw form (Freud, 1925, 1940a; Bion, 1982/1992, p. 192). Through the work of mourning, our sense of reality becomes clear. Our speech becomes sincere and convincing. The mirror is not blurred. The reality is not veiled. The non-decision of this conflict that founds the human psyche is of psychotic order (Bion, 1957/1967).

Kott (1971/1976) concludes that Alcestis, when read as a tragedy, ends with a mock resurrection; when read as a comedy, it ends with a deadly marriage. The play begins with Apollo comically targeting Death with his bow and arrow because it is "his custom". It ends comically with Heracles putting Alcestis in Admetus' hands and him looking away like Perseus looking away from Medusa in terror. Terror hides behind this comic scene. In the face of death, everything becomes ridiculous and mundane. What can we say? We feel glad that we are alive. We project guilt (due to our aggression against the person who died and abandoned us) onto others around us and feel that they blame us. When we go to a funeral, we are careful to be on our best behaviour; we must not give any reason to be criticised. That is why the agon between father and son (Pheres and Admetus) over Alcestis' body, about who is responsible for her death, is so chilling. Meanwhile, we fear that the deceased will return to take us with him to the Underworld.

When we feel helpless, we gather together with others – we become 'us' – in order to find reality and be convinced that our finding is true and suitable to be internalised. The chorus of a tragedy represents this gathering, this 'us'. The Demos is the witness of our experience and its meaning.

In a recent production of the play,[2] the chorus – men of the city – began after the funeral to climax the tension through frantic choreography and martial music. In the centre of the stage, there was a massive triangular mound of dirt that had been dug out and compiled by two members of the chorus. The top of the mound remained open. On the top of the mound, on the edge of trauma, Admetus, a helpless king, now sits as if it were a throne. He is in pain, on the verge of the abyss.

One by one, the men of the chorus suddenly started swirling around this mound that had an open mouth on top, threatening to suck you in, to trap you inside. A mounting tension? A horrifying object, which will become your grave if it pulls you in, and you will be gone? It is the opening from which Death appears on stage at the beginning of the play. Death had come to do work, he said to Apollo. The work of death? Throughout the play, the mound was gaping open. Death is not the end. Mourning brings the end. Did the mound represent the navel of a perpetual repetition of a fear of breakdown, a psychotic defence against annihilation (Winnicott, 1974)? The ambiguity of a daemonic repetition does not separate before from after, inside from outside, the self from the object.

The men's swirling choreography is reminiscent of the elusive clouds that Alcestis saw swirling in the sky, looking for reality. One by one, the men of the chorus charge to conquer the mound, but they fall as if they are colliding with an invisible wall, an unknown limit. The men of the chorus do not fall off the world into the abyss. They are not estranged. They struggle; they fight for life with madness but close to life, also near death and psychosis but against them. They make meaningless noises like children who repeat the incomprehensible noises they hear in a violent family scene. They throw, they thrust their bodies into battle in a manic transgression of boundaries, a frantic dance of the emotions of life. The boundary, however, is there to be found/created.

What is the boundary? It is reality that puts a limit on our omnipotence. It is the reality of the object that is on its way to becoming objective when it is attacked to be destroyed, yet it survives.

Critchley (2019) comments: The object of a tragedy is not the tragic hero but the city-state. The hero is 'the problem', not the solution. He is 'an enigma', not the answer. The man in the tragedy acts and, at the same time, is on the receiving end of the action. Both innocent and guilty. Both incomprehensible and monstrous. Euripides shows us that tragedy means scepticism. It dissolves all certainties. It finds its expression in the question: 'What shall I do?'. Such questions are not the beginning of logical argumentation but the end of any logic. It is a tragic coupling of human with the divine.

Admetus sits on the top of the mound. The throne represents an institution, a counter-traumatic barrier. It negates the nothingness of death. It links people to the skies of the divine. However, underneath the institution, a primitive world of fragmented primitive elements menaces. These are our ghosts, lost parts of self and objects that are liberated when the frames of our institutions are disturbed. The dance of these elements shapes the institution. All are cast on stage in an emotional storm of interactions. If the storm ceases, they cease to exist. And the institution will fall to pieces. The institution needs one crisis after another.

We can think of an institution as a statue (e.g. Moses of Michelangelo) which shows the embodied movements that made it (Segal, 1990). When the traces of our experiences are inscribed, their time is embodied. A dance expresses movements of time that make a statue. And as the madness of the dance of the chorus rages on, we imagine that, on a different stage, Heracles fights Death like crazy, like a baby fighting to win life. Or we imagine making love like crazy to fight the numbness and feel real.

After the funeral, Admetus, in despair, despises his return and his palaces without Alcestis' presence. He does not know what to do. And he wishes that he were dead. He envies the dead and longs to inhabit their house, Hades. His mother brought him into life with a heavy fate: to die young. He did not die, but he is now thrown into vortexes of unthinkable pain by the realisation of his loss. With anguish and profound shame, he wants to vanish off the face of the earth. Faced with the violence of his emotions, he is in vertigo. His fear of breakdown is a defence; it is a chance to be present and live, for the first time, as a subject of the unthinkable experience of annihilation and to begin a re-organisation of defences. Admetus makes a painful comparison of how his life with his wife began and how it has now ended up.

The capacity to feel guilt is a profound step of development. The psyche attaches an annihilating, economic situation of the trauma to a conflict, that of object loss (castration or separation). The survival of the external object is essential in this process (Freud, 1940b; Winnicott, 1963/1990).

When Admetus returns from the funeral, he notices the empty bridal bed, his children crying, the slaves bewailing, and the floor covered in dust (940–950):

> Now I understand. For how shall I endure entering this house? Whom will I greet, by whom be greeted, to win pleasure in my coming in? Which way shall I go? For the desolation within will drive me out of doors when I see my wife's bed empty and the chairs in which she sat and in the house the floor unswept and the children falling about my knees weeping for their mother, while the slaves bewail what a mistress they have lost from the house.

The detail of Admetus noticing the unswept floor is an example of Euripides' "domestic realism", but it is a poetic and useful image (Iacov, 2012, pp. 321–323). An interpretation is that being in shock because of the loss when returning from the funeral, the mourner's gaze stops on a perceptual detail of the house. Perception is overinvested in, and time stops. And life stops. Without links of meaning of a present perception with the past, the mourner feels numb. He does not feel real and alive. He does not feel at home any longer.

In contrast to such an interpretation, Kott (1971/1976) ridicules the mention of dust as laughable: Euripides' Alcestis is a good 'housekeeper'! A feminist interpretation sees women changing hands: from the father to the husband, from Heracles to Admetus. Alcestis is silent beneath a veil of oppression. Confined, she enters a marriage, alienated in a patriarchal world. She sacrifices herself (Rabinowitz, 1993).

But who is this stranger under the veil? Is she the new woman who let the perfect child of an idealised mother die? Or is it someone who refuses to leave the primary object and grows up to become a woman? In rites of passage, the symbolic death of a child that transitions to the next stage of adulthood signifies the real imminent death of the parent. Admetus' parents refuse to die willingly. Young people grow up to take their parents' place and go on with their lives. There is time, there is death, the end of time. That is reality. End of story (Iacov, 2012).

What does it mean to be alive? Parsons (2009) writes:

> Winnicott distinguished two different ways of living. One is based on compliance, and is organised around fitting in with reality and adapting to it. The other is based on a relationship to reality that Winnicott called "creative apperception". The unfamiliar word 'apperception' means the perception of something in relation to one's past experience, and thus the perception of the inner meaning that it has for oneself.

Outside the continual psychic work of aliveness, there is a larger timelessness. "The natural boundaries of the primal scene and death, Eros and Thanatos, represent our passage . . . from non-existence into existence and out again". How is one really present to live the experience? "The present is a moment in the passage of time, and aliveness depends on inhabiting it with as much freedom of movement as possible between it and both past and future. But the present moment is also timeless" (Parsons, 2009).

Euripides has the couple live years of happiness and have children before the day arrives when Alcestis will keep her promise and die in her husband's place. In the myth, the promise of sacrifice and the wedding ceremony happen on the same day. In the tragedy, the return from death and the (second) wedding happen on the same day. Iacov (2012, p. 277) reads Alcestis as a "fable drama".

> It maintains the basic structure of the pre-literature fable where a misfortune/ deprivation (Alcestis' death) is restored (the resurrection of the queen). However, the difference from the fable lies in the fact that, in the play, blood relations are disparaged and the role of genuine friendship (divine, spousal or that of companionship) is highlighted.

Also, 'friendship', as the ingredient that unites the city, is highlighted, I would add. Yet, is the stranger, the object, a friend or an enemy?

Why is it that by loving the object, one must die?

This question is the most tragic underlying current in Alcestis. By loving her husband, Alcestis is diminished. While she marvels in front of him, she herself fades away. She diminishes her subjectivity. She dims the light of her existence. The libido that is invested in the object drains narcissism; it depletes her ego of life. This is Alcestis' choice, the most tragic one.

I hypothesize that Alcestis' and Admetus' cult was dedicated to existence and the fear of non-existence which is an organized defence analogous to the fear of breakdown (Winnicott, 1974, p. 107).

Euripides' Alcestis is not one of our clinical cases. We have grown accustomed, however, to Euripides' profound diagnoses of the most primitive areas of the human psyche. Does Euripides utilise the veiled Alcestis to trace the depletion of narcissistic investments of the psychotic self?

Alcestis, like Dido in Virgil's Aeneid, transforms from a self-governed subject to a passive thing that expresses itself through silence (Panoussi, 2005; Iacov, 2012, p. 40). Alcestis is alive but does not exist as a subject. Could it be that Admetus is quite literal in his conversation with Heracles (518–521): Admetus: *"There is a double tale to tell of her"*. Heracles: *"Do you mean that she has died or is still alive?"*. Admetus: *"She is and is no more. It causes me grief"*. Heracles responds that there can be no two ways about this matter. One is either alive or dead. If one, however, is to have the right to be alive and live well, she must conceive the continuity of life and death without refuting their difference (Alford, 1992, p. 130).

Ancient Greeks did not believe that in another life, they would be rewarded. They believed that their heroic deeds would be remembered in the songs and celebrations of the future generations. Immortality is an affair of the living who keep alive in their mind the memory of the dead. Mourning is both a painful recognition of reality and a joyful celebration of the life of the dead.

The refutation of the end of time is a psychotic attack against the sense of self. Euripides discusses the division between being and non-being (528): Heracles: *"Existence and non-existence are deemed to be separate things"*.

Pasche (1971, p. 696)[3] shows us the breakdown of investments towards the object and narcissistic investments. It is a scaly lining of narcissism with anti-narcissism, a psychotic solution where the object is the enemy that constantly threatens the individual to suck it in and trap it. The diffusion of the drives leaves destructivity inside the ego. The subsequent destructive real violence against the object is the only exit from anxiety. Pasche advises us to follow Perseus' example and use the shield against the attacks from the object we are petrified to face.

In Alcestis, Euripides mentions Medusa with the scaly snakes instead of hair. A version of the myth speaks of Admetus discovering scaly snakes coiled in the bridal chamber on the first night of his marriage: a bad omen sent by the goddess Artemis, who was angry with him for neglecting to make sacrifices in her honour during his wedding ceremonies.

Marriage, virginity and death are linked in ancient myths and tragedies (Persephone, Antigone, Ifigeneia, Alcestis). Their link is the primal scene, from where the time begins, and the mythical subject emerges as a historical being, inside time, that moves towards its end, the death.

The drama's transitional space is the shield, where contradictions coexist; they do not compromise, and they are not split. With Alcestis' plot, Euripides offers us a mirror that resembles Perseus' shield so as to create a condition where reality is a reflection next to us, and we can face it in the paradoxical transitional space.

Christina, a late adolescent and a university student, fell passionately in love with a young man. At that time, her twin brother drowned in the sea. It was apparently an accident, but she thought that it was a suicide. Christina abandoned her studies, returned home, and remained inside her room in complete isolation for two years. She continued to be passionately in love even if she had no real communication with the young man. At the same time of her life, her aliveness, her presence, her realness, grew dim. She felt she was trapped. Her love object was the enemy. Loving him meant that she herself would die. Did she identify with the object that left her, and she also abandoned herself? It was something more than that. She felt that if she was not fully alive, she would not have to fear death. Since she was a child, she struggled tooth and nail to defend herself in the middle of violent attacks by her paranoid father against her brother and her mother. She sat quietly in the corner, in a state of half-existence, waiting for the storms to pass. The storms felt endless. It seemed to her that they never ceased; they were not subjected to time. She then split herself into two parts. With one part, she lived inside the world of objects. With her other part, she made up stories. Now, she remained isolated in her room all the time, hooked up to the internet. She hardly existed.

In the transitional space, contradicting parts of the self coexist and can meet. The agons of words that Euripides utilises in his tragedies is an example of how contradictions can coexist. The agons show the spontaneous gesture, the true self in action. The true self can say 'no' and take a distance in order to ensure that the object is not experienced as an excessively realistic medusa.

Here, I must note a word used by Phrynichus, who had also taught his version of Alcestis. He uses the word 'athamves', which means 'fearless' in the face of that which is dazzling (Chantraine, 1968–1980/2022). Maybe in the face of the bedazzling object, you are left speechless and terrified. You may then dim the light of your existence.

Euripides deals with the finite nature of existence (death) and with reason (irrationality) by making a distinction between the boundaries (of the impossible omnipotence) that we cannot transcend and the boundaries (of prohibition) that we must transcend in order to change. Change is not painless. It is a feat and requires courage. Mourning, symbolisation, and internalisation require perseverance. The tragedy of Alcestis has a happy ending but requires that we pay the price of recognising the boundaries of the human condition. The solution that Euripides suggests, as does psychoanalysis, is the representation of the lost object.

The drama of Alcestis is a convincing testimony that death is personal and reality inescapable. The painful emotions of mourning and the manic defences against them testify to that. Thus, it is possible for Heracles to perform a real feat, even while presented in this comical manner: he fights death. Resurrection, the representation, of the lost object is indeed a feat.

Through valiant battle, we extract meaning (representations, affects) from the experiences we repeat. This meaning creates a corresponding realisation of a new emotional experience that we share with others. The "raw" physical death is defeated by psychic and social life. T.S. Eliot (1949), in his version of Alcestis, "The Cocktail Party", says: "Ah, but we die to each other daily . . . At every meeting we are meeting a stranger". Will the stranger bring us life or take us to death? When we psychotically fear that the stranger will trap us, we kill him inside daily with our splitting defences in order to escape. And he returns from outside again with a threatening perception. If we experience early the trauma of falling outside the world, we can never feel at home again.

When we have the courage to do the work of mourning, the person we have lost returns to life inside us as a representation. The visiting stranger initiates the plot that unravels the myth of the character into a living story. He brings new music, and it matters not if it is out of tune like that of Heracles. He brings the flowing time towards the end. The space that has finite boundaries. The object.

Admetus now sees (940): "*Now I understand*". An example of this kind of learning is the child that throws the object, which then returns. It does what Winnicott (1941) termed 'object-lesson' when he observed the scene where the emerging infant tells its mother 'No' through actions and defines itself as a subject. The infant throws the object, and the mother must return it again and again until the infant stops doing that. This process must be carried out. The infant lives an experience that has a beginning, a middle, and an end. The mother holds the time of the course that the experience runs before being recorded by the infant as a memory trace. It is a process of making a representation that is also an embodiment of the time of the experience.

In theatre, this holding is done through the staging in which we define an intermediate space of playing, where a sample of psychic life is implemented in reality. The tragic plot is a shield; a game that transforms the psychotic defence of splitting in a paradoxical transitional space that expels and makes the menacing object disappear and reappear. It destroys it. The object survives and is on its course of becoming real, objective, and beyond omnipotence (Winnicott, 1971).

Carson (2006, pp. 8–9) writes:

There is in Euripides some kind of learning that is always at the boiling point. It breaks experiences open and they waste themselves, run through your fingers. Phrases don't catch them, theories don't hold them, they have no use. It is a theatre of sacrifice in the true sense. Violence occurs; through violence we are intimate with some characters onstage in an exorbitant way for a brief time; that's all it is.

Notes

1 The direct line quotes are taken from Kovacs, D. (1994). *Euripides: Cyclops, Alcestis, Medea*. Cambridge, MA: Harvard University Press.
2 Directed by Katerina Evagelatou and presented in the summer of 2017 in the ancient Epidaurus theatre.
3 I am indebted to Vassilis Dimopoulos for bringing to my attention the relevance of Pasche's concept of anti-narcissism to Alcestis' drama.

References

Alford, C. F. (1992). Greek tragedy and the place of death in life. A psychoanalytic perspective. *Psychoanalysis and Contemporary Thought, 15*(2), 129–159.
Bion, W. R. (1967). Differentiation of the psychotic from the non-psychotic personalities. In *Second thoughts. Selected papers on psychoanalysis*. New York: Jason Aronson. (Original work published 1957)
Bion, W. R. (1992). *Cogitations*. London: Karnac. (Original work published 1982)
Carson, A. (2006). *Grief lessons: Four plays*. New York: New York Review of Books.
Chantraine, P. (2022). Dictionaire Ètymologique de la Langue Grecque: Histoire des Mots. Klineckshiek. In G. Papanastasiou, D. Christidis (Eds.), G. Darlas & A. Petrou (Trans.), *Greek*. Thessaloniki: Aristoteleion Panepistimion Thessalonikis. Institute of Hellenic Studies. (Original work published 1968–1980)
Critchley, S. (2019). *Tragedy, the ancient Greeks and US*. London: Profile Books.
Eliot, T. S. (1949). *The cocktail party*. New York: Harcourt, Brace and Company Publications.
Euripides. *Euripides, with an English translation by David Kovacs*. Cambridge, MA: Harvard University Press.
Freud, S. (1919). The uncanny. *S. E., 17*
Freud, S. (1920). Beyond the pleasure principle. *S. E., 18*.
Freud, S. (1925). Negation. *S. E., 19*.
Freud, S. (1930): Civilisation and its discontents. *S. E., 21*.
Freud, S. (1940a). Splitting of the ego in the process of defence. *S. E., 23*.
Freud, S. (1940b). An outline of psycho-analysis. *S. E., 23*. (Original work published 1938)
Green, A. (1986). On the relation between madness and psychosis. In *On private madness*. Madison, CT: International University Press. (Original work published 1980)
Iacov, I. D. (2012). Euripides, alcestis, volumes A, B. In *Greek*. Athens: MIET.
Kott, J. (1976). Gott-essen. In A. Varikokaki-Artemi (Trans.), *Greek: Theofagia. Essays on ancient tragedy*. Athens: Exantas-Nimata Publications. (Original work published 1971)
Kovacs, D. (1994). *Euripides: Cyclops, Alcestis, Medea*. Cambridge, MA: Harvard University Press.
Lesky, A. (1925). *Alkestis. Der Mythos und das Drama*. Wien: Hölder-Pichler-Tempsky.
Panoussi, V. (2005). Polis and empire. Greek tragedy in Rome. In J. Gregory (Ed.), *A companion to Greek tragedy*. Oxford: Wiley-Blackwell.
Parsons, M. (2009). Après-coup, Avant-coup: Death and the primal scene. *EPF Bulletin, 63*.
Pasche, F. (1971). The shield of perseus or psychosis and reality. In D. Birksted-Breen, S. Flanders, & A. Gibeault (Eds.), *Reading french psychoanalysis*. London and New York: Routledge.
Rabinowitz, S. N. (1993). Anxiety veiled. In *Euripides and the traffic in women*. Ithaca, NY and London: Cornell University Press.
Segal, H. (1990). *Dream, phantasy, art*. London and New York: Routledge.
Topouzis, K. (1993). Euripides, Alcestis. In *Greek*. Athens: Epikairotita Publications.
Winnicott, D. W. (1941). The observation of infants in a set situation. *International Journal of Psychoanalysis, 22*, 229–249.
Winnicott, D. W. (1971). *Playing and reality*. London: Karnac.
Winnicott, D. W. (1974). The fear of breakdown. *International Review of Psychoanalysis, 1*, 103–107.
Winnicott, D. W. (1990). The development of the capacity for concern. In *The maturational processes and the facilitating environment*. London: Karnac. (Original work published 1963)
Winnicott, D. W. (1996). The manic defence. In *Through paediatrics to psychoanalysis*. London: Karnac. (Original work published 1935)

Chapter 7

Euripides' Iphigeneia in Tauris
Bringing the stranger back home[1]

We are watching Euripides' tragedy *Iphigeneia in Tauris*. The stage philosopher presents many levels of irony in a masterful manner in order to introduce the fear of strangers to metaphorical thought through the horror of castration and fear of death. He presents the discovery of otherness as the most traumatic rupture in human development. He uses examples of transformations through which people represent a traumatic raw reality, cladding it in images so as to make it appropriate for thinking. He presents uncanny horrible scenes of massacre that offer us an acute sense of the self. He stages the work of mourning the loss of omnipotence after the shock of discovering the otherness of the object. Like the seismic shock that Iphigeneia saw in her dream the previous night.

The horror of the bloody massacre of strangers

What do we praise as an audience in Iphigeneia in the Land of the Taurians? What do we praise when Artemis' priestess, and the chorus of Greek slave women serving her, mourn her own bodily sacrifice at the hands of her father in Aulis so that the thousand ships could set sail for Troy as Calchas the seer had counselled him? *"For you once vowed to sacrifice to the torch-bearing goddess the most beautiful creature brought forth that year"* (20–21). What do we praise when Iphigeneia and the chorus mourn the *bloody massacre* of strangers that are sacrificed in the temple where Iphigeneia, the priestess of Artemis, makes the preparations sprinkling and purifying them? What do we praise in the face of the horror of the unfamiliar images of castration and death while Iphigeneia and the chorus nostalgically mourn their homeland that they miss?

We praise the confirmation of our sense of being in the world. We praise the fulfilment of the mission. We obeyed the command that was given to us at the beginning of life to enter a long process of internalisations, face the horrors of the journey, and make ourselves a home for the stranger (Kennedy, 2023). In the face of castration, loss, and the threat of personal death, we become fervidly optimistic with a passion for life, a passion for being an autonomous thinking subject. All of these are transient, and beautiful. They have the beauty of clarity, the result of the work of mourning (Freud, 1916). The tense is future perfect. It is the time

DOI: 10.4324/9781032712864-8

of re-establishment. We sing of horrific images of sacrifices, of old familiar and presently unfamiliar castrations, the living offering up their blood. In an acute manner, we experience our sense of self as clear. We know that we are present here.

We come into the world with an innate capacity to seek the other and to participate in an adventure of conquest: to re-establish our land or origin. We are motivated by the desire to find (again) the object of desire, to recognise it, to be recognised by it, and to begin mutual exchanges that will be beneficial to both as well as to the context of our relationship. With every step of differentiation, we do not annihilate our primary autoerotism and narcissism. We transform them, but we keep our roots in them. We abandon the original illusion of primary autoerotism and narcissism, but our parents replace the immortality of its perfection and become the standards we strive to achieve. And when we are disappointed by them, too, we imagine that we are descended from noble, superior ancestors. We long for heaven.

When we leave our homes, we become refugees in the outside world. It is as if we have been abducted by the native indigenous people. And we long to return home, to our family home, to relish in sweet sleep. We want to return to our place of origin, which is always of a noble descent. We wish to surrender to sleep.

"*Dark straits of the sea, dark*" (392–393). The chorus of Iphigeneia in Tauris sings about the gadfly that stung the cow, which was Io transformed, and overwhelmed her with lust so that she flew over the waves, beyond Europe, to the lands of Asia.

We sing with drastic words that act, touch, taste, and feel. We do things with words. It is with words that we re-establish our country of origin. We restore our roots of origin. We feel the pain of being uprooted and the longing for return. Is it possible that we lose our roots and become strangers to ourselves? Can we travel to the farthest reaches without falling off the world? Can we return home? Or have we lost our Nostos, our way home? This is our deepest fear. Will we recognise our own strangers when we meet them again? Will they recognise us as one of their own? Will our unconscious wild strangers find a home (become integrated) in ourselves?[2]

At the time when ancient tragedy flourished, human sacrifice had not been entirely abandoned (Meraklis, 1984/2014, p. 20). Plutarch mentions that before the naval battle of Salamis, Themistocles sacrificed three beautiful prisoners of war, obeying the prophecy that many Athenians had believed. The 'Pharmakoi' were sacrificed in the Thargelia festival. During this festival, the people performed a purification sacrifice of a man and a woman who had been condemned to death for crimes they had committed. They were led around the city wearing a wreath and a string of figs. Accompanied by a flute, they were led outside the city, where they were put to death. Afterwards, their dead bodies were burned to ashes.

In the works of Euripides, we find the most frequent mentions of human sacrifices. In *Iphigeneia in Tauris*, the barbarians sacrifice Greeks. Iphigeneia and the chorus denounce the sacrifices (465): "*the rites which the custom among us declares to be unholy*". However, the Greeks performed the exact same kind of sacrifices, and Iphigeneia herself had been a victim of one. The sarcasm of this contradiction and the presentation – instead of an evasion – of the subject gives the words a sense of acute realism. Painful realism is also given by the fact that when *Iphigeneia in Tauris* was performed in 414 BC, the Greeks (the Athenians) were being slaughtered in Sicily.

The plot

The play was written before its counterpart, *Iphigeneia in Aulis*, which was the last play that the poet's psyche penned. It takes place in Tauris of Scythia. Iphigeneia narrates the prologue of the play. She tells us that while everybody thinks she is lost, she was saved by Artemis, who put a deer on the altar to be sacrificed in her place. Artemis brought her to Tauris as a priestess in her Temple, where human sacrifices are performed. Greeks are captured and sacrificed in the land of Tauris. And it is Iphigeneia who performs the purification of the men before their slaughter.

Iphigeneia had an ominous dream the previous night. However, she narrates it, awake now in the morning air and light in order to undo it. Then, Orestes and his friend Pylades arrive at the land following Apollo's command that he should bring the statue of Artemis to Athens in order to be saved from the Erinyes that haunt him after having murdered his mother. Orestes is on a mission. He should do the work that is needed for Artemis's statue to return home. We can think that Taurian Artemis represents an archaic, cruel maternal superego to be internalised, appropriated, by Athenians.

Orestes and Pylades are captured by the barbarians and are brought to the Temple to be purified by the priestess before they are sacrificed. There, at the last moment, Iphigeneia and Orestes recognise one another. Iphigeneia thinks that it is herself that should be sacrificed, while Orestes thinks that both they and Pylades should be saved. King Thoas, who hates strangers, particularly Greeks, is deceived by Iphigeneia, who tells him that the statue of Artemis should be taken to the sea for purification. The goddess Athena helps them escape and takes the statue of Artemis with them to Athens.

The prohibited and the impossible

When we come of age, we accept that there are things that are impossible to do (reality as a boundary of omnipotence) and things that are prohibited (symbolic castration as a boundary of deficiencies and differences that signifies reality). We struggle to transform the impossible of omnipotence into that which is prohibited. However, we retain a measure of legitimate infantile illusion in the unconscious. Otherwise, we resort to character and institutional pathological narcissism.

The unfamiliar is, in essence, the old familiar event of castration that signifies our first stranger, the mother, and then the oedipal father, as the third person in our psychic life. Mothers sing lullabies with violent scenes and narrate violent fairy tales. We do the same to ourselves as we grow up. Yet, we may overuse the horror of the unfamiliar and corrupt the confirmation of the sense of self with the many trends of production of 'born again' experiences in order to face early narcissistic traumas. Through inflammatory rhetoric and violent actions in stadiums and in the streets, where political conflicts are raging on, we heart-wrenchingly express the silent pain we carry from the time when pieces of our existence and subjectivity were amputated because of painful traumas. We express a fundamental pain of the self that hurts from the narcissistic trauma. We demand that what we believe is rightfully ours be returned to us. We demand that which does not exist, a utopia. Others around us experience disheartenment and the pain of the traumatised existence.

These destructive behaviours from the mob, however, do not happen like in a play, with metaphorical thought and a sense of the tragic and of irony. It is a reality show where existence is confirmed through trauma and through being left naked. It all starts out like a game but rapidly becomes very serious and dangerous, without, however, becoming more real. Real pieces of the human and material world are sacrificed in stupid, ridiculous, arrogant, and paranoid performances.

The sense of horror of the unfamiliar originates in the discontinuity of castration that reveals the void of unknown capabilities while simultaneously offering us the sense of self in an acute manner (Freud, 1919; De M'Uzan, 2007/2010).

Many forms between raw realism, perception, representation, and fantasy are mixed inside the experience of the unfamiliar that is brought on by a new encounter with the object. The primal scene of the sexual intercourse of the parents is the prime example of the place where perceptions and fantasies are mixed (we hear half words, utterances, sighs, breaths, strange sounds, we see blurry shadows and unclear motions, we imagine images of threat of castration and violent sadomasochistic torture).

In every new encounter, the otherness of the stranger seeks recognition. The mother, hopefully, introduces herself and the world gradually, in doses manageable by the infant's immature ego. The mother introduces the father. She warns the child to be careful and not allow to be passivised. Out there, in the world that it sets out to explore, the threats of castration, loss, and death lurk. The question is whether the mother presents the stranger to the child as a raw, literal external reality or introduces him with her metaphorical thought as another self. The question is whether through alternations of contact and distance, fear and reassurance, hope and anxiety, the recognition will occur, the action will be perfected, and time will be fulfilled.

Orestes and Pylades show up at the courtyard of Artemis' temple at the break of dawn, with precautions, warning one another of the dangers lurking in this foreign land (67–68): *Orestes*: "*Look out, take care that no one is in the path*". *Pylades*: "*I am looking, and turning my eyes everywhere, in examination*".

Everyone believes that Iphigeneia was sacrificed by her father on the altar of Aulis so that the wind would fill the Greek sails and take them to Troy, where the generals would find their glory. Yet, was the wild part of the girl that was preparing to marry Achilles sacrificed? Was it rescued by Artemis, who had requested the sacrifice in the first place? Iphigeneia disappeared during the sacrifice, and a slain female deer appeared on the altar. Was the deer that was slain the untamed part of the girl? She was tricked. She was taken to Aulis as a bride, "a wretched bride" for Achilles.

Could it be that, on an existential level, what was slaughtered on the altar was her capability of seeking another person, her mate with whom they would become a couple? Was it an early cruel maternal superego that attacked her capacity to grow up, to become a woman? Did it stop the winds from filling the sails of her development? This early cruel superego's action "affects the most precious and the most desired objects, including the body itself, and the wished-for baby, representatives of fertility, creativity, and thus of sexuality, and life itself" (Chabert, 2007, p. 258). We can think that in this tragedy, Artemis identifies with such a cruel maternal superego.

Artemis took Iphigeneia away from home, following aerial routes, much like Io had done (29–30): "*conducting me through the bright air*". She settled Iphigeneia in her temple in the land of Tauris, where she anointed her priestess.

There was a temple of Artemis in the Land of the Taurians, too, not only in Athens. In Athens, Artemis was celebrated as the benign virgin hunter who protected pubescent girls and women who had just given birth! In fact, pubescent girls were sent to live in the dormitories of Artemis' temple at Brauron, near Athens, for a while in preparation for the imminent change. In the Land of the Taurians, the other side of the pubescent girl and the woman who has just given birth is presented and performed: here, strangers are sacrificed. Violence is projected outside the maternal body and its babies and is absorbed by the third person, the father. Expecting pregnant women dream of violent battles, accidents, murders, and sacrifices. This is normal and temporary for those stages of development. It is normal and temporary, provided that the mothers can perform the silent work of mourning personal and transgenerational traumatic losses.

The question posed once again by Euripides with *Iphigeneia in Tauris* is whether the primitivism of the relationship with the primary mother will be salvaged or whether their union will settle in with identification, like a fortified temple of Artemis where strangers – all those who represent the father, the triad, stranger anxiety and castration – are sacrificed. The father is not only the person who introduces us to the oedipal superego who sets the boundaries – beneficial prohibitions – and threatens us with castration. The father also helps us retain contact with the primary mother, the ultimate stranger inside us (with morphological regression of thought through images, in dreams, in playing, in art). Iphigeneia happened to have a cruel, remote father and a dark fate (864): "*Fatherless was the fate I received, fatherless*".

Ancient Tragedy borrowed from Homer's *Odyssey* the recognition as a crucial turn in the plot. In Euripides' *Iphigeneia in Tauris* Orestes' recognition by Iphigeneia is an important example of recognition according to Aristotle's *Poetics*. The scholars observe that perhaps Euripides believed that the Athenians needed to bring the statue of the barbaric Artemis back home, re-found their city, shoulder the responsibility for their world, and recognise their fears of persecution and the bloodshed of sacrifice that constituted the city's war situation. The last moment

Orestes is recognised as a brother, another self. Is this enough to end the war? Euripides does not think so. However, he recognizes that the war situation in his city reinforces primitive individual and social defenses. We can think of adhesive identifications as primitive defenses against the unbearable pain of separation that raises an 'autistic' fortress, a fortified temple constructed by chronic neglect, despair, and apathy that turns the self to stone. You can't be heard by a rock as Nina Simone sings in her Sinnerman. Iphigeneia enters the Temple, and then Orestes and Pylades enter the scene cautiously. Orestes: "Look out, take care that no one is in the path". Pylades: "I am looking, and turning my eyes everywhere, in examination". They have nowhere to hide. When the autistic defenses crack, a light enters, and then fears of persecution begin. Recognition is an act of reclamation. It is linked to internalisation. It is also a process of being in the world.

Iphigeneia in Tauris reminds us of some patients who cannot be accessed because they cannot listen or feel, perhaps due to chronic apathy as a result of despair. Euripides creates a sense of urgency in the 'act of reclamation', waking us to mindfulness and meaning, offering realisations to barely experienced preconceptions, that are at risk of becoming atrophied, a barbaric wasteland (Alvarez, 2010). However, when people wake up to mindfulness, then the Furies also wake up to persecute them.

Orestes is a stranger in this barbaric land. He reminds us of Odysseus, who comes to reclaim his own land. When a stranger enters a scene, he shakes the fantasy of omnipotence. Then things begin to happen. The stranger that enters a scene brings the new, the random, the chance. They do not enter a place. They enter a moment, a living occurrence. This is a dramatic situation; action occurs in real-time. It should not be wasted. The barbarians that inhabit the land, like Suitors in Odyssey, keep missing it. They sacrifice the strangers. They do not have the capacity to recognise, take in, and use the object. They waste it. Nothing happens. No meeting, no recognition, no wedding; nothing happened until Odysseus arrived at the palace of Ithaca and Orestes at the Temple of Artemis.

The question is whether the temple of the Taurians will become for Iphigeneia a closed autistic fortress, untransformed and concrete, a retreat, structured with adhesive identifications with the pre-oedipal Great Mother Artemis. This is a fortress of silence, whose immobility stresses the contradiction with its opposite: the name of King Thoas (from the Greek word '*theo*', to run fast, to always be ready).

I hypothesise that the statue of Artemis and the sacred fortress of her temple represent some functions of our character traits and institutions (character traits of a society). We can think that our institutions allow us to separate from the primary mother without destroying her and facing annihilation anxiety. They may be transitional places full of life and multiple meanings. They may become temples where recognition and appropriation of the 'stranger' are realised. Or they may become rigid autistic defensive structures which result in a relentless persecution of the Erinyes when they crack. Or, they may function with fetishistic relationships that cover destruction and psychosis. They may also rely on our adhesive identification with the great Mother, and on our placing her inside us as an altar of private worship, on which we sacrifice the link with the object.

Hubris and Ate

Iphigeneia's lament (203–235) lyrically expresses the recognition and reconciliation with the Hubris and Ate with which the previous generations have burdened her personal development.

> From the beginning my fate was unhappy, from that first night of my mother's marriage; from the beginning the Fates attendant on my birth directed a hard upbringing for me, wooed by Hellenes, the first-born child in the home, whom the unhappy daughter of Leda, by my father's fault, bore as a victim and a sacrifice not joyful, she brought me up as an offering.

She now remembers the introduction of the father who failed to separate her from the primary mother.

As soon as she begins her lament, she remembers her little brother Orestes, whom she left as an infant, a tender sprout in her mother's bosom; him who would one day take the throne and become king of Argos. With the memory of the newborn breastfeeding on his mother, Iphigeneia informs us that the bloody images of castration are connected with a traumatic primal scene and a violent, raw introduction of the father.

At night, Iphigeneia dreamt that the pillar of her house, the male child, Orestes, survived the earthquake that destroyed the entire house, yet he was to be sacrificed. Iphigeneia was preparing him for the sacrifice, as she did with the strangers at the temple. She sprinkled him with holy water and lamented and felt the horror.

In the morning, she mourns with profound grief for the fact that she is a stranger in Pontus, without a polis, without a husband, childless, forgotten by all. Nobody awaits her return. Nobody believes in her nostos any longer. Now, Iphigeneia is not where she should be, where the life that befits her is going on. She does not sing for Hera; she does not weave the forms of Athena and the Titans on the loom. Instead, she blesses the slaughter of the strangers, covered in blood and tears. The strangers here are the Greeks. She is sacrificing Greek men in this foreign land. Full of love and hate, she is saddened by their loss, but she also avenges her own sacrifice at the hands of her people. Her mourning has not been resolved; her ambiguity is casting veils of mist upon the 'eyes' of recognition.

The institution of sacrifice in this temple, however, is based on another much more fundamental sacrifice performed by the congregation of Greeks in Aulis: the sacrifice of the primary mother. In Euripides' *Hecuba*, the Greeks sacrifice Polyxena on the demand of the ghost of Achilles. The ghosts of the dead brothers (comrades) live on in the mobs and demand sacrifices of the living, whether we are in ancient Athens, Tauris, or Gaza. It is the feminine essence of existence that is sacrificed by the masses, which are animated by receiving her infinite powers that stem from the sacred mother–infant relationship.

Femininity comprises the rock of un-represented experiences. It entails passivity. We fear that we will surrender entirely to the passions of the woman who gave birth to us. Her passions intrude violently and asymmetrically in the infant's world. The other has the primacy from the beginning. We feel longing for our primary mother. In some cases, we crystalise the essence of the feminine existence into an idol, a xoanon. How difficult is it then for us to remove our femininity from the temple of private worship (character traits, institutions, cultural morals, and customs), to recover it, to appropriate it, and set it free in psychic circulation between the foreign land of the unconscious, the conscious and the public domain, where its rightful place is?

Orestes and Pylades arrived at the break of dawn, just when sleep would end, in order to steal, to appropriate Artemis' xoanon and take it to Athens. It was Apollo who requested it. He gave Orestes an oracle stating that if he wants to escape the Erinyes that persecuted him after the murder of the primary mother, he must steal the statue of the wild, barbarian Artemis and bring it to the city of civilisation. He must embark on an adventure of internalisation, recognition of the reality of the foreign, primitive maternal element inside of him. He must forgive it and let it go. He must bring it back home. Now, incapable of mourning, he is persecuted and losing his mind. Apollo, much like a paternal element, helps Orestes bring back the primary motherland inside of him. Apollo seeks the return of his sister, Artemis. Mirroring this, Orestes will also find his own lost sister again. He will recognise her and achieve her return. Euripides employs the symbolic capacity of language (symmetries, reflections, condensations, transpositions) in order to mitigate the terrifying impact of encountering the stranger. The descriptions of the sacrifices are familiar/unfamiliar images of horror that introduce castrations, differences of the object, and the many levels of symbolisation – from the most raw and unrepresented to the most symbolised, abstract, representational elements of affects and thoughts. Boys and girls are taken away from their families to be initiated into the world of objects. The question of every change is the transitional space from the primal to the more differentiated. Before landing on the next position, we are up in the air, nowhere. We constantly experience changes.

We have many prospects. We may introduce the stranger, the drives of our soma, the maternal object, and the object of sexual desire, and establish a fundamental border of our psychic life (with normal primary repression or splitting), separate, that is, the 'compatible' conscious contents from the 'incompatible' ones, the familiar from the 'foreign' land inside us. We may emerge from the primary union and progressively differentiate ourselves with every new meaning that we create by allowing the intervention of our mother as another self, whom we invest with meaning so that we can make the transition to a new relationship in reality.

Or we may literally kill the primary mother inside us, remove the foundation of ourselves, uproot the core of our emotional cohesion, and go mad. Then, the

Erinyes will constantly persecute us. We may live awaiting the Barbarians. We may constantly deceive the primitive king inside us. We may constantly be persecuted by the threatening father every time we make a motion of appropriation and integration of the elements of the foreign motherland.

We may escape castration with a perversion: deny reality and retain the fantasy of omnipotence by identifying with the Goddess – great Mother – and thus be the ones that sacrifice the strangers. We may return to nature, become native wild men, and denounce our civilisation. We may return, through poetry, to the hallucination and the metaphorical connection of what can be felt to what can be conceived. We may say: I will be the hallucination you will have when you see my marks in (messages I will send you from the foreign lands with) "the cool breeze of spring and the dew of winter", in circular times.[3] You will host what you see in your gaze. I will find you once again as a baby in your arms, when I was the reason for your worship, I was you, and you were me, and I established a core of emotional continuity of the sense of self so that I can be an autonomous self away from you. Good containment also means separation and differentiation, Bion says.

Euripides offered us a similar containment. He sent Athena as the deus ex machina, who, through her drastic (performative) words, made things happen. She offered things cogency and put them in their rightful place. This, however, happened with substantial irony, as we know that this chaos will never become a cosmos, an order. In the end, with her drastic discourse, Athena made repetition become the past and re-established the public space of the city. Athena said so with the imposingness and the prestige of a protective force! And lo and behold it was done.

The fugitives were not persecuted by the barbarian king. Orestes, Pylades, and Iphigeneia took the statue of Artemis on the journey back home after their own expedition (to Troy and Tauris). As instructed by Athena, they placed the statue of Artemis in a temple in Attica, close to the sea. This was the Temple of Tauropolis Artemis. From then on, Artemis would be celebrated every year thus: the priest would touch a sword on a man's throat, drawing a little blood as a substitute for Orestes' sacrifice. Iphigeneia would become a priestess next to the hills of Brauron and would be buried there upon her death.

When Athena told all this to the Athenian contemporaries of Euripides, the temple already stood there. All the locations she identified also existed and had their specific meaning at the time. Her discourse declared the re-establishment of the homeland, of the sense of self, of being in the world, of the common sense of co-belonging in the common space. And that became language in a future perfect tense. These places, these hills, and these temples bearing the same names still exist today (Rafina, Brauron, Temple of Artemis). And when the tragedy is performed again today, our homeland, our language, is re-established. We re-establish our sense of self with the connections that language allows.

One day, the daughter of the soldier who had died in the Asia Minor war heard her grandmother (the grieving soldier's mother) sing. And then she suddenly interrupted her song and said to herself, "Language, you whore, you fooled me again (putana glossa, pali me xegelasses)".

Notes

1 The direct line quotes are taken from Euripides. (1938). The complete Greek drama. In W. J. Oates, E. O'Neill Jr. (Eds.), & R. Potter (Trans.) *Two volumes. 1. Iphigenia in Tauris*. New York: Random House.
2 Micael Parsons examines this question in his unpublished paper "Where is the stranger at home? The case of Odysseus".
3 From a modern Greek folk song of foreign lands.

References

Alvarez, A. (2010). Levels of analytic work and levels of pathology: The work of calibration. *International Journal of Psychoanalysis*, *91*(4), 859–878.
Chabert, C. (2007). The Malaise of culture and the problem of the superego. *Canadian Journal of Psychoanalysis*, *15*(2), 238–260.
De M' Uzan, M. (2010). The uncanny or I am not who you think I am. In B. B. Dana, F. Sara, & G. Alain (Eds.), *Reading French psychoanalysis*. London and New York: Routledge. (Original work published 2007)
Euripides. (1938). The Complete Greek Drama. In W. J. Oates, E. O'Neill Jr. (Eds.), & R. Potter (Trans.), *Two volumes. 1. Iphigeneia in tauris*. New York: Random House.
Freud, S. (1916) On transience. *S. E.*, *14*.
Freud, S. (1919). The uncanny. *S. E.*, *17*.
Kennedy, R. (2023). The evil imagination. In *Understanding and resisting destructive force*. Bicester: Phoenix Publishing House.
Meraklis, M. G. (2014). Euripides' two iphigeneias and the theme of sacrifice. In *Greek. In Potamianou A. Psychoanalytic approach to ancient tragedy*. Athens: Nea Hestia Publications. (Original work published 1984)

Chapter 8

Euripides' Iphigeneia in Aulis
Triumph in sacrifice[1,2]

A tragedy is a valid mirror of the human condition. It presents, on stage, as actions, the repressed and split-off experiences that return to be represented and integrated. It presents the subject's unbreakable bonds of tragicality with the unconscious. The tragic subject undertakes the responsibility of his fate, which has been defined by the mysterious forces in the past. A tragedy recognises – does not shy away from – the emotional storm that inescapably breaks out every time living people meet and are really present. The presented words and actions are precise, drastic, crucial; they differentiate, and they do not confound the acting and speaking subjects but instead render them real, alive, and visible in transitional spaces of tragic paradoxes. A tragic plot gives time to words and emotions so that they can speak their truth and make it objective. A play takes time because it is an act, not a fantasy. It is a composition of things that begin to occur when people meet. Iphigeneia comes to Aulis to meet her father and his army, who plan her sacrifice. Her tragedy presents the return and recognition of unfamiliar, frightening, somatic-psychic experiences; the experiences are created anew in search of a novel interpretation and integration.

I wish to examine *Iphigeneia* as a tragic sacrifice of the individual that fantasises about uniting with the entirety of the large group in order to both 'be saved' and 'save' it from the dissolution that threatens it at the moment when she is integrated as a unit. Iphigeneia is summoned to Aulis, unaware of the fact that she has been selected to be sacrificed. However, she decides to recognise her emotions, not deny them, to be present at the beginnings of her violent primal experiences, and personally choose the meaning with which they will be registered in her history. Her sacrifice reminds soldiers that they go to war not only to kill but also to be killed. Men need to recognise the girl inside themselves, assume the feminine position towards the father, and be loyal to him. Iphigeneia's sacrifice, like the war against the common enemy, unifies the people of her country.

The Greek army has gathered in Aulis. Everyone is anxious to set sail and destroy Troy, to slaughter, to take women as slaves and spoils of war, to avenge the insult that was the abduction of Helen. The shrine of Artemis is there, in Aulis. A shrine of sacrifice is always built in a place of violence; it envelops the violence and brings it back to mind. The Greek general Agamemnon, however, has killed the sacred deer of Artemis, which is the perfect depiction of the autonomous body that emerges as

DOI: 10.4324/9781032712864-9

a form in the forest, like a girl's body that rises from the anal stage, lustrous, clean, clear, phallic, and enviable. Thus, the goddess punishes the Greeks by withholding the winds. Standstill. Nothing happens. Time stops. Nothing is liberated; nothing is born. Every now and again, noise breaks out. A turmoil in the army that is in danger of turning into a mob. The pounding of hooves, not as a triumph of life but as a threat that a wild wave of passions will sweep everything. The sound-making gates of the psyche are open. Chaos threatens to obliterate the world (order). Wild, violent scenes between couples that bewail when they learn the truth.

Calchas' omen states that in order for the winds to fill the Greek sails, the gods want Agamemnon to sacrifice Iphigeneia. The general sends word to Clytemnestra to bring their daughter to Aulis, where she will supposedly marry Achilles. He instantly regrets this and sends a letter ordering them to return home. Menelaus intercepts the letter and attacks Agamemnon, accusing him of renouncing the responsibility of being a leader. The army is about to explode and dissolve into idleness. A civil war may destroy the unity of the large group. Odysseus is plotting.

Iphigeneia arrives. When Achilles learns the truth, he promises Clytemnestra to do everything in his power to prevent the sacrifice. The maniacal notion of war has, however, enticed everybody. Everything lies under a merciless light. You cannot find a place to hide, to take time, to perch, to turn to yourself and reflect. At one moment, the camp is full of violent emotions and crowds of people, and the next moment, everything is void. No one is there to look after you. Everyone is untrustworthy. In the blinding, dazzling light of the day, you cannot see the object.

The girl addresses her father and then her mother with heart-breaking pleas of unbelievable affection to save her (1216–1219):

And about your knees, as a suppliant, I twine my limbs – these limbs your wife here bore. Do not destroy me before my time, for it is sweet to look upon the light, and do not force me to visit scenes below.[3]

As a version of Achilles in Hades, from how he is depicted in the Odyssey, she wants to go on living even if it is an inglorious life. She does not want a glorious death. Achilles represents the explosive violence of her emotions, as well as the inglorious emptying of the self, the sad shadow of a child that is left all alone when it has been caught in a violent family scene that has passed like a storm; the parental couple retreats to its bedroom with everything beastly having been tamed.

In her glorious sacrifice, Iphigeneia finds a meaning. She becomes one with everybody. She removes herself from the notion of a separate individual, as well as from the notion of a couple, of wedlock. She decides that she will not be alone in a world of Hubris, without cohesion or meaning, but that she will offer herself for sacrifice and, thus, offer both meaning and cohesion to us. The world around her is incomprehensible, full of arrogance and destructiveness. She decides to take on the evil so that the world may be absolved. She is the subject of the fantasy of sacrifice. She walks to the altar on her own and unites with the large group. The kings and the army stand around her. Is it a revival of an incestuous union ceremony? In the end, a messenger announces to the mother that it was a deer that was sacrificed. Iphigeneia was taken by the goddess. What does remain? A bitter, desolate range with several dark shacks, useless and meaningless. In the darkness of the night, you cannot see that the object is lost.[4]

André Green (1969) notes: None of them thought, "let's not go to Troy, it is not mandatory". The gods' oracle was neither telling them to go or not to go. It was telling them that if they wish to go, they must sacrifice Iphigeneia. Their catastrophic obsession was Hubris. The general that would spill the blood of so many children must pay for the Hubris in advance by first sacrificing his own daughter. The daughter is sacrificed for her father's desire so that the operation of vengeance and profit will be successful.

The sacrifice of Iphigeneia by Agamemnon is tragic. The human subject is a law unto itself. She emerges from the primary union as a separate and autonomous self: she makes a spontaneous gesture that changes the world. A baby is actually born on the verge of annihilation. Literally helpless. If its mother does not take care of it, it will really die. Fear of death is a reality for the human infant that registers.

We know that existence is finite and the only absolute truth is change. Yet, we need to believe in absolute truths, in our ideals. We believe that if we achieve these ideals, they will protect us and bring us happiness. By definition, we never reach our ideals. Faith in ideals is necessary for us to continue trying by sacrificing personal satisfactions. We need our illusions and our disillusions. First, we believe, then we know the reality. Deception is common in animals, including the weakest one: man. If, however, we refute the bonds with which we form meaning, if we avoid creating and finding truth, then we do not live inside the experience. It does not touch us; it has no effect. In the tragedy of *Iphigeneia*, everyone runs from the truth.

In Greek, Iphigeneia's name means 'born in strength'. She is split in two. She is in contact with reality. And she is born again by being united with her paternal Ideal. Iphigeneia is the person that becomes powerful, distinguishing the reality from the impossible (1370): "*It is hard for us to persist in impossibilities*". She uses the Ideal as a shield to deflect the fears of persecution and annihilation. In the end, with her sacrifice, Iphigeneia accomplishes a delusion. She becomes one with her Ideal. She saves the army, the large group, Greece! And she saves herself (1375–1376): "*I am resolved to die; and this I want to do with honour, dismissing from me what is mean*".

We are born open to the body and the outside world in a galaxy of a primordial psycho-sensory multi-subjectivity, and only gradually and painfully, and always incompletely, do we become autonomous individuals (Bleger, 1967/2013). There is a time when illusion is a legitimate reality. The mother, with suitable doses of presence and absence, allows the child to create an intermediate space of transitional objects between the internal and external reality. The infant gradually discovers that the world is beyond its omnipotence. It existed before the infant was born and will continue to exist after it is gone. When we participate in a large group, our experience of being inside a primordial womb of multi-subjectivity is revived.

Bollas (2018) reminds us of LeBon's studies according to which the organised large crowd makes decisions according to its own unconscious, in a manic way, in contrast to the unconscious of each individual. Erlich (2016) discusses the large group dynamics: It is worryingly unfamiliar to see a large group transforming beyond individuals. Becoming something similar to a primeval, prehistoric creature that pulsates, a dinosaur moving slowly on vast ranges seeking prey, all the while being careful not to be attacked by another predator. Its motions may be slow, monotonous, boring, and purposeless until suddenly, there is an explosion, and the beast begins to charge towards unknown directions at breathtaking speed. The leader of a large group is in danger of losing his sense of direction or falling victim to its ravenous mania. Participation in a large group fills individuals with anxiety, especially when they are becoming a separate unit and form the belief of having control over their lives.

Bollas (2018) examines how, in our modern times, we put emphasis on instant connectedness that replaces the need to be a separate subject that reflects and gives meaning to our being in the world. We can think that today, we cannot find a safe place to rest, full of pleasure and meaning. We do not find pleasure in waiting. We exhaust ourselves; we are not saving our strength.

The chaos that lies in the foundations of the large group is expressed through the aphonia, confusion, and bewilderment of some of its members who become really attuned to the discovery that reality has no meaning; it is not at all harmonious or rational. Instead, it is arhythmical and lacks metre. Man by himself is not a measure of anything, nor did he come into the world for a reason. Fear that the individual will become enmeshed in the large womb of the group may prompt a member to retreat into himself, to autistically lay low, to isolate in an attempt to escape. Strangely enough, isolation leads to the other extreme, the sacrifice of individuality and the loss of the self inside the mass.

Bion (1961) described the tragic essence of human existence as the innate conflict between two fundamental motions: as an animal that belongs to the herd, which is only capable of existing within a womb with others, and as an individual with its own subjectivity that can only find fulfilment in an autonomous course.

According to Freud (1914): "The individual does actually carry on a twofold existence: one to serve his own purposes and the other as a link in a chain, which he serves against his will, or at least involuntarily".

The newborn is dependent on an environment mother, an external object that can be good enough or may fail in a devastating way. The fantasy of the primary mother may be an interpretation of the infant's experience of coming into the world helpless, without meaning or purpose, like an unwilling simple link of a chain.

Iphigeneia is dangerous when she becomes a subject. By willingly sacrificing her autonomous existence, she becomes enmeshed with the whole. In order to harness the tremendous forces of the large group (the army), Agamemnon becomes authoritarian. He identifies the group with the terrifying primary mother (Artemis), and by also identifying with her himself, he acquires her properties (Winnicott, 1950/1986).

The Superego houses the tragic realisation of this reality. It transforms this realisation into an Ideal and internalises it as an end in itself, the sacrifice for the large group that also takes the place of the primary mother. The Superego includes prohibitions of reality and ideals. It is shaped by the identification with the Superego of the parents and connects the individual with the chain of previous generations and community requirements. In order to feel secure, we sacrifice a portion of our possibilities of happiness. Freud (1930) noted that we are unhappy for the sake of civilisation, because the drives are repressed. They do not, however, stop working on the foundations of society, constantly threatening them with dissolution. In order to defend against the unthinkable agony of annihilation, individuals and groups organise a defence, the fear of breakdown, a chaos, a civil war. Then, wars and sacrifices become necessary. Fears of breakdown, organised chaos, civil wars, wars, and sacrifices are defences of psychotic order against the agony of annihilation. People take destruction into their own hands.

In 1921, Freud studied the phenomena of the large regressed group and linked them to infant development (primary identification). Apart from the mob, he described large groups with structure and hierarchy, like the church and the army, which work towards a clear goal. Finally, he addressed the manner in which a leader creates a group of followers that follow his ideals and morals by usurping their ideals and their need to believe in them. The leader risks becoming the enemy of the people, as he is in danger of attracting all the aggression that individuals repress inside in order to coexist as a group. Moreover, the group threatens to change their leader (Freud, 1912–1913, 1921, 1930, 1939).

Humans create and fear chaos. They try to bestow order and assign meaning to the world and, thus, resort to unconscious compromises that seem to be funny for the conscious when, in reality, they are tragic. A girl saving Greece appears to be funny; however, the realisation of her being simply an involuntary link in a chain of generations is tragic. The transformation of such an involuntary link to a voluntary social bond is tragic.

Social bonds are bonds of tenderness and a transformation of autoerotism, love for the self and our double, the other that we like. In spite of our differences, on a deep visceral level, we are like that person; we have bonds of friendship and sympathy with them. This transformation creates, and at the same time discovers, the other person inside us, as well as our self inside the other person (Denis, 1982/2010). The other is another self.

Iphigeneia salvages the social bonds of tenderness by becoming enmeshed with the 'us' of the group. Being both liberated and a liberator, she escapes by waking up from a nightmare. A nightmare brings an end to the fear of persecution; it interrupts what you are experiencing. It follows the simple reasoning that only that which does not exist is safe. What is Iphigeneia trying to escape from with her death that resembles waking up from a nightmare? What she salvages is the link of meaning connecting the generations and the community. There are many ways of not existing; for instance, physical death, denial of reality, idealisation of the object, etc. By following the paternal Ideal, Iphigeneia decides for herself, opting for her self-sacrifice. It appears that at the moment of her conversion, when she decides to be self-sacrificed, Iphigeneia defeats her own death.

When we make a movement of internalisation, we need another (external) subject to envelop – with a fantasy – the somato-psychic elements we are reviving so as to interpret them and integrate them into the self. If internalisation is obstructed, we create a nightmare. Persecuted by our fears, we run in search of a refuge where we can hide and save what we are trying to internalise (as well as the self). However, if the refuge (the containing object) is not sufficient, we wake up in order to save both the elements that we are attempting to internalise and the self.

The dream is a temporary refuge that we create for the self to spend the night in. We build it with sensory, motor, emotional, and perceptual elements that we process psychically. The self is 'drawn into' the plot of the dream; it does not wander uncommitted to a relationship with an object; it finds a place to go to and stand. The sense of self is precarious and paradoxical. It constantly changes, but in the morning, when we wake up, it maintains its continuity and cohesion, its identity. The artistry with which we build a dream, as well as the lack thereof, are indicative of the quality of the complex work of imagination.

"To die her inevitable death then, the death that they all want so much. To die it herself by her own volition" (Hatzis, 2000). Hatzis links Iphigeneia's sacrifice with the sacrifice of a Greek fighter in the modern civil war in Greece (1945–1949). After the Second World War, after the war against the external enemy ended, the civil war exploded in modern Greece.

Iphigeneia (she who is born in strength) says, in a way, to the soldiers who are restless while they wait to go to battle: Be patient, be passive, assume a feminine, receptive position, rely on your normal primary masochism, like a girl that becomes a woman, learn how to wait, save your strength. When the omens become favourable, you will need all your strength to fight and not to spare yourself.

Some scholars insist that an explanation is necessary regarding how a girl reaches the decision of self-sacrifice. There is a link missing; what did transpire in her psyche? How is it possible for one to kill one's self? I think that the insufficient link here is the function of the paternal boundary. The difficulty to transform the wish/fear to castrate (kill) and be castrated (killed) by the father was the secret that the girl shared with her father and her little brother. By sharing a secret of this insufficiency, Iphigeneia 'assigns' the change of the organisation to patriarchy to the little boy – Orestes – that accompanies her to the camp in Aulis. When he grows up, Orestes will come to her rescue – rescuing himself from sacrifice, by being recognized (internalized) as a brother, at the same time. He will have endured the persecution of the Erinyes all the way to the land of the Taurians after having murdered his primary mother. He will have undertaken the task of bringing the statue of Artemis to Athens in order for the city to integrate her archaic powers. These powers belong to the city, not to any leader. No one will identify with the primary mother – out of fear of – and become a dictator.

Iphigeneia sets out on a chariot, along with her mother, on the long road from her childhood home to the public stage of Aulis. There she will present herself, bringing forth both herself and her body to the present, on-site, on stage, to encounter all the things that return from the unconscious so that they can be recognised and internalised. In the end, after the painful encounter with the other self, the unfamiliar saviour, the tragedy presents us with the clear gaze of the subject that accepts the responsibility for her fantasies and actions.

Let us, finally, consider the tragedy from Agamemnon's point of view. He undertakes the responsibility of commanding an army in a campaign of abduction, domination, and the return of spoils and sex slaves. However, he feels alienated from the troops. He resembles the captain in Conrad's (1910/1993) novel *The Secret Sharer*. The captain encounters the unfamiliar stranger, his alter ego, who returns as an old acquaintance of his unconscious. He confronts him and leaves him where he belongs, in the past, in a foreign land. Thus, in the end, he manages to feel that he is the captain and that nothing can stand between himself and his ship.

Euripides' tragedy concludes when the wind fills the Greek sails, the ships sail towards Troy, and Agamemnon becomes a leader with nothing standing between himself and his army. What was it that returned as an unfamiliar acquaintance from the past that brought with it the stillness of the winds and the threat of disorganisation for both Agamemnon and the troops? We all respond to this question by self-analysis.

When an individual (or a group) forms into a separate unit, it fears that the outside world will persecute it, and its formation will dissolve. It is then that an adequate father intervenes to take the child to the outside world, introduce it to social bonds, and alleviate its acute paranoia. The fear of breakdown threatens the camp in Aulis. This fear is a psychotic defence against the unthinkable anxiety of annihilation. It actively repeats the chaos experienced by the helpless infant when the environment-mother is unreliable and fails to help the infant develop into an individual with continuity and cohesion, become a person (with the psyche inhabiting its body), and connect to reality (Winnicott, 1974, 1988). The mother who 'lies' to the infant does not offer meaning. She leaves her infant exposed to the raw reality that raises an excess of rage and agony. The leader who lies fails to contain people's anxieties. She defensively creates chaos. She commits Hubris.

Euripides opens paths for us to very early layers, to the place where the psyche emerges, close to non-meaning, to places where the scores with the gods are never settled. The slaying of the sacred deer and the daughter's sacrifice is not the cause and the solution but an attempt, rather, to create a narrative, a transference chronicle, a (private and public) registry of our history, from the achronicity of the compulsion to repeat early extreme failures of the holding environment.

It is necessary that our potential connections with the previous generations and the community that is transmitted by the Superego of the parents are realised in the experience of the relationships inside the family, as well as with others in the community. The Superego has its roots in the Id, in the source of the drives. The Id is defined by the body but is also undefined because there is no subject of the drives there. When fantasies are shaped, then it can say: 'I am their subject'. Where the Id once was (and the roots of the Superego as well), the subject will now stand. It will internalise and accept its responsibility, its drives and ideals.

The subject is something that will be completed in the future, following a landmark that will set the potential free. We will become the subject of our fantasies, that is, the interpretations of the experiences that we create. We are not free to choose. But we can become responsible for the way we understand, interpret, and register the traumatic badness of the world. The idea that we are a cohesive being with an autonomous self that possesses free will is an illusion.

We need to believe there is meaning and order in the world as well as cohesion in the self. Losing control over our destiny is terrifying. Being aware of it gives us a sense of the tragic. We emerge from the primary union; we become subjects; we act and change the world. Troy will never exist again. There is constant change. We always make agreements with others regarding what is reality. At the same time, we ask: What do the people say? In the tragedy of *Iphigeneia*, the chorus, every now and again, commends somebody on their choices. The assembly of the city, the chorus, legitimises the subject.

Notes

1 Michael Cacoyannis' cinematic adaptation of Euripides' *Iphigeneia in Aulis* set the tragedy at the traumatic time of the restoration of Democracy in Greece, in 1974, when Cyprus – as a daughter of the mother land – was sacrificed in order for the foundations of a new regime to become safely rooted.
2 The direct line quotes are taken from Euripides (1891). In E. P. Coleridge (Trans.), *The plays of Euripides* (Vols. II). London: George Bell and Sons Publications. 1891.
3 Euripides. In E. P. Coleridge (Trans.), *The plays of Euripides* (Vols. II). London: George Bell and Sons Publications. 1891. www.perseus.tufts.edu/hopper/text?doc=Perseus%3Atext%3A1999.01.0108%3Acard%3D1211
4 In Cacoyannis' film, the tragedy ends with the Greek ships setting sail into the night, lighting the way to doom, while Clytemnestra shoots a look of unbearable pain and mortal envy to those sailing on the wind that her daughter's loss brought.

References

Bion, W. R. (1961). *Experiences in groups*. London: Tavistock.
Bleger, J. (2013). *Symbiosis and ambiguity: A psychoanalytic study*. London and New York: Routledge. (Original work published 1967)
Bollas, C. (2018). Meaning and melancholia. In *Life in the age of bewilderment*. London and New York: Routledge.
Conrad, J. (1993). *The secret sharer and other stories*. London: Dover Publications. (Original work published 1910)
Denis, P. (2010). Primary homosexuality: A foundation of contradictions. In D. Briksted-Breen, S. Flandres, & A. Gibeault (Eds.), *Reading French psychoanalysis*. London and New York: Routledge. (Original work published 1982)

Erlich, H. S. (2016). Bion and the large group. In H. Levine & G. Civitarese (Eds.), *The W. R. Bion tradition. Lines of development. Evolution of theory and practice over the decades*. London: Karnac.

Euripides. (1891). *The plays of Euripides* (Vols. II, E. P. Coleridge, Trans.). London: George Bell and Sons Publications.

Freud, S. (1912–1913). Totem and taboo: Some points of agreement between the mental lives of savages and neurotics. *S. E., 13*.

Freud, S. (1914). On narcissism. an introduction. *S. E., 14*.

Freud, S. (1921). Group psychology and the analysis of the ego. *S. E., 18*.

Freud, S. (1930). Civilisation and its discontents. *S. E., 21*.

Freud, S. (1939). Moses and monotheism. *S. E., 23*.

Green, A. (1969). *Un oeil en trop. Le complexe d'Oedipe dans la tragédie*. Paris: Minuit/ Series "Critique".

Hatzis, D. (2000). Studies. In *Greek*. Athens: Rodakio Publications.

Winnicott, D. W. (1974). Fear of breakdown. *International Review of Psycho-Analysis, 1*, 103–107.

Winnicott, D. W. (1986). Some thoughts on the meaning of the word democracy. In *Home is where we start from*. Harmondsworth: Penguin. (Original work published 1950)

Winnicott, D. W. (1988). *Human nature*. London: Free Association Press.

Chapter 9

Sophocles' Philoctetes
From somatic pain to trading[1]

Philoctetes led seven ships of warriors from Thessaly in the campaign of the Greeks against the Trojans. Along with the rest of the Greeks, he made a stop at the island of Lemnos. There, he went too close to a temple of Athena and was bitten on the foot by a venomous snake. His wound would not heal, and he suffered immensely. He cried out in horrible pain, which brought terror to the troops. Odysseus convinces the Greeks to abandon him on the island. The Greeks continue their expedition towards Ilion, while Philoctetes remains alone in Lemnos, forsaken, abandoned for ten years, almost for the complete duration of the Trojan War. He has no companions to become an echo of his experience. Inside him, the war between the most primitive forces is constant and merciless. Ten years have passed, and the Trojan War still will not end. The oracle then states that the Greeks cannot conquer Troy without Heracles' invincible bow and arrows. Heracles has gifted his bow to Philoctetes.

Philoctetes was the penultimate of Sophocles' seven surviving tragedies. It was taught in 409 BC. Philoctetes lives in extreme loneliness on an island that is void of inhabitants. He has only his pain. He clings to his physical pain as an envelope to unify his fragmented bodily self and contain his fear of disintegration. Finally, an adequate holding world is made through political negotiations. We can think of politics as a work of culture, a transitional phenomenon which links internal with external reality and consoles us.

What does the fact that Philoctetes went too close to Athena's temple mean? What boundary did he violate? A symbolic barrier? Philoctetes, son of Poeas and Demonassa, is, according to Homer, the hero who had been given Heracles' bow and arrows in gratitude for lighting the pyre on Mount Oeta to rid him of the pain due to Deianira's tunic that ate away at his flesh. Heracles asked Philoctetes to keep his place of death a secret. Philoctetes vowed to never speak of it. However, he gave in to being questioned, climbed Mount Oeta, and stomped his foot on the ground where Heracles' pyre had been lit. He had not spoken, but he had broken his oath. For this Hubris, he was punished with a horrible wound from the snakebite on his foot. He ended up being confined to Lemnos, a desolate island. He is without a polis. Without his comrades, his destructiveness prevails. It threatens his self and his object with fragmentation. The desert island, like the group of his comrades

DOI: 10.4324/9781032712864-10

who deserted him, like an abandoning mother, 'contained' him with extreme pain, like Deianira 'contained' Heracles with a death bearing (aggression turned inside) poisoned tunic. He is in pain, he moans, and he leads a non-negotiable existence with hatred, rage, and unbearable pain.

It is mourning that is not achieved and idealisation (the invincible bow) that is not let go. Sophocles' Philoctetes is clinging on to physical pain uncompromisingly. He defends his existence with a pain that reaches the human limits. He envelopes his story not with meaning but with pain. This is a constant somatic pain that is lived as an intolerable repetition of raw sensory bombardment, beyond meaning, beyond the human capacity to be lived as an experience by a subject who thinks about it (Winnicott, 1949/1996; Ogden, 2023). An unbearable pain is beyond our capability to receive a response of understanding from an object. It is beyond the opportunity given to us by our link to the other person who feels our pain. It is beyond the purpose of transferring our pain to them.

Schmidt-Hellerau (2011) refers to Elaine Scarry's (1987) study of physical pain in tortures. Physical pain cannot be expressed. It cannot be put into words. It unmakes the world of meanings that contain the self. Schmidt-Hellerau examines how, in states of unbearable physical pain, the world of objects and the self shrinks. The self withdraws in the locus of pain, where language becomes a scream. The scream is an aggressive act that defends the self against attacks from outside. It is not enough to think of the human being in terms of the conflict between love and hate, we need to also think of the realness and aliveness of the soma.

Philoctetes struggles to make his physical pain a psycho-somatic experience. He forms a combination of masochism and narcissism. This, however, can be a deadly combination. Philoctetes chooses to keep both his torture and his bow. When a child feels physical pain, she must repeat the experience by inflicting similar pain on somebody else to see the other suffer and reflect on the other's pain through fantasies and emotions. Through this reflection, the child can recall her own experience of physical pain and render it psychic. If the object, as an external subject, agrees to temporarily house the child's pain and experience it on her behalf, if the other self is touched and hurt in the child's place and survives, then the pain will transform from physical to psychic.

Leon made an announcement stating that in six months, he would stop his analysis. In a subsequent session, we created and shared a transference experience based on the reconstruction that in six months, his analysis will break down like his world had broken down when he was eight years old and heard the news that his father would soon die from a very aggressive cancer. Is this an adequate time for a child to be prepared to be on his own? The next day, he began to make some incredible sounds: oououaaaaagggggtttt. With an agonising madness, he made these sounds as if something was eradicated (expelled) from inside. He said that he felt an intense somatic pain, an intolerable burning inside his throat. He tried to speak, but he suddenly interrupted his speech with these raw howls. I thought this howl was the rejection of an unbearable psychic pain that he felt when he realised his helplessness and his dependence on me as an external object. He felt my interpretation as a traumatic intrusion. He revived the trauma of being close to his father, who was clinging to him when he was suffering from cancer. Leon then felt that he did not count as a subject. He felt expelled, alone, with nobody to listen to him. He tried to expel his body and its pain. But this pain was the only real thing he had to hold on to and maintain its object-related source.

Did Philoctetes' cries have the power to convey meaning, to make things visible, and to set a stage? Are they battle cries or an appeal for negotiation? In the course of his tragedy, Philoctetes sets the work of mourning in motion (recognition and negotiation of reality). His cries begin to convey meaning, to set a stage because the sound-producing sources of the psyche remain alive within the language. Auditory fossils come to transference relationships in everyday life. They appear in condensed forms that comprise the somatic poles of affects (McDougal, 1989). They are gateways to traumatic experiences of despair but also of sexuality and destruction. The use of language as a bridge between the physical and the psychic field renders these experiences capable of obtaining access to meaning-making processes.

The Greeks send Odysseus and Neoptolemus to take Heracles' bow and arrows from Philoctetes, even by deception if need be. Philoctetes refuses to hand them over the weapon and does not want to reconcile with the men who had so cruelly abandoned him helpless ten years previously. Odysseus tries to talk Neoptolemus into deceiving Philoctetes. He advises him to tell Philoctetes that he himself had also been deceived by Odysseus, who held on to his father's, Achilles', weapons, and that is why Neoptolemus left the battle in anger to return home to the isle of Skyros. Thus, Philoctetes would feel that he was not the only one that had been deceived and angry and that Neoptolemus was in the same position.

Philoctetes would think that Neoptolemus felt the same pain as he did. A pain concerning the loss of something that was absolutely necessary, without which he could not exist. The thing that was absolutely necessary for Philoctetes was his grip on his physical pain. Through this grip on the physical pain, he would keep both his existence in a suffocating cohesion and his object in prison (Potamianou, 2001). He fears that he will fall to pieces if he loosens his grip on the pain and lets the object go.

Transference, like tragedy, presents the process of integrating unrepresented elements and transforms this repetition into a story. However, the possibility of losing one's grip is becoming real in the tragedy of *Philoctetes*. Philoctetes' immobile nature is expressed through his epic persistent refusal to mourn the traumatic loss of omnipotence and accept reality. Then, however, it transmutes to the tragedy's dialectic, which means that the object and its meaning are introduced.

Neoptolemus protests greatly but is ultimately convinced by Odysseus to take part in staging this deception. He is convinced when he hears Odysseus speak of the glory he will achieve when Troy is sacked with Philoctetes' bow and arrows. Neoptolemus deceives Philoctetes but immediately begins regretting it. Odysseus intervenes once again, arguing intensely in order to convince Neoptolemus.

Out of nowhere, a merchant appears. The presence of Odysseus as a resourceful negotiator who likes winning poses the question, 'What is best for us?'. The intervention of the role of a 'merchant' introduces the sense of profit with the word 'virtue' ('χάρις'), which is a term of political practice (gratitude for a benefit). It means collaboration. Here, it is both ironic and ambiguous: Neoptolemus is grateful to the merchant for aiding him in deceiving Philoctetes by making him believe the lie even more. But it is Philoctetes who will profit the most from the entire staging; he will come in contact with the truth. In order for the truth to be felt, it is clad in 'lies'; to know reality means to transform it. The reaction to the pain of mourning is at stake: Will the cry 'war' be chosen or the negotiation of accepting reality?

The life exchanges with other people mobilise and free Philoctetes' developmental possibilities and allow his rigid autistic defenses to be transformed into a 'common coin', something that is 'current' through being commonly discussed and sanctioned. Through the tragedy's process, Philoctetes' internality and femininity/receptiveness obtained depth, as did his capability to intervene, to accept interventions, to bargain, to mitigate polarisations, and to include complex contradictions of a resourceful and treacherous Odysseus. To create a transitional space of politics where contradictions can be tolerated and co-exist.

An old man exiled from the polis confronts a young man, Neoptolemus, who tries to find his place in his polis. The issue is that of an honest fight versus cheating. Will the young man be disappointed by the defeated old man? Will he identify with him and become alienated from himself? Vernant and Vidal-Naquet (1972) examine the paradox of an adolescent who becomes an adult, a fighter. He goes through the rites of passage. The adolescent does not participate in battles yet. He guards the boundaries; he uses deceit and lies in ambush. Philoctetes lives in a cave, on the boundary between human life and an animal (body) wild world. Philoctetes, finding himself in an impasse, asks the question that we always hear in ancient tragedy: "What shall I do?" (1063, 1350). Both he and Neoptolemus choose to return home. However, Philoctetes is integrated again into the human world. This begins when he hears, for the first time after ten years, people speaking Greek, and he comes again in contact with language. He begins to be cured by regaining his flexibility when he is immersed in the flexible accuracy of the Greek language. Language shapes us because it helps us find/create an object.

Odysseus leaves in anger when Neoptolemus ultimately returns the bow to Philoctetes. Heracles appears as a deus ex machina and convinces Philoctetes to give in to the plea of the Greeks and go to Troy to bring victory. Philoctetes is convinced to go to Troy, where they will take care of him and cure him. Schmidt-Hellerau (2008, p. 719) uses the concept of the lethic phallus in order to study how trauma can result in "a specific pathology in which disease is used as a trophy and a means to bind the object in an ongoing caretaker relationship".

The play ends with a wish for a good journey. In Troy, he kills Paris with his arrows and proudly takes part in the ultimate deceit. He hides inside the Trojan Horse in the final attack against Troy.

With Heracles' epiphany, "Sophocles makes it clear that only in the fictive context is a revolution, a happy ending, possible. In reality, it is human obstinacy and malice that win out". Mortals can be narcissistically wounded and fall off their world. Then, the world becomes incomprehensible (Zimmermann, 1986/1991, pp. 84–85).

The infant's word is an order of meaning, a cosmos, an environment-holding mother. She takes in and works through the infant's anxieties. She returns them to her infant in meaningful forms, along with the way she processes them. The infant internalises maternal care and makes a psychic space. Salonen (2022) writes:

> In finding another human being, the infant simultaneously finds himself as a metaphor for the latter. This early configuration, the primary identification, will create a preliminary frame of reference for the psychic representation and elaboration of elementary drive phenomena that would otherwise discharge directly as stark drive-instinctual deeds. The collapse of this vital constellation signifies extreme psychic trauma: a strange world of cosmic stimulation outside primary identification without hope and consolation. On the other hand, recognizing another human being at this elementary lever of psychic functioning may restore integrity and the capability of genuine thinking.

The processes of object finding/creation are affected by painful somatic experiences (illnesses, medical procedures, abuses). Physical pain leaves traces on the object that the person rediscovers in the psyche's motions of recognition and self-recognition. Language comprises the medium of recognition of these traces. As the elements of physical pain are intertwined with psychic movements, it is possible that they are transformed into psychic pain through the relationships and processes of object formation. In the analysis, and Greek tragedy, we hear the things that lie beyond thought – the pre-psychic, sensory, motor, and perceptual elements of physical pain experiences – because words retain the somatic rhythm of auditory images regardless of their source.

Note

1 The direct line quotes are taken from Sophocles (1898). *The Philoctetes of sophocles. Edited with introduction and notes by Sir Richard Jebb.* Cambridge. Cambridge University Press. 1898.

References

McDougal, J. (1989). *Theaters of the body: A psychoanalytic approach to psychosomatic illness.* New York and London: W.W. Norton.
Ogden, H. T. (2023). Like the Belly of a bird breathing: On Winnicott's "mind and its relation to the psyche-soma". *International Journal of Psychoanalysis, 104*(1), 7–22.
Potamianou, A. (2001). *Le Traumatique. Repetition et Elaboration.* Paris: Dunod.

Salonen, S. (2022). A stranger in exile: Metapsychological remarks on sophocles oedipus at colonus. In *Presentation at 9th Delphi international psychoanalytic symposium, on 25–28 August 2022*. Delphi.

Scarry, E. (1987). *The body in pain: The making and unmaking of the world*. Oxford: Oxford University Press.

Schmidt-Hellerau, C. (2008). The lethic phallus: Rethinking the misery of Oedipus. *Psychoanalytic Quarterly, 78*, 719–753.

Schmidt-Hellerau, C. (2011). Lethe and remembering: Self-preservation and the death drive in Freud's psychoanalysis. In *Presentation at the hellenic psychoanalytic society, on 30, september, 2011*. Athens.

Sophocles. (1898). *The philoctetes of sophocles. Edited with introduction and notes by sir Richard Jebb*. Cambridge: Cambridge University Press.

Vernant, J. P., & Vidal-Naquet, P. (1972). *Mythe et Tragedie en Gréce Anciennne*. Paris: François Maspero.

Winnicott, D. W. (1996). Mind and its relation to the psyche-soma. In *Through paediatrics to psychoanalysis*. London: Karnac. (Original work published 1949)

Zimmermann, B. (1991). Greek tragedy. In *An introduction*. Baltimore, MD and London: The John Hopkins University Press. (Original work published 1986)

Chapter 10

Sophocles' Antigone
The tragic staging of the political[1,2]

Sophocles' play is a paradigmatic staging of the political in a tragic plot. This staging is relevant today in the time of unmanageable complexities and loss of orientation. Freud took from the tragic poets the unique concept of man's necessity to go on stage, express and publicly present his private suffering (Steiner, 1984). To come in contact with the other inside of him through the other outside.

Death is a necessity determined by nature. Mourning is a human need. It is a personal, profound, internal, painful work, and it is also, always, a public affair. Creon prohibits this process for the next of kin of Polynices and for the community. The work of mourning is not a drive; it is a need. The drives should be prohibited. Needs of the ego should never be let down, says Winnicott.

Antigone goes out into the agora and clashes mortally with Creon, who expresses the law of the state. Antigone expresses the 'morality of common blood', the unwritten law. It is easy to misinterpret this conflict as a strife between divine and human law (Topouzis, 1997).

A philosopher, Hegel saw a conflict between Antigone's duty to her family and Creon's to the polis. A poet, Goethe saw that such abstractions cannot be cut off from personal violent passions. Creon is severely affected by *atē* (bewilderment). He turns a deaf ear to all. He is absorbed in his role as a ruler of Thebes. Only when Teiresias cursed him did Creon come to his senses. After great suffering, he realises that he acted wrongfully, and he changes (Zimmermann, 1986/1991, p. 67).

In fact, the tragic poets took the position that seers had in the city in order to speak about the areas of human experience that lie beyond the order of politics, written law, and reason. The poets help us recognise and integrate into politics these domains that lie beyond meaning (Manolopoulos, 2022).

The construction of a supernatural reality comprises a mirror of a vague recognition of the unconscious processes (Freud, 1901, p. 259). Freud (1912–1913, p. 93) also writes:

> If the survivors' position in relation to the dead was really what first caused primitive man to reflect, and compelled him to hand over some of his omnipotence to the spirits and to sacrifice some of his freedom of action, then

these cultural products would constitute a first acknowledgement of Necessity (Anagke), which opposes human narcissism.

Man must respect these unknown forces that bind him to the yoke of necessity, lest he commits Hubris. The tragic subject personally undertakes his fate, which was defined by the mysterious forces long ago. He does not evade it; he endures it (Williams, 1993, p. 146). A tragic position is achieved with the separation and the emergence of the subject from the primary union, the encounter with the inevitability of reality, and the necessity of suffering the shock of the loss of omnipotence. In order to be able to endure the shock, the subject employs transitional objects and the phenomena of the Third reality, the area in which we live our experiences. It is the realm of the culture, an intermediate space between the psychic and social reality (Winnicott, 1971).

The tragic and the political begin when the subject emerges from the primary union, and the boundaries between phantasy and reality begin to form. In the area of transitional objects, contradictions are not resolved through compromises. They become paradoxes that are connected with the tragic and the political action.

Castoriadis (2008, pp. 219–220) refers to a lengthy excerpt that was added to the *Seven Against Thebes* tragedy from an unknown author 70 years after 470 BC when it was written by Aeschylus.

> This lengthy excerpt ends with a Stasimon in which the chorus is divided into two parts, with each part singing on its own accord . . . The Athenians . . . dealt with the two opposing positions without feeling that they should radically side with one or the other.

Democracy is a 'tragic' regime because it is self-referential: we are responsible for our choices and their consequences. As a political institution, tragedy is an institution of self-restraint. It reminds the Athenians that there are limits that are unknown beforehand to the subject, who acts responsibly, accepting the dangers of his actions. One of the meanings of Antigone is the problem of democracy, of political action.

> Tragedy allows us to see the uncertainty that prevails in this field, the constantly fragile and unfinished nature of causes and motives, on which we base our decisions . . . They are a warning against Hubris, even when it is hidden behind superior motives and speaks a totally reasonable and rationalised language . . . Even when you believe that your actions and decisions are based on the best motives in the world, it is possible that you are making monstrous decisions.

Creon is not a monster, and Sophocles' Antigone is not a horror show. It is a tragedy.

The poet tells us that a city needs to have a sense of the tragic. It needs to be able to transform and stage the ambiguities of demonic repetition as tragic paradoxes in which the contradictions coexist and are tolerated in the political sphere. A dictator is not capable of achieving the tragic position of enduring the shock of the loss of omnipotence. He does not have a sense of the tragic. He stages horror shows in reality or melodramas; he attacks people's capacity to know (transform) reality. Both gods and humans obey Necessity. It is the Necessity of abandoning your omnipotence and recognising the limit of reality. It is the necessity to make meaning. It is obedience, in the sense of commitment to a real self and not of conformity to a false self. It is the capacity to be a thinking subject with a sense of identity and a sense of orientation, not lost in the wilderness.

Antigone is her true self. She obeys the Necessity to make meaning. She feels compelled to build a resting place, the final one for Polynices, a meaning to envelop his story. Otherwise, the deceased will have a horrible death: he will lay unburied, unbefriended, without the right to belong to the human canon. The universe that surrounds him will not become a cosmos (world), a meaningful order, or a law, in the eyes of the living. He will not live in immortality. From Homer to the tragic poets, immortality is an affair of the living; it is given through their work of mourning and their living memory.

Our psychic constructions work night and day to find and create our world. Freud began to build his world through his mourning and his dreams following the death of his father. A dream is the way the mind works when we are asleep and awake. Dream work is identical to unconscious thinking, as a part of the reality principle, to assist the work of a true – not a pathological – transformation of frustration, as Bion would say.

The rules of the world that surrounds us are hard to explain; they are something profound, visceral, and primal. An ethos is created from the first spontaneous gestures of the infant's true self that emerge from the primary union and the mother's specific responses that offer meaning and communication value to its gestures. Ethics begins in infancy (Freud, 1895).

Without ethics, we are stripped, orphans, of meaning, with no world to contain us. The word ethos in Greek is connected to ethics, law, habits, customs, and character. In Homer, the word ethos meant the natural habitat, the place where both beasts and men would take refuge from predators. Antigone's ethics is the struggle to make meaning, integrate it, and fight against the forces that destroy meaning. Antigone, after her clash with Creon, is without a polis. She then needs to re-organise a cosmos, an ethos to which to belong.

Out of the surrounding nature, man constructs a world, an order of meaning. In the 'Ode to Man', Sophocles depicts the Chorus' anguished movements between man's extension of possibility to the very limits of the material world and of homecoming to his hearth (Steiner, 1984).

It may be necessary for us to construct meanings that clad the naked truth in order to make it more tolerable. But we may also need to retreat, sever the bonds of truth with others, and return to where our being began, to non-being, to non-meaning. It takes a lot of courage for spontaneous gestures and words to get out and roam the streets of the city, our true self in action, the one that tyrants fear (Winnicott, 1958/1990).

> Creon: What do you mean? I shudder to hear you!
> Teiresias: You will understand, when you hear the signs revealed by my art. As I took my place on my old seat of augury where all birds regularly gather for me, I heard an unintelligible voice among them: they were screaming in dire frenzy that made their language foreign to me.
> ...
>
> nor does any bird sound out clear signs in its shrill cries.

The seer says: Think. It is horrible when your environment does not give you signs of mutual recognition, signs to construct a meaning that will contain your story, signs with which you can build a world from the universe, a cosmos, an order, a place of ethics. Thoughts need a subject to conjure them (Aisenstein, 2019). But what happens if the city that surrounds us ceases to have a meaning, ceases to constitute a world? If we cease to comprehend? If we are bewildered? If we lose our sense of direction? If we cease to have the capability of achieving our tragic position? If our polis loses its sense of the tragic?

Haemon warned Creon, his father, that he would be a ruler of a wasteland. Following Antigone's conviction, Thebes is consumed by a profound sadness, a dark sky, a dark day.

George Seferis, in his poem *Thrush III – The light* (Trans. by Sherrard Philip and Keeley Edmund), calls Antigone 'the dark girl' at the time of the Greek civil war when brother killed brother determined to either conquer the maternal land or turn it to a wasteland (Kapsalis, 2022). Antigone is linked by Sophocles to Kore, who returned every year from Hades and was reunited with her mother, Demeter, and her grandmother, Rhea, so that from the reunion of the women of three generations, the earth became fertile and blossomed again. This does not happen in Antigone's play. Seferis speaks of "Angelic and black light" (Kapsalis, 2022). This is the light of mourning, the dawning, and the denial of reality.

The developing girl separates from – but never entirely erases – her roots in the mother. Antigone is not a heroine. She is a tragic subject. She yokes the yoke of necessity. She becomes a separate subject who can think her thoughts, expecting the response of the internalised maternal object in agony (Aisenstein, 2019). She achieves a tragic position.

A young woman was involved in violent confrontations with the police that caused fallings and injuries. They happened every year in a festival of political action that took place outside her city before the summer break. In her analysis, we found out that her confrontations constituted an altar of sacrifice, a stage for identifying, updating, and integrating some significant past traumatic losses in her family. The location where her confrontations occurred was the place where her older brother had been involved in a fatal car accident when he was a teenager. This location was also connected with still another place outside her childhood hometown where her father and some other men had been ambushed and killed during the Cyprus War in 1974. Since then, they had been missing, and her hometown was under Turkish occupation. "The missing has no home to return to", she said, "after a short imprisonment in a dark cell, between life and death". Her injuries were a 'human sacrifice' so that her feelings of guilt could become more real, and her lost objects – for the loss of which no subject had assumed responsibility – could be located and, thus, cease to be 'ghosts' that were nowhere and lost, but rather be buried, and mourned. Her confrontations with the police and her imprisonment acted out, defined, and contained a space, like choreographies. "If this hadn't happened, we wouldn't have had 'the story'", she said. She tried to make a story, a place, a home, for the missing to return to.

Antigone does not change throughout her play. Her values are absolute. In extreme circumstances, the importance of the mother for the internal life is refuted. Antigone defines herself as the daughter of the father. She is not the daughter of a mother. She is not the mother of a child. She is the guardian of the tomb (Britton, 2002). She ultimately descends to the 'heart of darkness', the horror of the void, the destruction of meaning. She is sentenced to be confined in a stone cave. Like Niobe, with rain as tears and stone for a body, in a time that has stopped between life and death, in eternal grief. It was in this grave made of stone that Haemon died embracing her body, becoming with her the eternal idealised couple.

Creon is not a tender father. He rejects the blood bonds with his son; he only serves the city. He is furious, unchanging, like a rock. Without innerness. Without space for forgiveness. Man's innerness is formed from bonds of psychic bisexuality, from primary identifications with both parents. These are primary bonds of love, friendship, and tenderness between a parent and the child, between siblings and friends. It is a basic foundation of links, the matrix of 'common blood'. From this deep psychosomatic subterrain, we draw the material of emotional experiences, as well as the material of phantasies with which we give meaning to them.

Sophocles' *Antigone* includes the core of ugliness, the Hubris, the unyielding confrontation of forces of destruction, the cave of the death drive, the horror, the void. It also presents the beauty of coherence, rhythm, harmony, and form. The play holds a mirror in front of us in order to live, reflect, and witness an experience: the Hubris and its devastating crash. The play helps us integrate the unthinkable and make it a tragic plot. Creon's political decision provokes the plot. The plot begins to unravel by Antigone at the crack of dark dawn. It forms a meaning to envelop the story. It ends with Creon sitting still in horror on a stone cave, an un-representable centre of the story, the stillness of the death drive (Segal, 1990).

The chorus, representing us, the people, narrates on stage our political actions, words, phantasies, and passions. The plot of the struggles with all these makes the polis, a bundle of our projections. The polis is a highly subjective object, which we constantly attack to destroy. It survives, and through our work of mourning, it is transformed into a more real, external objective, and useful object, in Winnicott's terms.

In tragedy, like in playing, emotional experiences and unconscious phantasies are staged in reality and can be shared. Antigone is a paradigm of how a society can stage the unknown individual and group unconscious forces for elaboration and integration in the political sphere. The tragedy ends when the chorus declares that one's capacity to think precedes happiness. The ruler who persists to be the only one who is right is condemned. Castoriadis (2008, p. 219) reminds us of Heraclitus: "Thought is common to all". In order to find our reality, we gather with others in a transitional (tragic, political) space, where we create and live our experiences together, learning from them and becoming who we are.

> Antigone is defined from the beginning of the tragedy as a sister.
> Antigone: Ismene, my sister, true child of my own mother.

Ω κοινόν (koinon) αυτάδελφον (autadelphon). Koinon (common). The poets create the common, a community, with their voice, offering coherence and continuity to that which is foreign, the constitutive ingredient of identity. Autadelphon (one's own sibling) means from the same womb. Man is born in a primordial womb of intersubjectivity with an innate need to seek the other self (Ogden, 2004). With a primary aloneness and a primary intimacy, Antigone shows us that sympathy is mutual recognition of the human similarity of the other self on a profound internal level, despite the differences (Ferenczi, 1932/1988; Miller, 2019). *Antigone* also demonstrates that man is characterised, in the depths of his psyche, by a combativeness, a relentless struggle for life, an essential conflictuality. She fights to express her spontaneous gesture, her true self in action. To be able to weave a plot with meaning around the rock of the unrepresentable. To abandon her Hubristic pathological narcissism, to internalise her drives, omnipotence, and bisexuality. To accept her interiority. To open up to the other person, to the outside world, while still remaining an autonomous thinking subject. She fights while she knows that the result will always be incomplete.

Notes

1 This chapter is based on my presentation at the Festival of Athens for an Epidaurus workshop with the title "Poesies and Metapoesies". A version of that speech was also included in the volume published by IPA Committee on Culture in 2023 on the occasion of the 53rd IPA Congress with the title "The Mind on the Line of Fire".
2 The direct line quotes are taken from Sophocles. *The Antigone of Sophocles. Edited with introduction and notes by Sir Richard Jebb*. Cambridge. Cambridge University Press. 1891.

References

Aisenstein, M. (2019). *Désir-Douleur-Pensée: Masochism Originaire et Theorie Pychanalytique*. Paris: Ithaque.
Britton, R. (2002). Forever father's daughter: The athene-antigone complex. In J. Trowell & A. Etcegoyen (Eds.), *The importance of fathers. A psychoanalytic re-evaluation*. London: Brunner-Routledge.
Castoriadis, C. (2008). Ce qui fait la Gréce, 2. La Cité et les lois. Séminaires 1983–1984. La creation humaine III. In E. Escobar, M. Gonticas, P. Vernay (Eds.), & Z. Castoriadis (Trans.), *Greek*. Athens: Kritiki Publications; Paris: Edition du Seuil.

Ferenczi, S. (1988). *The clinical diary of sàndor ferenczi* (J. Dupond, Ed., M. Balint & N. Z. Jackson, Trans.). Cambridge, MA: Harvard University Press. (Original work published 1932)
Freud, S. (1895). Project for a scientific psychology. *S. E.*, *1*.
Freud, S. (1901) The psychology of everyday life. *S. E.*, *6*.
Freud, S. (1912–1913). Totem and taboo: Some points of agreement between the mental lives of savages and neurotics. *S. E.*, *13*.
Kapsalis, D. (2022). The children of Oedipus. Pieces of the mosaic for antigone. In *Greek. Festival of athens and epidaurus*. Athens: Festival of athens and epidaurus.
Manolopoulos, S. (2022). Psychoanalysis and Euripides' suppliant women. In *A tragic reading of politics*. London and New York: Routledge/Focus.
Miller, P. (2019). Working through the body-ego in the analytic process. *EPF Bulletin*, *73*, 134–141.
Ogden, H., T. (2004). The analytic third. *Psychoanalytic Quarterly*, *73*(1), 167–195.
Segal, H. (1990). *Dream, phantasy, art*. London and New York: Routledge.
Sophocles. (1891). *The Antigone of Sophocles. Edited with introduction and notes by Sir Richard Jebb*. Cambridge. Cambridge University Press.
Steiner, G. (1984). *Antigones. The antigone myth in Western literature, art and thought*. Oxford: Oxford University Press.
Topouzis, K. (1997). Sophocles' antigone. In *Greek*. Athens: Epikairotita Publications.
Williams, B. (1993). *Shame and necessity*. Berkeley and Los Angeles, CA: University of California Press.
Winnicott, D. W. (1971). *Playing and reality*. London: Tavistock.
Winnicott, D. W. (1990). The capacity to be alone. In *The Maturational processes and the facilitating environment*. London: Karnac. (Original work published 1958)
Zimmermann, B. (1991). Greek tragedy. *An Introduction*. Valtimore and London: The John Hopkins University Press. (Original work published 1986)

Chapter 11

Aeschylus' Prometheus Bound

From suffering to thinking[1]

Prometheus Bound was probably, one of Aeschylus' later plays, following *Seven Against Thebes* but preceding the *Oresteia* trilogy. Its central theme is the concept of an incessant struggle against an unjust, merciless father. The punishment of the Titan by the father of the gods is inexplicably cruel. From the pain, the Titan struggles to create, suffer, and contemplate his passionate experience.

Aeschylus is the creator of the trilogy that consists of *Prometheus Bound, Unbound,* and *Pyrophorus* (Fire-Bearer), from which only the first survives. Only a single line survives from *Prometheus Pyrophorus*. The Athenians worshiped Prometheus the Fire Bearer as a benefactor and a protector of craftsmen, and built an altar to him in the Academy. We know that *Prometheus Unbound* follows *Prometheus Bound*. We assume that this sequence produces a transformation. Heracles sets Prometheus free. Omnipotence is internalised, and a forgiving paternal authority prevails. Something similar also took place in the third play of the Oresteia trilogy, where the Erinyes are transformed into Eumenides through the persuasive words of Athena. In the 5th Century BC, it was believed that Zeus pardoned Cronus and forgave the Titans. Through the act of reconciliation, the new world is now governed by justice and the harmony of antitheses after an era of ferocious violence. After the act of forgiveness, the father is no longer the law; he now represents the law. The new world order, that of Zeus and the Olympian gods, will hence be governed by justice.

Aeschylus warns us that the technology invented by Prometheus will bring arrogance and destruction to humanity if it is not freed from its shackles. The poet-prophet created an Apocalyptic work. The wrath of a god that wishes to obliterate mankind is posed at the beginning of the play. It is this god that Prometheus defies. At the end of *Prometheus Bound* comes the horror. The Earth trembles from Zeus' thunderbolts. Prometheus and the chorus of the daughters of Oceanus are thrown into Tartarus, the furthest reaches of Hades. The collapse of the world means that no one will survive to keep a memory trace of us. This is the agony of extinction. In no other myth, not even in that of Oedipus, did mankind so clearly see its fate and its struggles (Dreyfus, 1967, cited in Potamianou, 1980).

The plot

Zeus and the Olympian gods rose up to dethrone Cronus, the son of Uranus. Fighting on Cronus' side against them were the Titans – the children of Uranus and Gaia. The Titans supported the ancient world order that was founded on the power of Kratos (brute power) and the enforcement of Bia (violence). Prometheus, with his mother, the soothsayer Gaia, fought alongside Zeus, utilising the power of craftsmanship, invention, persuasion, and deception. Following his undisputed victory, Zeus wanted to wipe men – whom he considered vulgar – off the face of the earth and create a new mankind instead. Prometheus felt compassion towards mankind and opposed this. He stole the fire from the gods and taught men how to use it. He taught them all arts (technes) of life and language, a tool for making meaning. However, truth is dangerous. Even though mankind is saved, its Saviour is cruelly punished, as he has committed Hubris by giving a gift to men before they could conquer it: "*I caused blind hopes to dwell within their breasts*" (252).

The illusion of omnipotence is legitimate in infancy. In the core of existence, our tragic fate is inscribed. Human life begins with a prolonged dependence of the infant on the care of an environment mother. We struggle to integrate and become responsible subjects for our fate, our demon, our infantile experiences, and the traumatic failures of the holding environment.

"*Of my own will, yes, of my own will I erred – I will not deny it. By helping mortals I found suffering for myself*" (266). This is how the tragedy begins. Prometheus is bound to the rock by Hephaestus, under Zeus' command and the instructions of Kratos and Bia, the silent violence. At the edge of the world, on Mount Caucasus, on the shores of the ocean, in desolation and silence, Prometheus hangs motionless above the abyss. The plot of the play takes place on the edge of the unthinkable. The magnificence of the place hides the threat of annihilation.

Prometheus knows that men develop by working through conflict. Yet, he needs to learn through suffering how to think of what he knows. He psychically constructs the original circumstances of his unthinkable anxieties. His initial speechlessness brings to mind the preverbal infant that can only comprehend its own story through sensory intensity (pain).

Prometheus desperately hangs on the pain, which he addresses towards the gaze of the object, in order to get a response so as to not plunge into nothingness. We are still in a pre-historical and pre-political era. Omnipotence is not yet internalised by the subject. The object is not yet external, outside the subject's omnipotence, capable of being used. When this is achieved, then history and politics can be instituted in a society. This is never quite achieved. It is a continuous struggle.

We, the spectators, must see Prometheus' pain eating away at his liver by day, only for it to be reborn by night. Prometheus invites the world to witness his experience, to see him suffer:

> O you bright sky of heaven, you swift-winged breezes, you river-waters, and infinite laughter of the waves of ocean, O universal mother Earth, and you, all-seeing orb of the sun, to you I call! See what I, a god, endure from the gods. Look, with what shameful torture I am racked and must wrestle throughout the countless years of time apportioned me. Such is the ignominious bondage the new commander of the blessed has devised against me.
>
> (88–96)

"*In shackles of binding adamant that cannot be broken*" (4–6), Prometheus is an obstructed runner. We can think that his obstruction is the immovable object that does not see and listen to him and does not take in and contain his infantile fears of death (Bion, 1959/1967).

The creation of experiences is Prometheus' matter and moving force. Kitto (1971) writes: The prologue ends, and the play begins; a play in an immobile state. All movement is internal. There is no action until the end of the play. The chorus of the Oceanides – the daughters of Oceanus – Oceanus himself, Io, and Hermes, all come on stage in turns and in sympathy for Prometheus. It is the law of increasing tension and not the law of logical sequence. Aeschylus dramatises a situation rather than events. He stirs preverbal emotional experiences that words cannot sufficiently represent or integrate. These experiences must be created and staged anew so that the subject may be present to live and comprehend them.

The chorus, Oceanus, and Io arrive simply to develop Prometheus' internal drama. Aeschylus does not merely explain how things occurred. These are not just things that led to the present situation. They are now a part of Prometheus' thinking. Prometheus' drama reminds us of the actual traumatic situation, where raw perceptual images, that have not been sufficiently psychically processed, prevail.

In times of transition – with social and political upheavals – like the one in which Aeschylus lives, early traumas that words can neither represent nor contain are revived. Inside an actual traumatic situation, we lose the sense of time. We feel that the traumatic violence continues in the present and will never end. How can we introduce time? We need to endure suffering the experience for as long as it lasts. When time passes, it becomes a teacher: "*But ever-ageing Time teaches all things*" (981). Time starts to pass when we begin to mourn our lost omnipotence.

Even among intense conflicts and enemy crossfire, we can experience, think and speak. Aeschylus introduces the friendly Oceanus, who thinks politically and tries to persuade Prometheus that it is in his best interest not to be so stubborn. Yet Prometheus warns him not to get involved because he may be cruelly punished. Zeus is unsparing and invincible.

Prometheus does not heed Oceanus' advice to adjust to modern times. He reminds Oceanus that he has left the stream that bears his name (Ocean) and the rock-roofed caves of the sea to "come to this land, the mother of iron" (301). It is from this unbendable, indestructible metal that Prometheus is made of.

Kitto (1971) notes that after Oceanus is sent back, the chorus sings of roaming around the world and presents all the nations lamenting the fate of Prometheus, who has to suffer Zeus' cruel tyranny. It places all the peoples of the world together in a wide congregation. It seems that mourning work creates links of meaning between people. Words transmit meaning in our neighbourhood from mouth to mouth. Also, with their music, rhythm, and somatic roots, they reach remote areas of human life.

Prometheus remains silent and falls into despair as he finishes his monologue. In the next scene, Io appears. Her powerful presence makes Prometheus dare to speak. Persecuted by the gadfly that is sent by the vindictive Hera, Io, who has been transformed by Hera into a cow as a punishment for becoming the object of Zeus' desires, wanders maniacally. Zeus, despite being the one who seduced her, now abandons her to her fate. Io narrates her terrible persecution and leads the play's rhythm to its climax. Our resentment towards tyranny – as an audience – also climaxes.

Aeschylus revolts and invites us to revolt, too. Prometheus finally reveals to us the secret that he had been hiding in his silence. The chorus listens in absolute terror. Zeus will be overthrown by a son from a new marriage, who will be stronger than he is. Suddenly, Io leaves the stage, hounded by her gadfly. Then, the space is open for the next scene. Zeus then sends Hermes to make Prometheus tell him which marriage will be so devastating for him. Prometheus does not answer. He resists. He is thrown by Zeus into Tartarus together with the chorus.

Kitto observes: The lonesome hero is everything. It is not what he does but what he feels and who he is. His experience is everything. There is no action between the prologue and the final destruction. It is a drama of revelation, not of action.

In the end, Prometheus calls upon his revered mother:

> Indeed, now it has passed from word to deed – the earth rocks, the echoing thunder-peal from the depths rolls roaring past me; the fiery wreathed lightning-flashes flare forth, and whirlwinds toss the swirling dust; the blasts of all the winds leap forth and set in hostile array their embattled strife; the sky is confounded with the deep. Behold, this stormy turmoil advances against me visibly, sent by Zeus to frighten me. O holy mother mine, O you firmament that revolves the common light of all, you see the wrongs I suffer!
>
> (1080)

Pathei-mathos. Learning from (suffering an) experience

In *Prometheus Bound,* we observe the cruelty of the state (kratos) that has been awarded the licence to utilise lawful violence as a defence against the (paranoid) fear of disorganisation (chaos). Zeus, like any new immature ruler, becomes tyrannical to establish order.

Grimal (1991, p. 376) writes:

> [Zeus] swore by the Styx that Prometheus would never be released. Heracles, however, subsequently shot the eagle with an arrow and released Prometheus. Zeus was pleased that this exploit added to his son's fame, but to show that his word was not to be taken too lightly, he forced Prometheus to wear a ring made from the steel chains and to carry a piece of the rock to which he had been attached. At this time the Centaur Chiron had been wounded [suffering from a perpetual, ever-present torment that would never cease] by one of Heracles' arrows and wanted to die. As he was immortal, he had to find someone who would accept his immortality. Prometheus performed this service for him.

You cannot really die until a son or a daughter kills you, feel their guilt, do their work of mourning and undertake (in memory) your immortality. You need to believe in your immortality in order to be committed to public life.

Aeschylus, being a democrat, presents Prometheus' disobedience as the trigger of the psychic conflicts that will lead to psychic transformations concerning the relationship with the superego. Ultimately, obedience becomes a commitment (the chain of the bonds becomes a ring of commitment) and ceases to signify submission. The state becomes organised through institutions, which, like the superego, preserve in capsules of time and transmit the creative fire of culture to the next generation.

The hero is immobilised and maintains his cause only via dialogues with visitors. His torture is constant and perpetual. Loss is irretrievable, and suffering is inevitable. Vulnerability, a fundamental aloneness of human existence, is experienced on stage. Ultimately, what becomes obvious is the inescapable necessity that opposes his narcissism: to transform his pain into suffering, to suffer his experience, think about it, and learn from it.

Aeschylus does not simply speak of fire, but "flashing fire, source of all arts": the essence of imaginative thinking, the creative light that burns in the core of language, arts and tools, knowledge and use of objects, as well as their destruction. Prometheus' play illustrates the 'stealing' of knowledge and the guilt of appropriation. Prometheus' tragic transformation implies the internalisation of omnipotence (Potamianou, 1980).

Meg Harris Williams (2013, pp. 233–234) cites Keats, who "spoke of the spark of identity that came from the gods and enabled man to convert a vale of tears into a vale of soul making". She argues that Prometheus' myth, as presented by Aeschylus, is a foundational myth.

> Fire and its acquisition is understood to be . . . a metaphor for a mental attribute . . . (Fire) is an endowment, not something generated by man himself, hence is associated with the world of gods or higher powers . . . Fire, like language, demarcates the prehistoric point at which we became recognizably ourselves, and humanity grasped the way to survive . . . We may take "fire" to represent the

ambiguous spirit of creativity and destruction . . . (through which) the external world becomes infused with meaning by the internal world.

Prometheus is split. He is omnipotent and good. He does not want anything to do with violence, weapons, and war, despite being a rebel. In the end, liberation comes through the weapons of Heracles. The split is undone. Integration occurs. Liberation is achieved when Prometheus is able to imagine the effort, the challenge, and undertakes the struggle (Potamianou, 1980). That is what Prometheus learns. He needs to be subjected to – endure – the resistance of the object, feel an emotional storm and create with it an experience through which only he can know (feel) it and foresee their common future. Aeschylus' essence of the tragic is condensed into two words: pathei-mathos. It speaks of the capacity to suffer, endure, not to evacuate an experience, to hold it in time, and learn from it. The chorus laments:

> I mourn your unfortunate fate, Prometheus . . . One other Titan god before this I have seen in distress, enthralled in torment by adamantine bonds – Atlas, pre-eminent in mighty strength, who moans as he supports the vault of heaven on his back.
>
> (399–435)

Prometheus explains (436–440) that he remains silent because painful thoughts devour his heart. Prometheus is the 'giver' that has helped the evolution of men; he has endowed them with the gift of thinking. Prometheus keeps a secret concerning Zeus. Despite the threats that Zeus throws against him, through his messenger Hermes, Prometheus resists:

> There is no torment or device by which Zeus shall induce me to utter this until these injurious fetters are loosed. So then, let his blazing lightning be hurled, and with the white wings of the snow and thunders of earthquake let him confound the reeling world. For nothing of this shall bend my will even to tell at whose hands he is fated to be hurled from his sovereignty.
>
> (989–996)

Zeus is ever-present on stage, albeit invisible. He remains unsparing. Prometheus also remains unwavering in his refusal to speak. Prometheus knows a secret, and he tries to understand the meaning of it: In the future, Zeus will marry Thetis and will have a son that will be stronger than himself who will dethrone him. Prometheus thinks/struggles to place Zeus within time. Who is the son that has not yet been born? Who is the new political subject? Williams (2013, p. 250) explains that it is not Prometheus but the Promethean (quality of forethought foresight) within each individual that is expected to be born.

The soothsayer Gaia revealed to Prometheus that the war between the gods will be won not by those who will use brute force and violence but by those who use the powers of crafts and deceit (209–215). Prometheus learns that he himself is part of the system. It is with his ruses that Zeus prevailed. And now he is teaching his ruses to the mortals. Men are all too willing to learn. But will they become responsible subjects for these ruses? Zeus (superego) knows best. Ruses are not enough; Violence is also needed for the unruliness of the drives to be harnessed.

Io is the second person in the tragedy. Her appearance accentuates Zeus' callousness and Prometheus' rigidity and immobility. Io is expelled from her home under Zeus' command. She falls into a mania and roams the world. She cannot find a place to stand, which is in sharp contrast to Prometheus, who is bound and does not have space to move. Like Prometheus', her condition is unbearable; she prefers to die rather than continue. Much time will pass before she is set free. Prometheus is immobilised, but his words, like Io, fly all over the world. The words we speak are free to go on their journey in peoples' thoughts once they become public.

The rock of the untranslated

Prometheus is bound to the rock of the unexplained. Franz Kafka (1971, pp. 475–476) wrote about the myth of Prometheus when he was endlessly struggling, in vain, to gain dominance outside before achieving the tragic position internally: "*The legend tried to explain the inexplicable. As it came out of a substratum of truth it had in turn to end in the inexplicable*".

What is inexplicable is the passion. The passion links him to the object through which the pain becomes suffering, and he becomes a subject of it. What will become of Prometheus? Would he become one with the rock, one with his iron, unyielding Titanic nature? Or would he be freed? Many generations later, a descendant of Io, the son of Zeus, Heracles set him free using his bow. What is it that is set free? I presume it is human creativity that is set free.

In our social existence, the chains of achronicity of repetition compulsion are transformed into bonds of psychic work, creative thinking, work of culture, political thinking, and historisation. Yet, the links of thinking always hold an unrepresented piece of rock, a preverbal trauma, a source of pain and passion for revenge, an unexplained enigma, a sheer horror. In every psychic formation, there is an inexplicable piece of perception that has escaped transformation. These traces return following a natural course towards expression, demanding to be included in processes of symbolisation. They are grains of historical truth that lie in the heart of repetitions (in psychic and social life). With every processing of the trauma and with acceptance of guilt for the internalisation (theft) that overturned the world order, we become capable of practical life, utilisation of tools, technology, and the arts. We acquire skills.

A college student, 19 years old, was terrorised by an intrusive maternal object, which filled him with food, sexual arousal, rejection, meaninglessness, and the fear that she would not survive. He defended himself against this traumatic terror by terrorising his girlfriends and his analyst, making them feel that something horrible would happen to them and that they could not stop him from causing them this fear. At times, he experienced reality in a very raw, unsymbolised, psychotic way.

His breakdown started after the separation from his girlfriend. He felt like a limpet that was violently detached from his rock. He began his analysis with feelings of hate and rage against the mother, as she was constructed in the analytic field. He then began to suffer painful experiences of being punished by a severe superego every time he allowed himself to feel that he was entitled to live, to fall in love, to know, and to grow up. He was letting others know how much he suffered because of unjust treatment by persons of authority. He met great difficulties in his path to internalise his sexual and aggressive maturing body. The working through early conflicts and traumas enabled him to begin integrating psychically certain recording technologies (visual equipment) that represented parts of his body (greedy mouth, eyes, and genitalia). He became more confident in using words to rebel against (put a stop to) the tyranny of his internal terror. In the analytic field, the mouth-to-mouth exchanges of words and ideas began to be used to understand and communicate experiences. In a dream, he saw that a girl was playing with him at a party, putting a camera between his lips to take a picture of his teeth and tongue and then moving it in and out in a pleasurable way. Like a small child, he had to first put in his mouth everything new he encountered in the object world, to experience, test it, and take it in. Then, he could implement it in reality as a new capacity. He was able to implement his growing capacity to know in external reality. The camera was no longer "an influencing machine" (Tausk, 1919/1933). The dream work had libidinised the traumatic experiences of parts of his body (eyes, mouth, genitalia) and transformed them into a kind of deus ex machina.

Defined by love and motivated by necessity, man constructs tools in order to perfect his somatic functions (Freud, 1930). The utilisation of tools offers us satisfaction in operating, in concluding an experience, and in its outcome. Tools hold the traces of memory from the history of the evolution of society, where the elements of civilisation intertwine with psychology, biology, and inorganic matter.

After the first nuclear test by Robert Oppenheimer, the American Prometheus, in Nolan's film, we hear the phrase "I am death". Hallucinating the wish and the fear of death, I misheard: "Let there be death". Like Prometheus and Oppenheimer, we worry about the future of our world. Does anybody care? Does anyone ever listen to anyone?

When Io appears on stage and narrates the injustice she suffered by Zeus, who seduced her and then abandoned her, we, the spectators of the tragedy, feel that tension is mounting and begin to feel authentic anger against the authoritarian power. When we watch a tragedy in an ancient theatre together with thousands of others, we feel a powerful sense of community. A sense of being surrounded by friends and having a cultural experience makes a reliable environment that cares for us. The required work of culture can happen when the persecutory anxiety that is felt as unforgivable can be mediated by the group concern.

I think that Prometheus seeks this group concern. He is cross-examined by Oceanus, the Oceanides, Io, and Hermes. He is heard by all nations. He wants the truth to be documented and known. He goes public. He seeks an ethos, a world to contain him, a moral community. He wants to be acknowledged and be believed.

This is what Oppenheimer expected from the committee that cross-examined him. He searched for his judge, whom K. could not find in Kafka's Trial. He sought for a court and politics; both these are theatres.

Note

1 The direct line quotes are taken from Aeschylus (1926). *Aeschylus, with an English translation by Herbert Weir Smyth, Ph. D. in two volumes. 1. Prometheus Bound*. Herbert Weir Smyth, Ph.D. Cambridge, MA: Harvard University Press. 1926.

References

Aeschylus. (1926). Aeschylus, with an English translation by Herbert Weir Smyth, Ph. D. in two volumes. 1. Prometheus Bound. Herbert Weir Smyth, Ph. D. Cambridge, MA: Harvard University Press.
Bion, W. R. (1967). Attacks on linking. In *Second thoughts. Selected papers on psychoanalysis*. New York: Jason Aronson. (Original work published 1959)
Dreyfus, R. (1967). *Tragiques Grecs, Eschyle-Sophocle*. Paris: Bibliothéque de la Pléade.
Freud, S. (1930). Civilisation and its Discontents, *S. E., 21*
Grimal, P. (1991). Dictionary of Greek and Roman mythology. In B. Atsalos (Ed.), *Greek*. Thessaloniki: University Studio Press.
Kafka, F. (1971). Prometheus. In N. Glatzer (Ed.), *The complete stories*. New York: Schoken Books.
Kitto, H. D. F. (1971). *Greek tragedy*. London: Associated Book Publishers.
Potamianou, A. (1980). Psychoanalytic thoughts on aeschylus' prometheus bound. In D. Anzieu, F. Carapanos, J. Gillibert, A. Green, N. Nicolaidis, & A. Potamianou (Eds.), *Psychanalyse et culture grecque*. Paris: Les Belles Lettres.
Tausk, V. (1933). On the origin of the "influencing machine" in schizophrenia. Psychoanalytic Quarterly, *2*, 519–556. (Original work published 1919)
Williams, M. H. (2013). Playing with fire: Prometheus and the mythological consciousness. In V. Zajko & E. O' Gorman (Eds.) *Classical myth and psychoanalysis*. Oxford: Oxford University Press.

Chapter 12

A plea for a new political subject

I imagined this book as a dialogue between the tragic poets, commentators, scholars and psychoanalysts, and certain modern poets. I imagined an exchange of original ideas about unconscious comicotragic aspects of human life. I explored seven of Euripides' plays, two of Sophocles' and one of Aeschylus'. I chose them as stories in which dramatic personal, family, and political passions are intertwined. I followed Freud, as well as the Freudian (narcissism) and Kleinian (depressive position) roots of Winnicott. I also followed Bion's roots in Freud's work on pleasure and reality principles and Klein's concept of projective identification. Finally, I included a few clinical vignettes to show how ancient dramas inform our psychoanalytic work. Of course, I could not think of Greek tragedy and psychoanalysis outside the culture in which I now live.

I do not study ancient tragedy in order to prove what we know from psychoanalysis. I study it in order to think about human life. I think of ancient dramas as comicotragic stories of human life in times of transition, like the one we live in today. In spite of all our technological progress, we feel confused. We do not understand. Reality is incomprehensible. Wild passions erupt. Our world is incoherent, our reason inadequate, our politics incomplete.

Freud understood the richness of the poets' insights into human life (De Romilly, 1970). Aristotle, in his Poetics, recommended to the poets to choose themes in which the passions are generated in relationships of love, where, for example, brother kills brother, son kills father or mother, mother kills children, etc. However, the most tragic solution today is to kill all feelings and withdraw in an impasse of impossible links, in apathy, lethargy, and near death. We split off or repress our anger. Out of fear of death, we stop being alive. We feel disheartened in front of the climatic change, unregulated artificial intelligence, and destructive wars. We feel de-moralised, not held by a caring culture, an ethos. We have lost our belief in our immortality.

The study of ancient tragedy and psychoanalysis can help us contemplate the links between infant development and society. Human (psychic and social) life develops from the dependence of the infant on maternal care. We cannot take for granted the infant's capacity for hallucinatory realisations. We need to take into account the nature of the external object, that is, the capacity of the mother to contain

DOI: 10.4324/9781032712864-13

the infant's fears of death and hold the shared experiences and symbolisation processes in time. The infant needs to destroy the object, and yet the object must survive in order to become external, objective, and useful. The primacy of the (m)other, the struggles for her psychic survival, and the terror of her non-survival lie at the foundations of human life. In human life, traces of nonsurvival of the object are revived. Our fate, our demon, is created by our infantile experiences and the traumatic failures of the holding environment (Abram, 2022, pp. 59–70).

In ancient tragedy and psychoanalysis, we become responsible for our fate. Aristotle defines tragedy by the effect it has on us. Tragedy is an emotional experience we create and live when its poesis (making) is directed towards us; it finds us and occurs in us (Lear, 1992, p. 328). Also, in life, out of the traces of past traumas, we create and live with others authentic experiences, commit ourselves to them, represent them, and keep them in our memory.

Necessity and responsibility

Central to any tragic plot is the shattering of the omnipotence of Hubris and the emergence of a tragic subject that "yokes the yoke of necessity", and personally accepts that what will befall it has to happen because of an ageless planning of 'mysterious' forces (Williams, 1993).

These forces are timeless and spaceless. They are unconscious. They come from an unknown past. Medea's revenge "is imposed upon her by her own nature. She must will it by necessity" (Schlesinger, 1966/1983, p. 295). Lesky (1966/1983, p. 21) examines the issues of decision and responsibility in Aeschylus' tragedy. Eteocles, in the last part of his Theban trilogy, encounters a turning point (653) when he learns that he will have to face the attacker at the seventh gate of the city, his brother Polynices. He knows what will happen the next morning. Yet he has to take up the fratricidal fight. Aeschylus stages the curse that causes a crime to be renewed from generation to generation. The persons in the drama personally undertake what has to happen. They create an experience in which they become responsible for a past failure (hamartia).

Winnicott (1960) explains: We become a subject that is responsible for how our past traumatic experience is acted, experienced, has meaning assigned to it, and is registered now in our psyche.

For Aristotle (in *Poetics*), hamartia refers to the tragic error that leads to a chain of actions that culminate in a catastrophe. Irma Brenman Pick introduced the idea of the tragic position to describe situations where defences mounted have led to real harm to the world (Weintrobe, 2023). Human life is marked by a hamartia: We are born helpless and with an innate need to seek an object and be beguiled by its words and actions. This need is expressed in the transference, a structuring force, and a structural fault (it provokes the intervention of the object). We create experiences through which we assume responsibility for the failures of the past.

Words transmit meaning with their content from mouth to mouth. Also, with their music, rhythm, and sensory-motor roots, words reach remote areas of psychic and public life. Three girls, 3–5 years of age, stayed with their grandparents for a weekend while their parents were on a trip. At some point, they all went out and took the external staircase to the street to go to the nearby playground. Suddenly, one of the girls started to cling to the grandmother and began crying. I suppose that she was overwhelmed with anxiety that she would not be held and would fall down the stairs to her demise. Soon after, the other girl also wanted the grandmother for herself, and it was not long before they all began to cry. The more the grandparents tried to console them, the more they cried. Their ailment was incurable because the grandparents were not the real parents. The children wanted the real thing. They did not see the grandparents as substitutes but as replacements, which made it acutely clear that the real parents were missing. The grandparents had two options: either to try harder to give more love than they really had, which would result in giving up and breaking down, or to put an end to their escalating crying. Then the grandfather raised the tone of his voice and imposingly said: "Heeyp!" The girls stopped crying. It was as if the grandfather angrily said: "Stop terrorising us!" When they reached the playground, one suddenly said: "Heeyp!" Immediately, the other responded: "Heeyp!" And the third joined in: "Heeyp!" and continued these singing voices in a jazz rhythm. They sang and rhythmically repeated "actions, movements, changes of space and time" in Austen's words. They created their own appropriate meter, their own intersubjective matrix. Thus, they met at the same place and time, feeling real, alive, and present in the experience. Not everything was lost. Someone inside and also outside listened and responded (spoke back) to them.

This episode reminded me of Tom Main's (1957) classical paper. Main described a psychiatric ward that treated some special (highly invested with the staff's therapeutic zeal) patients. In this ward, one by one, the nurses began to break down. They acted like the mothers or the nannies in a park that, one by one, tried hard and failed to console a baby in despair. The baby was excessively distressed and cried its heart out because its holding mother had temporarily disappeared. We can hypothesise that the mother's representation in the baby's mind was going to die at any moment, and no one could rescue her. The baby needed the mother herself and could not use a substitute. The more the strangers tried to console the baby, the more they became precisely that: strangers. The harder they tried to give more love than they had, the more they failed and broke down and felt disheartened.

We observe something similar in social institutions. One by one, members take the role of the rescuer, and they fail in their frenzied efforts to rescue the group from an imminent reality. Their fear of breakdown is a defence of psychotic order against the fear that the object (the institution) will not survive and the self will be annihilated. We can think that the ailment of our culture today is that we cannot mourn and find substitutes, and thus, we resort to replacements. The ailment is that people, unlike the little girls with their grandparents, do not have the passion to meet, experience, and think. Us humans and our polis are phenomena of nature, Aristotle said. We are political animals. We need to meet and share with others the passion to be alive, real, and present in our experiences, as well as the passion to give meaning to the shared experiences. We need to imagine together the institutions with which we will find our city. We do not know the limits in advance, yet if we violate them, we will commit Hubris. With this sense of the tragic, we make decisions, right or wrong, and we proceed.

Castoriadis (2007) writes: By politics, we imply the activity that aims to institute society itself. In Ancient Greece,

> "civic affairs and the law become, for the first time, the object of explicit collective – and I would also add rational – activity, in the sense that the activity itself is discussed. It is discussed, not so much concerning its procedural aspect regarding the means or technical matters . . . Politics . . . are integral to the fact that the community decides to take its affairs into its own hands . . . This is what we can term the first birth of politics, the primal moment of history . . . : everybody has a say regarding the law".
>
> (Castoriadis, 2007, pp. 94–95)

In our democratic social institutions, we should use Euripides' sense of irony and the tragic. Some spectators of Euripides' comic-tragedies laugh, and others feel fear that everything will be lost. At some point, both pleasure and pain come together, and then spectators feel a deep sadness and a sense of catharsis; we reach a depressive position, and this has a liberating effect on our creativity.

Alford (1992) argues that the ancient tragedy makes a plea for a new political subject. Politics and tragedy began together. The same people attended both. The ancient tragedy tells us how the city deals with its antinomies. The tragedy itself is an antinomy, an unresolved polarity between wild and tame. Zimmerman (1986/1991, pp. 6–9) notes: There is a reciprocal relation between poetry and public life. In Aristophanes' *The Frogs*, Dionysus, despite preferring Euripides, gives the throne of the best poet to Aeschylus, basing his decision on the poets' political views: "The pollicisation of the City Dionysia in the late sixth century helps to explain why the festival was so important to the fifth-century democracy. After the Persian Wars it became a political instrument par excellence". The essential function of the Great Dionysia was to promote a sense of pride and solidarity in Athenians and display to their allies and visitors the glory of the city.

De Romilly (1970) explains: The tragedy was, from the start, tied to the activities of the citizens. Ancient tragedy began to flourish after the victory at Salamis against the Persians and died after the war against Sparta ended with a devastating defeat. It was a period of 80 years full of destruction and a spring of creativity. When the Greeks defeated the Persians, they regressed to the original way of dealing with their aggression, the civil war. Bell (2023) comments that the capacity to recognise inside us the potential for destruction is a fundamental precondition for modern political thinking.

Belfiore (1992, p. 374) emphasises that what matters most profoundly and fundamentally for our existence as human beings is whether we, like Iphigeneia, will recognise our brothers in time to avoid killing them.

> (Euripides), like Aristotle, thought of the Iphigeneia in Tauris as a play about philia, and about relationships that are political in a broader sense. According to

Aristotle, human beings are political animals because it is their nature to live in communities of philoi, and the person who is by nature not political is "a lover of war" (Politics 1.1253a3–7).

The struggle against tyranny

Prometheus is the prototype of the subject who, through suffering, moves from the Titanic nature to human life, from pre-history to history, from pre-politics to politics, from physical to mental powers, from omnipotence to the sense of the tragic. He reaches the tragic position. He undertakes the work of mourning that comprises both dirge and revelry. Meg Harris Williams (2013, pp. 236, 240, 249–250) notes: Prometheus' play is set at a transitional moment in humanity, "the change from Titan values of strength and force to Olympian-Athenian values of justice and order". It marks the growth of imaginative thinking. Necessity shapes the way change happens and, hence, the meaning of things.

> Creativity is the life-force; a law beyond any temporary formulation . . . Prometheus' "binding" becomes the binding force of thought . . . Shelley redefined Foresight as Poetry, which can see the shadow of the future cast before, and making use of myth and metaphor, can symbolise ideas that mankind will be able to formulate discursively or put into action centuries later.

Man always evolves through thinking about himself. "This can only be effected by converting pain into suffering: integrating split projections transforming somatic 'beta' into mental 'alpha' elements which are suitable for symbol formation".

Prometheus' omnipotence is internalised, and a forgiving paternal authority prevails. Similarly, at the end of Oresteia, the blood-thirsty persecutory Erinyes (Furies) are transformed into judicious Eumenides through Athena's words of persuasion. However, the violent nature of the Furies is still lurking. Fear enforces the law.

Tyranny can be more appealing than democracy. Engle and French (1951, pp. 261, 272) write:

> Plutarch . . . has Solon say to Aesop. "You may think the city ruled by one man is best off, yet in a social group you think it a virtue for everyone to join in the conversation". . . . (However), self-government is self-restraint. If a people are to govern themselves, they must be able and willing not only to rebel against the arbitrary authority of others, but also to submit to the legitimate authority of the laws that they themselves make and of those whom they choose to enforce them.

Politics, democracy, history, and tragedy are all children of Homer's poems. The myth in Homer's poems is the bearer of collective interpretations of human life. Tragedy is addressed to an audience that vibrates passionately in desire to experience and think. Men pass through the fundamental drama of suffering the shock of the loss of omnipotence and emerging from the primal union to the transitional space. Working through the loss of omnipotence enables them to reach a tragic position. The shock of loss of omnipotence introduces the transitional objects and phenomena.

In the transitional space, unintegrated contradictions are paradoxically tolerated. There is always a tension between ambiguity and paradox in Euripides' tragedies (Segal, 1968/1983, pp. 245–248). Benjamin (1925/1988, p. 103) states that the demonic is for the tragic what ambiguity is for the paradox. Ambiguity belongs to the demonic repetition compulsion (Freud, 1920). Paradox belongs to transitional space (Winnicott, 1971).

Heaney (1990, pp. 27–29) observes that both the wounded hero, the young negotiator, and the members of the group (army) face the conflict between integrity and political expediency. The victim of injustice and his perpetrators are devoted to their irrationality, the first to his pain, the second to their group's basic assumption. They gradually begin to exchange places. In order to negotiate, they first need not to know. They need the void that will allow them to think on their own instead of provoking reactions and complying with them. The merchant is a true messenger in this way.

> Merchant: Old Phoenix and the two sons of Theseus /Are on the high sea after you./ Neoptolemus: Why this time? To snatch me or negotiate?/ Merchant: I Have no idea. I am telling you all I know./ . . . I am only a trader and have to trade/ In whatever's going. Like information.

How does this ancient merchant speak to us today? Zajko and O' Gorman (2013) explain: Myth projects a sense of timelessness. It is a mode of expression. The focus shifts away from the story towards what the story is doing. The meaning of any individual story changes depending on where it begins and ends. The storytelling allows the truth to emerge. It creates the past and opens the future. Freud argued that there is an interdependence between myth and psychoanalysis. Every myth has a grain of historical truth, an actual traumatic event, in its core. Potamianou (1985, p. 287) points out:

> It is true that myth was originally related to sacred action, and there was a time, traces of which can be found in the *Odyssey*, when the term myth had the meaning of action as well as that of discourse.

We need myths to believe in. Our beliefs meet our feelings and make an emotional experience that has meaning. If we can suffer our experiences, our myths are felt true to us. Their meaning envelops the story that is acted on the stage. Tragedy, like playing and transference, is a true story that becomes real.

In Prometheus' myth, there is an inexhaustible 'thing' of repetition. An unchangeable iron lies at the heart of his titanic nature. The act of pain that mimesis doubles (makes it a suffering) on stage belongs to a transformation that gives a story to historical truth. The story narrates our struggle against tyranny. Kaplan (2023, pp. 83–84) emphasises that rebels do not have to bargain or make concessions. They remain pure in their ideals. Herington (1965/1983) comments that Aeschylus fearlessly and honestly shows "a picture of archaic power-god which . . . has taken on political overtones".

Our struggle against the tyranny humanises us; it gives us strength for living, passion for thinking, self-respect in the place of arrogance, respect for the subjectivity of the other, freedom, and justice. Friendship and mercy also humanise us. All these qualities make the new political subject who struggles to live inside history and politics without losing contact with personal and collective pre-history and pre-politics.

The wish to change. The desire to take revenge

Tragic subjects struggle between their loyalties to family and society. However, polis cannot be separated from oikos. Civilisation flourishes when both loyalties are prevalent. The conflict between Creon and Antigone is between city and house and also between man and woman. Antigone struggles to live in a world in which power and justice do not coincide. She fights to be seen. She becomes the "bride to Hades", the world of the unseen. She moves into the darkness of her cave, a place of contact between life and death (Segal, 1981/1983, p. 171; Alford, 1992, p. 180; Kaplan, 2023, p. 480).

In *Alcestis*, death may happen at any time, but friendship may resurrect. Friendship is a life factor. It springs from the matrix of likeness (Winnicott, 1958/1990; Burnett, 1965/1983, p. 271). The opposite of this is Winnicott's idea (1963, p. 192) of an "anti-life factor derived from the mother's depression". This situation is related to a society's common pool of guilt and desire for reparation. The true gesture of reparation presupposes that one should reach one's own personal guilt and sense of responsibility because of one's destructive drives. Otherwise, the reparation is false (Winnicott, 1948/1996).

Critchley (2019, p. 127) describes the tragic as a situation where things collapse, get distorted, perverted, and split. Orestes has an illness that is transmitted to his city and us, the spectators. Medea is a force of nature beyond language, meaning, and logic. She knows the pain she is going to cause but she feels that her passion is stronger than her mind. The women (Hecuba, Phaidra, Medea) take revenge; they make the others suffer as they have suffered. In Greek, change (allage) and other (allos) have the same etymological root. However, the verb 'to change' (allasso) also means 'to take revenge' (Kovacs, 1998, p. 159). In a tragic situation we cannot think in terms of dialectics (thesis – antithesis – synthesis). We can think of Winnicott's theory of unintegration – integration – disintegration. We can think of an anti-dialectical splitting of the ego (Freud, 1940) in which we recognise and, at the same time, we deny the recognition of reality. Tragedy struggles to restore the process of recognition. Dodds (1951) thought that ancient Greeks were in love with irrationality as a defensive retreat to avoid the burden of identity.

Medea's passions of despair and rage make her a pure force with no meaning. Then, an oedipal father appears out of nowhere. Aegeus, the king of Athens, offers her asylum in Athens and asks her to help him have a child, an heir to the throne, his continuation. Then, Medea finds a meaning. Aegeus brings an oedipal structure. This episode is considered by Aristotle as 'alogon' (absurd). However, Schlesinger (1966/1983, p. 308) disagrees: "But there is a real relation between the journey of Aegeus and the Medea plot . . . Its nature is purely poetic, for what ties together these seemingly disparate actions is again the children motif". Infanticide is the ultimate revenge against a father.

The characters of Hippolytus' drama are absorbed by their passions. They are not available for transformational processes. They are not available in their city. Their emotions eventually become outgoing. However, speaking out to connect with the object is dangerous. Knox (1952/1983, pp. 320–321) says:

> But in the *Hippolytus* speech is presented as an explosive force which, once released, cannot be restrained and creates universal destruction. "To what length will speech go?" asks the Nurse, when she has finally succeeded in opening Phaedra's lips. It goes far enough to ruin all of them. It assumes many forms: Phaedra's delirium, the Nurse's cynical argument, Hippolytus' invective, Phaedra's letter, Theseus' curse.

Orestes is Euripides' invention. Its moving force is revenge. Orestes cannot form a public sphere. He forms the defensive chaos of a mob. Before he comes to public trial, Orestes faces the private indictment of his grandfather Tyndareus. Part of his 'tragedy' is that true tragedy is no longer possible. It is like a rehearsal that does not succeed in becoming a play. "Change is always pleasant", Electra says to Orestes, restless in his sickness (234). "Oh, yes", he answers, "for that has a semblance of health; and the semblance is preferable, though it is far from the truth" (235). Illusion and semblance dominate the play (Wolf, 1968/1983).

In *Orestes,* we see the perverted false meta-truth frame of today's politics. Illusion and semblance dominate Trump's populism/authoritarianism. He plays in a reality show. He cannot form a tragic plot. He forms a mob that attacks the palace. Trump is like the ghost in Ethan and Joel Coen's film *No Country for Old Men*. The ghost takes over the actor and causes real harm in external reality, not as mimesis inside a frame. Then, the play is no longer contained.

Thucydides (1910) (Book 3, Chapter 82, 2) makes a poignant diagnosis for humanity: "Such as have occurred and always will occur, as long as the nature of mankind remains the same". Human nature does not change. However, we cannot make good use of History. We know, and at the same time, we do not know; we are deeply split in our psyche and our society.

In contrast, in ancient tragedy, words are drastic; they act and thus are convincing. They mean what they say. They tell us who we are. You cannot disregard them. An oath can be broken only at incalculable peril, said Athena to Theseus in Euripides'

Suppliants. Euripides' Orestes and Sophocles' Philoctetes are sick because they cannot believe the spoken words. They do not want a symbolic substitute. They want the real thing.

Zimmerman (1986/1991, p. 106) links these tragedies with Thucydides' (3:82) account of the Pathology of deterioration of political conduct and the transvaluation of political ideas: "The customary meanings of words were changed as men claimed the right to use them as they would to suit their actions". Perhaps the poets and Thucydides speak of a pathology of human life that is inherent in language. This pathology is linked to the use of words in order to obstruct the employment of normal projective identification and communication with preverbal experiences (Bion, 1959/1967). Without their roots to the soma, words do not mean what they say.

The tyranny of meta-truth

Hesiod's Theogony narrates the regulation of the first revolution that changed the world: the agricultural revolution. Presently, we live in the fourth (the technological) revolution. Today, we worry about the effect that new technologies have on human life. We need new regulations for them. We worry that new technologies attack the capacity for an alive absence, a talking silence, a budding expectation, the creative pulse of life, the hesitation between sound and meaning, poetry, and thinking. We resort to a crazy dance of instant connectedness in order to make our unmourned lost objects exist. However, without 'written' (in individual and collective memory) traces, we have no sense of immortality. This worry is not new. In Plato's *Phaedrus*, Socrates speaks of Theuth, a god from Naucratis in Egypt, who, like Prometheus, discovered numbers, arithmetic, geometry, astronomy, and also the games of draughts and dice, but most importantly, letters. Theuth presented the new technologies to King Thamus so that they would be imparted to all Egyptians. Writing was the first important technology that changed our world. Theuth said that writing was an elixir of memory and wisdom. Thamus replied that letters bring forgetfulness to the souls because humans recall things to their memory by external characters and not from within themselves.

Postman (1993) studied the tyranny of technology. The manner in which new technology is integrated by the individual and by society is important. Society mobilises the arts to enable it to integrate technology. We, as a community of citizens, need to integrate our new technologies, investing them with symbolic meanings, unconscious fantasies, magical animistic thoughts, and rituals.

Tools do not offer us the libidinal constancy of an object. They give us a sense of control. However, if we use them in the context of a search for the unknown, we transcend from the utilisation of tools to the utilisation of the meaning that we acquire and thus promote knowledge. With our tools, we can turn towards constructive uses of the world or towards perverse solutions that deny difference and absence.

Tools may give us a false certainty. They may become fetishistic objects. Then, a totalitarian reasoning prevails. Nothing can be doubted, and nothing new can be born. The miracles of technology, the techniques of marketing, and the use of speech and icons for propaganda give us false certainty. They threaten us that by having them, we will face death. Then, they may become things in themselves, stripped of any symbolic meaning. And we become a false self who follows orders. Winnicott (1965/1990, p. 153) describes a boy who initially used a string, like a telephone, to deny separation. The string became a thing in itself that needed to be mastered. And the boy became addicted to the disavowal of reality that it offered (Winnicott, 1965/1990, p. 153). Without adequate meaning, we may keep, along with our technological achievements, the secret world of mysticism. We sacrifice the Master Builder's wife in the foundation in order for the building to remain standing (Ion & Anderson, 2005).

The fear is and has always been whether the tools use us as their slaves. With artificial intelligence, this fear becomes horrifyingly real. If we attempt to enslave the tools without allowing them to change us, we strip them of meaning, and we use them as subjective and not as external useful objects. Then, the tools become things in themselves that fill us with anxiety as we cannot master them. Then, we become addicted to the denial of reality that they offer.

We hope that our technologies enable us to use the outside world based on the capacity to make and use signs, a gift that was given to humans by Prometheus. His tragedy concerns the transmission of knowledge. From the very first stone tool to the internet, knowledge is nothing more than our links with the things that we know. Tools should not be acquisitions but bonds of knowledge with which we transform reality, external objects to be used.

Knowledge of truth does not lie in the arrangement and rearrangement of things in relation to one another. Labelling something does not comprise the truth. The truth is something that we do when we encounter the world that does something to us (McLuhan, 1989). Plato wanted to expel from his ideal state poets, particularly Homer and the tragic poets, as not politically correct. However, in his *Phaedrus*, he uses poetic language to discuss the position of rhetoric in the production of knowledge. He describes how, under a very tall plane tree, student and teacher put themselves in the process of transformation of reality, the desire for transmission, and the opening to the future. He depicts a light-hearted moment. However, we feel it is a pregnant moment, painful, and serious.

It is analogous to the moment we see a baby. We accept that we do not know, and we expect in faith a gesture of a true self, which has a basic rhythm, a primordial measure. With basic trust, the baby relies on the environment mother's capacity to hold open a window of time for their unfolding symbolising processes. However, ancient drama and psychoanalysis show us that we cannot take any of these things for granted.

Creating and living an experience implies public appearances of the self with the participation of the body. We link our felt body with meanings. We connect ourselves to the social world and the nature. Today, social media cultivate the meta-truth. We are relieved of the burden of meaning and the importance of objects. We become light-hearted but disoriented. Of course, we do not believe in 'grand narratives'. The only truth is change. However, meta-truth rejects any knowledge of truth in absolute terms. It relieves the individual of the painful processes of symbolisation and internalisation. It is a rigid system that cannot tolerate randomness. Fake news feeds the monster of populism/authoritarianism. Their rationale is based on the logic of the false self that complies. Meta-truth threatens the work of culture. It dismantles the process of making meaning. Nobody is held as an accountable subject. The subject is delegitimised.

Mimesis

In contrast to the culture of meta-truth, ancient Greek tragedy teaches us that the experiences of learning are realised through 'mimesis' (imitation) of praxis. In 304 BC, Aristotle discussed tragedy as mimesis of a praxis (action). The emphasis here should be placed on the experience. Mimesis can be thought of as a basic psychic work that happens on many levels of transformation, from beta to alpha elements, from soma to psyche, from unconscious to conscious, from the pre-psychic to psychic quality, from pre-history to history, from pre-politics to politics, etc. In ancient drama, mimesis means that the poet provides his audience with the capability to draw connections between what they are experiencing now and previous personal experiences.

Kosman (1992, pp. 64–68) examines the power of mimesis of praxis "to effect an almost magical salvation". It makes present the mysterious forces that come from the past. Aristotle describes the plot as "the soul of tragedy, the cause of its being what it is as the mimesis of an action". We can think that the story is contained in a meaning that gives the plot an end.

Woodruff (1992, pp. 89–93) explains: "Aristotelian mimesis is not the same as imitation or fiction or reproduction or representation or make-believe; it is not expression; and it is not even the making of images or likeness". Mimesis is the art of arranging for one thing to have an effect that properly belongs to another. It is an activity "that aims at producing effects that are normally achieved by other means". It is exciting and safe. It deceives the emotions but not the subject. We do not believe that all the experiences are actually happening, but we are made to feel the emotions that we would feel if we believed in them.

Woodruff (1992, pp. 89–93) comments that mimesis allows the inventions of fiction to have effects that are normally reserved for actual experiences. The poet makes actions that are convincing and affecting. They affect us as if they were real. They make the story "probable enough to trigger our emotions". Mimesis bypasses our consciousness. This disturbs Plato but not Aristotle, who, in his Ethics, emphasises that we are responsible for the impressions that we have. "Mimesis of O gives us the sort of impression we would have if we were having an experience of O; but that sort of impression is partly a product of our moral character". In other words, we are responsible for the way we perceive our impressions, the meaning we give, and how we register them in our human (psychic and public) life.

In the beginning was the action, the spontaneous gesture of the infant. The infant begins to emerge from a primary union with agonies of annihilation and primary identifications that precede the object relations (Freud, 1921). Gaddini (1987, 1992) and Salonen (2018, pp. 3, 114) examine the origins of primary identifications in the psychosensory area. The infant first finds the object and, at the same time, the self as a metaphor for the latter. In the original human frame of reference, a basic psychic configuration emerges from the infant's bodily contact with the mother.

There is no learning without the experiencing body that suffers the consequences of an action. The body is the first theatre. The first life events are somatic. The body learns itself; it changes, imitating the changes in the body of the other. The changes that we feel in our body give, as an idea that makes the other our object, something or somebody that has meaning for us. When we separate, mourn, and give meaning to our object, we emerge as a thinking subject.

Then, the relationship between a subject and another subject (ego relatedness) refers to the matrix of likeness in parent–infant relationships, playing, transference, and friendship. This becomes possible because of the state of Primary Maternal Preoccupation (Winnicott, 1956/1996, 1958/1990). In this state, the participants regress in order to feel themselves in the place of (identify with) the other. In order to find reality, we create doubles of ourselves that are similar and different from the object. The way we feel our body's change becomes a metaphor for the object, the influence of which causes this change.

We hope that inside our social group, the meeting points of mutual recognition between individuals form a 'contact barrier' made of alpha elements in a way that is analogous to what Bion hypothesised happens inside the psyche. A symbol is made of two pieces that are placed together and matched in order for the people who hold them to recognise each other. Recognition, from the Odyssey to ancient tragedy, psychoanalysis, and everyday life, is crucial. Alpha elements of meaning make crossroads where people really meet.

We raise our hand to hit the oedipal father who obstructs our path at the crossroads. On a deeper psychotic level, the obstacle that obstructs our path may be the monster of stupidity, arrogance, and omniscience (Bion, 1959/1967). A social group may become such a monster to take the place of a mother who is not open to receiving the projective identifications of the infant. Then, the social group cannot form a caring culture that can dream of the individuals' infantile primitive anxieties and return them to them in forms that are suitable for symbolisation. A society needs to have a sense of the tragic, in order to receive and elaborate the infantile (individual and collective) anxieties with their poetic language, the music of preverbal experiences.

Catharsis

Bernard Williams (1993) writes: We know that the world is not made for us, and we are not made for this world, that History does not tell us any useful story, and yet there is no place for us outside History. We must accept the fact that there is no redemptive solution that will show us that everything in the end will go well. In contrast to philosophers, we know that our ethical relationships with the world will never become understood.

We hope that our city has a sense of the tragic. A sense of the tragic enables politics to contain the anxieties of the citizens. Reading or watching a tragedy is a healing process. It brings a catharsis, where a piece of work of mourning is completed, a new depressive position is reached, emotions are clarified, and reality becomes clear. Catharsis does not mean purification or salvation. It means clarity. Tragedy holds the time of the experience of mourning. It holds a clear mirror (not a blurry one) in front of us.

Lear (1992, pp. 328–329) notes that Aristotle "defines tragedy in part by the effect it has on the audience: it is a mimesis of an action which by arousing pity and fear produces a katharsis of such emotions". Aristotle (1996) speaks about "mimetic pleasure". We do not derive pleasure from the beauty of the object we see on stage but from the act of mimesis. Lear (1992, pp. 515–520) explores Aristotle's belief in "an innate desire to understand, and a special pleasure that attends the satisfaction of that desire . . . It is because we gain a deeper insight into the human condition that we derive a special cognitive pleasure from tragedy".

Nehamas (1992, pp. 301–309) explores in Aristotle's *Rhetoric* and *Poetics* the structure of fields and practices of poetry in general and tragedy and epic in particular, against which Plato had argued vigorously. "In recognizing Oedipus or Medea in ourselves we recognize that what can happen to that sort of person can happen to us as well, since we have just come to recognize that we ourselves are the sort of person". Aristotle believes in the value of both rhetoric and fiction. However, the issue – that Plato raised – of the nature, the status, and the ethical character of rhetoric and fiction remains disturbingly unresolved.

Taplin (1978/1983, pp. 9–12) refers to Gorgias, the Sicilian sophist, who taught Rhetoric in Athens in the last quarter of the 5th century. Gorgias said: "the man who deceives shows more justice than he who does not; and the man who is deceived has more wisdom than he who is not". Following this idea, Taplin notes:

> The tragedian who succeeds in enthralling his audience does more justice by the effect this has on his audience than the playwright who fails to captivate them: likewise, the member of the audience who succumbs to the spell of the play will through that experience be a better, wiser man than the member who resists and remains unmoved.

The key word is 'to deceive' (apatan), which perhaps means that tragedy 'takes in' its audience. Gorgias considers emotions to be the heart of tragedy: "All tragedy I consider and define as discourse in metre. There comes over the audience of poetry a fearful horror and tearful pity and doleful yearning". These emotions are generous. Outgoing. Taplin concludes: "It seems to me that Gorgias is right that tragedy is essentially the emotional experience of its audience". By enthralling its audience, tragedy unites emotion and meaning so as to give us an experience. There is always a tension between emotions and meaning.

The hypothesis of a tragic plot is an interpretation based on the theories of the mind of the poet. It has an echo effect. Its meaning envelops the story that unfolds in the play. It pushes the envelope. It creates a corresponding realisation on stage. This is a realisation of an emotional experience that is created and shared between the persons of the drama and the spectators. Psychoanalysts, poets, and scholars examine the importance of such a realisation of an emotional experience.

The traumatised patients experience a pain that they cannot suffer. Pain envelops and holds together the fragmented self. Others, the audience, suffer the pain; the heroes are simply in pain; they wrap themselves in the pain until the time they achieve a tragic position. This means that they create and live now as an emotional experience, give meaning, internalise, and become subjects to – undertake the responsibility of – their past and the previous generations' past traumatic experiences (wars, sacrifices, genocides). They begin to suffer the pain when they give meaning to raw beta elements with alpha elements that make a story that becomes a memory. The meaning envelops the story, in which they find a place to put the self.

The tragic subject pleads to be given the time to struggle with its fate. Medea uses her forceful rhetoric to persuade Creon: Give me this day! Like the pilot of a warplane, when he is about to take off, she identifies her whole life with her mission. She pleads to be given the time to complete her experience. Give me this day! Everything happens in one day.

The poet inserts actuality into the mythical material. The poet inserts into the myth an action that has time embodied in it. Action offers conviction. The myth becomes a plot that is acted on stage. The tragic plot creates an experience made of actual events that unfold on stage as a sequence of moments of 'being' and 'becoming'. It delivers us alive, real, and present to the experience. Then, après coup, enables us to search for the meaning. Going through this experience has a liberating effect on our thinking. Working through the emotional storms of the plot, we emerge in a clearing. The fog of depression has been lifted. Emotions are clarified. We perceive reality more clearly. Catharsis is not purification. It is clarity.

References

Abram, J. (2022). The surviving object. In *Psychoanalytic clinical essays in psychic survival-of-the-object*. London and New York: Routledge.

Alford, C. F. (1992). *The psychoanalytic theory of Greek tragedy*. New Haven, CT and London: Yale University Press.

Aristotle. (1996). *Poetics. Translated with an introduction and comments by Malcom Heath*. New York: Penguin Books.

Belfiore, E. (1992). Aristotle and Iphigeneia. In A. O. Rorty (Ed.), *Essays on Aristotle's Poetics*. Princeton, NJ: Princeton University Press.

Bell, D. (2023). Psychoanalytic reflections on the conditions of possibility of human destructiveness. *International Journal of Psychoanalysis*, *103*(4), 674–691.

Benjamin, W. (1998). The origins of German tragic drama. In J. Osborne (Trans.), *Introduction George Steiner*. New York: Verso. (Original work published 1925)

Bion, W. R. (1967). Attacks on linking. In *Second thoughts. Selected papers on psychoanalysis*. New York: Jason Aronson. (Original work published 1959)

Burnett, A. P. (1983). The virtues of admetus. In E. Segal (Ed.), *Oxford readings in Greek tragedy*. Oxford: Oxford University Press. (Original work published 1965)
Castoriadis, C. (2007) Ce qui fait la Grece, 2. D' Homère à Héraclite. Seminaires 1982–1983. La creation humaine II. In E. Escobar, M. Gondicas, & P. Vernay (Eds.), & X. Giataganas (Trans.), *Greek*. Paris: Editions du Seuil; Athens: Kritiki Publications.
Critchley, S. (2019). *Tragedy, the Ancient Greeks and US*. London: Profile Books.
De Romilly, J. (1970). *La Tragedie Grecque*. Paris: Presses Universitaires de France.
Dodds. E. R. (1951). *The Greeks and the irrational*. Berkeley, CA: University of California Press.
Engle, B., & French, M. T. (1951). Some psychodynamic reflections upon the life and writings of solon. *Psychoanalytic Quarterly*, *20*, 253–274.
Freud, S. (1920). Beyond the pleasure principle. *S. E.*, *18*.
Freud, S. (1921). Group psychology and the analysis of the ego. *S. E.*, *18*.
Freud, S. (1940). Splitting of the ego in the process of defence. *S. E.*, *23*.
Gaddini, E. (1987). Notes on the mind-body question, *The International Journal of Psychoanalysis*, *68*, 315–329.
Gaddini, A. (1992). *A psychoanalytic theory of infantile experience*. London: Tavistock and Routledge.
Heaney, S. (1990). The cure at troy. In *Sophocles; Philoctetes*. London: Faber & Faber.
Herington, C. J. (1983). Aeschylus: The last phase. In E. Segal (Ed.), *Oxford readings in Greek tragedy*. Oxford: Oxford University Press. (Original work published 1965)
Ion, R., & Anderson, J. (2005). The myth of the masterbuilder. A psychoanalytic perspective. *Annual of Psychoanalysis*, *33*(1), 241–259.
Kaplan, D. R. (2023). *The tragic mind. Fear, fate, and the burden of power*. New Haven, CT and London: Yale University Press.
Knox, B. M. W. (1983). The hippolytus of Euripides. In E. Segal (Ed.), *Oxford readings in Greek tragedy*. Oxford: Oxford University Press. (Original work published 1952)
Kosman, A. (1992). Acting: Drama as the mimēsis of praxis. In A. O. Rorty (Ed.), *Essays on Aristotle's Poetics*. Princeton, NJ: Princeton University Press.
Kovacs, D. (1998). *Euripides: Suppliant Women, Electra, Heracles*. Cambridge, MA: Harvard University Press.
Lear, J. (1992). Katharsis. In A. O. Rorty (Ed.), *Essays on Aristotle's Poetics*. Princeton, NJ: Princeton University Press.
Lesky, A. (1983). Decision and responsibility in the tragedy of aeschylus. In E. Segal (Ed.), *Oxford readings in Greek tragedy*. Oxford: Oxford University Press. (Original work published 1966)
Main, T. (1957). The ailment. *British Journal of Medical Psychology*, *30*, 129–145.
McLuhan, M. (1989). *War and peace in the global village*. New York: Simon & Schuster.
Nehamas, A. (1992). Pity and fear in the rhetoric and the poetics. In A. O. Rorty (Ed.), *Essays on Aristotle's Poetics*. Princeton, NJ: Princeton University Press.
Plato. (2011). *Phaedrus*. Cambridge: Cambridge University Press.
Postman, N. (1993). Technopoly. In *The surrender of culture to technology*. New York: Vintage.
Potamianou, A. (1985). The personal myth: Points and counterpoints. *The Psychoanalytic Study of the Child*, *40*, 285–296.
Salonen, S. (2018). *Metapsychological perspectives on psychic survival: Integration of traumatic helplessness in psychoanalysis*. London and New York: Routledge.
Schlesinger, E. (1983). On Euripides' medea. In E. Segal (Ed.), *Oxford readings in Greek tragedy*. Oxford: Oxford University Press. (Original work published 1966)
Segal, C. (1983). Antigone: Death and love. Hades and dionysus. In E. Segal (Ed.), *Oxford Readings in Greek tragedy*. Oxford: Oxford University Press. (Original work published 1981)

Segal, E. (1983). Euripides: Poet of paradox. In Erich Segal (Ed.), *Oxford readings in Greek tragedy*. Oxford: Oxford University Press. (Original work published 1968)

Taplin, O. (1983). Emotion and meaning in Greek tragedy. In E. Segal (Ed.), *Oxford readings in Greek tragedy*. Oxford: Oxford University Press. (Original work published 1978)

Thucydides. (1910). *The Peloponnesian War*. London, J. M. Dent; New York, E. P. Dutton.

Weintrobe, S. (2023). From illusion to delusion: Reflections on the rising crazy. *EPF Bulletin, 77*, 254–277.

Williams, B. (1993). *Shame and necessity*. Berkeley and Los Angeles, CA: University of California Press.

Williams, M. H. (2013). Playing with fire: Prometheus and the mythological consciousness. In V. Zajko & E. O' Gorman (Eds.), *Classical myth and psychoanalysis*. Oxford: Oxford University Press.

Winnicott, D. W. (1960). The theory of the parent-infant relationship. *International Journal of Psychoanalysis, 41*, 585–595.

Winnicott, D. W. (1971). *Playing and reality*. London: Tavistock.

Winnicott, D. W. (1990). Communicating and not communicating leading to a study of certain opposites. In *The maturational processes and the facilitating environment*. London: Karnac. (Original work published 1963)

Winnicott, D. W. (1990). The capacity to be alone. In *The maturational processes and the facilitating environment*. London: Karnac. (Original work published 1958)

Winnicott, D. W. (1990). *The maturational processes and the facilitating environment*. London: Karnac. (Original work published 1965)

Winnicott, D. W. (1996). Primary maternal preoccupation. In *Through pediatrics to psychoanalysis*. London: Karnac. (Original work published 1956)

Winnicott, D. W. (1996). Reparation in respect of mother's organised defence against depression. In *Through paediatrics to psychoanalysis*. London: Karnac. (Original work published 1948)

Wolf, C. (1983) Orestes. In E. Segal (Ed.), *Oxford readings in Greek tragedy*. Oxford: Oxford University Press. (Original work published 1968)

Woodruff, P. (1992). Aristotle on Mimēsis. In A. O. Rorty (Ed.), *Essays on Aristotle's Poetics*. Princeton, NJ: Princeton University Press.

Zajko, V., & O' Gorman, E. (2013) *Classical myth and psychoanalysis*. Oxford: Oxford University Press.

Zimmermann, B. (1991). Greek tragedy. In T. Marier (Trans.), *An introduction*. Baltimore and London: The John Hopkins University Press. (Original work published 1986)

Index

Achilles 105
Admetus 83–89, 92
adolescence 4, 26, 32, 36–39, 59–60, 62–63, 116
Adrastus 67–69, 77
Aegeus 42, 45, 142
Aeneid (Virgil) 90
Aeschylus 2, 8, 126, 128–130, 136; *see also Prometheus Bound*
Aethra 28, 34, 67, 69, 73, 77
Agamemnon 104–107, 110
agons 16, 91
Aisenstein, M. 69
Alcestis 83–86, 88–92
Alcestis (Euripides): anti-narcissism in 6, 82, 90; change in 91; Chorus in 84, 87; death in 6, 8, 83–84, 86–89, 91–92, 141; drives in 86, 90; as "fable drama" 89; first performance of 82; guilt in 88; Hubris in 82–83; inescapable Necessity in 82–86; loving and being diminished in 90–92; maternal failures in 84; mourning in 87, 90; narcissism in 6, 90; overview 6–7; plot of 82–84; psychoanalysis and 85, 91; reality in 6, 82, 86–92; Resurrection in 86, 91; sexuality in 84; tragedy in 82; transitional space in 84–85, 91–92
Alford, C. F. 2, 7, 138
alogon (absurd) 142
Anaxagoras 48
André, J. 50
animistic thinking 143
annihilation anxiety 44, 54–55, 57, 62, 99, 108, 110, 146
Antigone 8, 119–124, 141
Antigone (Sophocles): Chorus in 121, 123; death in 8, 119, 121, 123, 141; drives in 119, 123–124; ethics of Antigone and 121, 123; faith in human life in 2; guilt in 123; Hubris in 120, 123–124; mourning in 8, 119; narcissism in 124; Necessity in 121; omnipotence in 8, 120–121, 124; overview 8; as paradigm 123–124; reality in 119–124; recognition in 8, 122, 124; staging of the political and 8, 119; supernatural reality in 119–120; sympathy in 124; transformation in 121
anti-narcissism 6, 82, 90
anxiety: annihilation 44, 54–55, 57, 62, 99, 108, 110, 146; about female nature 50; group dynamics and 107, 146; love of object/person and 90; persecutory 133; publication 61; separation 15; Sphinx and 72; about technology 144; tragedy and 147
Anzieu, D. 15
Aphrodite 28, 31, 33–36, 38
Apollo 82–83, 101
Argos 57–58, 61, 71
Aristophanes 138
Aristotle 1, 13, 20, 54, 78, 98, 135, 136–137, 139, 142, 145, 147
Aron, L. 19
Artemis 31–32, 36, 94, 96, 98–99, 101
artificial intelligence 144; *see also* technology
Arvanitakis, K. 6, 78
Asclepius 82
Asia Minor war 76, 102
Ate 100–102
Athena 68, 74–75, 96, 102, 139
Athens 66–67, 69, 71, 74–75, 78
Atlas, G. 19
Atropos 84
Austen, J. 12
authenticity 7, 48

Index

autoerotism 3, 15, 95, 108
autonomy 47

Bacchae 35
barbaric reality 41, 44–47, 50–51, 53–54
Belfiore, E. 138–139
Bell, D. 138
Bion, W. R. 12, 107, 146
bisexuality 26, 32, 38, 68–69, 72, 75, 123
Bleger, J. 19
Blume, H. D. 27
Bollas, C. 107
Breuer, J. 17
Britton, R. 61
Burian, P. 66, 70

Calchas 94, 105
Carson, A. 5, 92
Castoriadis, C. 120, 124, 138
castration 39, 94–98, 100–102
Catharsis 2, 5, 9, 146–148
changes 1, 21, 27, 61, 91, 101, 106, 111, 141–143
chaos 102, 105, 107–108, 110, 129, 142
Chekhov, Anton 60
Cherry Orchard, The (Chekhov) 60
Chorus: in *Alcestis* 84, 87; in *Antigone* 121, 123; as element of tragedy 14, 19; in *Hippolytus Crowned* 29–31, 33–34; in *Iphigeneia in Tauris* 95; in *Medea* 43–44, 46; of Oceantides 128; in *Prometheus Bound* 16, 128; replacement of 16; role of 14; in *Suppliant Women* 78
civil wars 105, 108–109, 122, 138
Clytemnestra 57–58, 63
Coen, Ethan and Joe 142
compassion 54, 57, 127
Conrad, Joseph 13, 110
creativity 13, 26, 29, 35, 50, 132, 138–139
Creon, King 8, 42, 46, 51, 67, 119–123, 141, 148
Critchley, S. 63, 87, 141
Cronus 126–127
Cypris 29–30
Cyprus War 122

dark side of life 2
death: in *Alcestis* 6, 8, 83–84, 86–89, 91–92, 141; in *Antigone* 8, 119, 121, 123, 141; birth of human society and 6, 21; fear of 34, 62, 87, 91, 94, 106, 128, 133, 135–136; in *Hippolytus Crowned* 26–27, 29, 31, 34, 36, 38–39; in *Iphigeneia in Aulis* 105–106, 108–109; in *Iphigeneia in Tauris* 94–95, 97, 102; in *Medea* 42–43, 46, 49, 51; mourning and 6; necessity of 15; in *Orestes* 57–58, 62, 64; in *Philoctetes* 113–114; in *Prometheus Bound* 128, 133; in *Suppliant Women* 66, 71–75, 77; technology and 144
deceive (apatan) 147
deception 48, 106, 115, 147
Delcourt, M. 41, 50
Demeter 67, 73, 74
democracy 65, 67, 79, 120
denial 26, 34, 69, 108, 122, 144
depression (fog of) 6, 77, 82, 148
De Romilly, Jacqueline 2, 14, 19–20, 48, 138
deus ex machina 27–28, 31, 44–46, 49, 52–53, 58, 63–64, 102, 116, 133
Dionysus 13–14, 41–42, 48, 138
disillusion 64, 75, 106
Dithyramb 14
Dodds, E. R. 141
double limit 14
dramatic point of view: concept of 11–13; interactivity of 19; meaning encountering sound and 13–17; overview 4; psychic staging and 17–22; psychoanalysis and 4, 11; reality and 11, 13–14, 17–18, 22; theatre as reflection of nature and 17; transference and 11, 19
dreaming and dream work 13, 17–19, 36, 52, 109, 121, 133
drives: in *Alcestis* 86, 90; in *Antigone* 119, 123–124; as demon 7; in *Hippolytus Crowned* 4, 26–27, 29–39; infant-parent 48; internalisation of 50; in *Iphigeneia in Aulis* 108, 110–111; in *Iphigeneia in Tauris* 101; in *Medea* 48, 50–51, 54; in *Orestes* 58; in *Prometheus Bound* 132; psychoanalysis and 18, 26, 48; reparation and destructive 141; in *Suppliant Women* 6, 68–70, 72–74, 76, 78–79; as threats 51; war against 29, 31–32, 37; *see also specific type*
Dupond, J. 19

Easterling, P. E. 33
Ego 3, 15, 17–18, 22, 27–31, 37, 42, 52, 62, 64, 68–69, 71, 90, 97, 110, 119, 141
Einstein, Albert 5–6

Electra 48, 57–58, 63
Eleusinian Mysteries 73–75
Eleusis 66–67, 71, 73–77
Eliot, T. S. 21, 92
emotions and language 14–17; *see also specific emotion*
Engle, B. 139
Erlich, H. s. 107
Eros 50–51, 78, 89
Eteocles 136
ethics 74, 121–122, 147
Euridice 77
Euripides 4, 16, 19–20, 27, 41, 45, 47–48, 52–54, 60–61, 65–66, 71, 75, 87; *see also specific work*
Evadne 68, 73–74
experience (emotional) 1, 3, 7, 11, 13, 16, 17, 22, 27, 29, 33–35, 63, 92, 123, 128, 136, 140, 147, 148

faith in human life and ideals 2, 106
fantasy: of Anna O 17–18; of audience 11; autoerotism and 3; creation and sharing of 13, 18; of hero 6; in *Hippolytus Crowned* 26–28, 31–33, 35–38; in *Iphigeneia in Aulis* 7, 104–105, 107, 109–111; in *Iphigeneia in Tauris* 99, 102; meaning and 1; in *Medea* 43–45, 49–51; narcissism and 26, 32; of omnipotence 99, 102; of omniscience 26; in *Orestes* 58–60; in *Philoctetes* 114; playing and 20; primal scene 16, 26, 38; psychoanalysis and 11, 18–19; reality versus 5; sensory images and 21; in *Suppliant Women* 72, 80; unfamiliar and, experience of 97
Fates 83–84, 100
fear: in *Alcestis* 87–88, 91; of apathy/ passivity 22, 34–35, 101; of Athenians 57; Catharsis and 147; of chaos 108; of death 34, 62, 87, 91, 106, 128, 133, 135–136; Euripides's use of 19, 138; in *Hippolytus Crowned* 28, 30, 34; in *Iphigeneia in Aulis* 106–108; in *Iphigeneia in Tauris* 94, 98–99; law enforcement and 139; in *Medea* 44–45, 50–51; in *Orestes* 58, 62; paranoid 69, 72, 79, 92; of parents 35; of persecution 7, 99, 106, 110; in *Philoctetes* 113, 115; in *Prometheus Bound* 128–129, 132–133; publication anxiety and 61; of reality 5; in social institutions 137;

of strangers 94; in *Suppliant Women* 74, 77, 79; of technology 144; in tragedy 53, 147; tyranny and 139; vignette, clinical 38
femininity 6, 69–70, 72–75, 79, 89, 100–101, 104, 109
Fenichel, O. 52
Ferenczi, S. 19
French, M. T. 139
Freud, S. 4–6, 12, 15, 18, 26–27, 35–37, 52, 69, 73, 107–108, 119–120, 135
friendship 79, 83, 89, 108, 123, 141
Frogs, The (Aristophanes) 138
future 13 17, 20, 36, 39, 47, 53, 57, 64, 71, 73, 89, 90, 94, 102, 111, 131, 133, 139, 140, 144

Gaddini, A. 146
Gaia 127, 131
Goethe, J. W. 119
Gorgias 18, 147
Greek civil war 109, 122, 138
Greek tragedy, ancient: deus ex machina in 45; Homer's *Odyssey* and 98; human struggle and 3; language and 14–15, 142–143; new political subject and, plea for 9, 135–136, 138; omnipotence and, loss of 68; plea for new political subject and 9; plot as analyst 2–3; poetics of 16; psychoanalysis and 1–4, 16, 135–136, 144; purpose of studying 135–136; reality and 9; *see also specific work*
Green, André 16, 52, 69, 72, 106
grief 5, 29, 43, 48, 68, 123; *see also* mourning
Grimal, P. 130
group dynamics 106–107, 110
guilt 5, 7, 18, 49, 61, 71–72, 86, 88, 123, 130, 132, 141

Hades 8, 34, 49, 77, 82, 88, 105, 122, 126
Haemon 122
hamartia 136
Hatzis, D. 109
Heaney, S. 140
Heart of Darkness (Conrad) 13
Hecuba 4
Hecuba (Euripides) 100
Hegal, G. W. F. 119
Helen 57–58, 60, 62–63, 104
Hera 129

Heracles 6, 8–9, 30, 57, 83, 85–86, 89–921, 113–117, 126, 130–132
Heraclitus 84, 124
Herington, C. J. 141
Hermes 128–129, 131
Hermione 58, 62–63
Hesiod 143
Hippolyta 4, 28, 33
Hippolytus 4, 26–39, 142
Hippolytus Crowned (Euripides): changes in action in 27; Chorus in 29–31, 34–35; as classic tragedy 35; connection between tragedy of Hippolytus in 35; death in 26–27, 29, 31, 34, 36, 38–39; denial in 34; deus ex machina in 27–28, 31; drives in 4, 26–27, 29–39; fantasy in 26–28, 31–33, 35–38; fear in 28, 30, 34; Hubris in 28; learning from experience in 4, 31–33, 38–39; maternal failure in 34; narcissism in 4, 26–27, 29, 32, 35–36, 39; omnipotence in 32–33, 38; overview 4; philosophical arguments of 28; plot of 28–31, 36; primal scene of sexuality in 26, 31–33, 39; primordial drive in 27, 31–33; reality in 31–33; recognition in 27, 34, 36, 38; repetition in 36–39, 41; sexuality in 36–39; theatrical space and 34–36; theme of 26, 34, 37; title's source 26; tragedy of 26; transference in 33, 37; transformation in 26, 38; visual effects in 27–28
history: adolescence and 60; Homer's works and 139; human nature in 1; in *Iphigeneia in Aulis* 104, 110; in *Medea* 44, 50–53; mimesis and 145; new political subject and 141; in *Orestes* 60; as performance 13; playing and 22; in *Prometheus Bound* 127, 133, 139; subjective 2, 13, 21, 51, 59; in *Suppliant Women* 71, 76; tragedy and 13, 20–22; in tragic plot/poetry 2, 20; Williams's (Bernard) view of 146
History of The Peloponnesian War (Thucydides) 78
history (subjective, psychic) 2, 13, 21, 51, 59
Homer 6, 54, 98, 121, 139
homosexuality 32
Hubris: in *Alcestis* 82–83; in *Antigone* 120, 123–124; in *Hippolytus Crowned* 28; in *Iphigeneia in Aulis* 105–106, 110; in *Iphigeneia in Tauris* 100; limits and, knowing our own 138; as mortal nature 82–83; omnipotence of 3, 136; in *Philoctetes* 113; in present public life 65; in *Prometheus Bound* 127; self and, sense of 1; supernatural forces and, accepting 119–120; in *Suppliant Women* 68, 71, 78

Iacov, I. D. 89
Id 110–111
illusion 4, 18, 22, 46–48, 60–61, 64, 75, 95–96, 106, 111, 127, 142
immortality 71–72, 75, 85, 90, 95, 121, 130, 135, 143
impossible things 96–100
incest 2, 39, 63; *see also* oedipal condition
inescapable Necessity 82–86, 130
injustice 33, 133, 140
internalisation 22, 45, 47, 50, 77–78, 99, 101, 109, 130, 132, 145
Io 129, 132
Iphigeneia 7, 22, 74, 94, 96, 98–100, 102, 105–110, 138
Iphigeneia in Aulis (Euripides): from Agamemnon's point of view 110; death in 105–106, 108–109; drives in 108, 110–111; fantasy in 7, 104–105, 107, 109–111; fear in 106–108; group dynamics in 106–107, 110; history in 104, 110; Hubris in 105–106, 110; human sacrifices in 106, 108–109; omnipotence in 106; overview 7; plot of 104–106; reality in 106–108, 110–111; recognition in 104; responsibility in 104–105, 110–111; social bonds and 108–109; as tragic sacrifice of individual fantasies 104, 106, 108–109; transference in 110; transformation in 94, 121; transitional space in 104; triumph in sacrifice and 7; war and 104–105, 108–109
Iphigeneia in Tauris (Euripides): Ate and 100–102; bringing home stranger in 6–7; castration in 94–98, 100–102; Chorus in 95; death in 94–95, 97, 102; deus ex machina in 102; drives in 101; fantasy in 99, 102; fear in 94, 98–99; femininity in 100–101; Hubris in 100; human sacrifices in 95–98, 100–101; impossible things in 96–100; irony in 94, 97, 102; massacre of strangers in

94–96; mourning in 94; narcissism in 95–97; omnipotence in 7, 94, 96, 99, 102; overview 7; plot of 96; prohibited things in 96–100; question posed by Euripides in 98; reality in 94, 96–97, 101–102; recognition in 98–101; responsibility in 7, 98; sexuality in 98
Iphis 68, 73
irony 50, 94, 97, 102, 138

Jakobson, R. 17
Jason 41–44–46, 51
Joseph (Biblical myth) 34
justice 8, 126, 139, 141, 147

Kafka, Franz 132
Kairos 12
Kaplan, D. R. 140
Keats, J. 130
Kitto, H. D. F. 32, 128–129
Klein, M. 18
Knox, B. M. W. 142
kommos 14
Kore 67, 73, 77, 122
Kosman, A. 145
Kott, J. 86, 89
Kovacs, D. 45

language: emotions and 14–17; as form of action 19; Greek tragedy and 14–15, 142–143; meaning and 12–17, 136–137; music of 14–15; myth and 2, 13–17, 53; in *Orestes* 48; psychoanalysis and 15; recognition and 16, 117; representation of words and 53–54; rhythm of 15–16; in theatre 17; in tragedy 21; true speech and 16; unconscious things and 37
Lear, J. 147
Lesky, A. 35, 136
lethic phallus concept 116
libido 90
Loewald, H. W. 19, 53
logos 2, 4, 68, 78; *see also* language
Loraux, N. 48

McDougal, J. 22
Main, Tom 137
masochism 4, 32, 109, 114
Mastronarde, J. D. 50
maternal failures 27, 34, 84
matricide 5, 57–58

meaning, creating 1, 12–18, 80
Medea 5, 41–55, 136, 141–142
Medea (Euripides): barbaric reality in 41, 44–47, 50–51, 53–54; Chorus in 43–44, 46; death in 42–43, 46, 49, 51; deus ex machina in 44–46, 49, 52–53; drives in 48, 50–51, 54; fantasy in 43–45, 49–51; fear in 44–45, 50–51; history in 44, 50–53; irony in 50; meaning of 47–48; metaphor of Medea and 50, 54–55; monologue of Medea in 51–52; murder of children in 45–46, 48–50; myth of Medea and 41–42, 48–50; new chain of meanings in 47; oedipal condition in 42, 45, 48, 50, 55, 142; omnipotence in 50, 52, 54; overview 5; plot of 43–47, 51; poetics in 47, 49–50; primitive elements in 51–52; psyche struggles and wounds in 5, 41; psychic constructions in 53–55; psychoanalysis and 41, 48, 53; reality in 41, 44–45, 47, 50–51, 53; recognition in 43, 45, 55; re-organisation of defences in 54–55; responsibility in 49–50, 53; restoration in, miracle of 54; revenge in 42, 45–46, 48–49, 51–52, 136, 141–142; thematic expressions in 52–53; tragedy in 41–42, 53–54; transference in 51–52, 55; transformation in 41, 46, 51–52
Medusa 42, 86, 90
melancholy 44, 46, 74
Menelaus 57–58, 61–62
mercy 141
meta-truth, tyranny of 143–145
metre 12–14, 147
mimesis (imitation) 15, 20, 140–141, 145–147
Money-Kyrle, R. 20
mortality *see* death
mourning 5–6, 8, 69–72, 76, 79, 87, 90, 94, 114–115, 119; *see also* grief
myth: of Demeter and Persephone 73; Euripides's poetic treatment of 48; of Hippolytus 26–27; language and 2, 13–17, 53; logos and 2; of Medea 41–42, 48–50; poets and 4; of Prometheus 130–131, 140–141; psychoanalysis and 4, 140; reality and 31–33; of suppliants and Oedipus 72; timelessness of 13, 140; as transitional space 3

narcissism 4, 6, 26–27, 29, 32, 35–36, 39, 61–64, 90, 95–97, 124, 130
Necessity 15, 121, 136–139
Nehamas, A. 2, 147
Neoptolemus 115–116
new political subject, plea for: Catharsis and 146–148; change and, wish for 141–143; Greek tragedy and 9, 135–136, 138; history and 141; meta-truth and, tyranny of 143–145; mimesis and 145–146; Necessity and 136–139; overview 9; responsibility and 136–139; revenge and, desire for 141–143; tyranny and, struggle against 139–141
No Country for Old Men (film) 142

"occurrences" 17
Odysseus 6, 13, 99, 113, 115–1166
Odyssey (Homer) 6, 98
oedipal condition 28, 32–34, 42, 45, 48, 50, 55, 60–63, 70–73, 142, 146
Oedipus Rex 21, 64, 71–72
Ogden, H. T. 16
O'Gorman, E. 4, 13
omnipotence: in *Antigone* 8, 120–121, 124; fantasy of 99, 102; in *Hippolytus Crowned* 32–33, 38; of Hubris 3; illusion of 127; internalisation of 8–9, 32, 124, 126, 130, 139; in *Iphigeneia in Aulis* 106; in *Iphigeneia in Tauris* 7, 94, 96, 99, 102; limit of 64, 87; loss of 2–3, 8, 50, 52, 54, 68–70, 79, 94, 115, 119–121, 128, 136, 139–140; in *Medea* 50, 52, 54; in *Philoctetes* 115; in *Prometheus Bound* 8, 8–9, 126–128, 130, 139; in *Suppliant Women* 72, 76, 79; threats to 20
Oppenheimer, Robert 133–134
orchestra 14
Oresteia 139
Orestes 5, 57–58, 60–64, 96–102, 109, 141–142
Orestes (Euripides): adolescence in 59–60, 62–63; anti-dialectical defences in 59–60; contamination of city in 5, 57–58; death in 57–58, 62, 64; deus ex machina in 58, 63–64; drives in 58; fantasy in 58–60; fear in 58, 62; history in 60; language in 48; murder of Orestes mother in 58; narcissism in 61–64; oedipal condition in 60–63; overview 5–6; plot of 57–58; private position in 59–60; public position in 59–60; reality in, fear of impending 5, 57, 59–60, 62–64; recognition in 7; revenge in 57–58, 61, 142; social fabric in, torn 60–64; transference in 60
original sin 69

paradoxes 47, 66, 68, 76, 85, 91–92, 104, 109, 116, 120, 140
paranoia 69, 72, 79, 110, 129
parent-infant interactions 15–16
Parsons, M. 16, 89
Pasche, F. 90
passion 7–8, 20–22, 43–44, 48, 50, 61, 67, 101, 105, 119, 132, 135, 137, 142
past 3, 5, 6, 11, 13, 19, 20, 33, 43, 47, 51, 55, 59, 65, 66, 69–71, 76, 89, 102, 104, 110, 122, 129, 136, 140, 145, 148
pathology of deterioration 143
Paul the Apostle 21
Pedder, R. J. 18
Peirce,? 17
Pelias 42
Peloponnesian War 67, 78, 82
Penelope 6426
Persephone 73
Persian Wars 138
persons of the drama 14; *see also specific character's name*
persuasion, art of 12, 17
Phaeacians 13
Phaedra 4, 26, 28–30, 32–33, 35–39
Phaedrus (Plato) 143–144
Pheres 83–84
Philoctetes 7–8, 57, 113–116
Philoctetes (Sophocles): death in 113–114; deus ex machina in 116; ending of 116; fantasy in 114; fear in 113, 115; Hubris in 113; meaning of 113; mourning in 114–115; omnipotence in 115; overview 7–8; physical pain in 7–8, 57, 114, 117; plot of 113–117; reality in 113, 115–117; sexuality in 115; tragedy in 115; transference in 115
Phrynichus 91
physical pain 7–8, 57, 114, 117
Pick, Irma Brenman 136
Pirandello, Luigi 18
Plato 85, 143–145, 147
playing 1, 11, 18–20, 22, 59, 68, 70, 92, 123, 140

pleasure principle 12, 75, 135
Plutarch 34, 95, 139
Poetics (Aristotle) 1, 20, 54, 98, 135, 136
poetry/poetics 16–17, 21, 47, 49–50, 53
poets as mythmakers 4
politics: definition of 70, 72; democracy and 67, 79, 120; Euripides's view of 65–66, 78; function of 70; institutions and, struggle to innovate 79; male-female conflict and 74–75; order of 75–78; social institutions and 138; theory of 65–66, 78–80; tragedy and 120; as transitional phenomenon of culture 78–79; transitional space of 6, 65–66, 77, 116; *see also* new political subject, plea for
Polymestor 4
Polyxena 74, 100
Pontalis, J. B. 18
Postman, N. 143
Potamianou, A. 140
present 2, 11, 26, 41, 59, 65, 82, 94, 104, 115, 119, 128, 137
preverbal experiences 5, 12, 16, 28–29, 37, 41, 44, 47, 49, 51–54, 128, 132, 143
pride *see* Hubris
primal scene 4, 6, 16, 19–21, 26–27, 31–34, 36, 38–39, 42, 45, 50, 73, 77, 89, 97, 100
Primary Maternal Preoccupation 146
primitive elements on stage 51–52, 77
private theatre 17–18
prohibited things 96–100
Prometheus 2, 8–9, 15–16, 126–133, 139, 140–141
Prometheus Bound (Aeschylus): background information 126; Chorus of the Oceanides in 16, 128; death in 128, 133; deus ex machina in 133; drives in 132; ending of 126; faith in human life in 2; guilt in 130, 132; history in 127, 133, 139; Hubris in 8, 127; learning from experience in 129–132; narcissism in 130; omnipotence in 8–9, 126–128, 130, 139; overview 8–9; passion in 132; plot of 127–129; reality in 132–133; rock of the unexplained in 132–134; from suffering to thinking and 8–9, 129–132; transformation in 8–9, 126, 130, 132
Prometheus Unbound (Aeschylus) 126
psyche 3–5

psychic acts 12
psychic constructions 12–13, 53–55, 121
psychic formation 12
psychic quality 12
psychic staging 17–22
psychic struggles 2, 5
psychoanalysis: *Alcestis* and 85, 91; dramatic point of view and 4, 11; Greek tragedy and 1–4, 16, 135–136, 144; language and 15; as live dialogue 19, 135; *Medea* and 41, 48, 53; myth and 4, 140; poetry and 16–17; stage and 3–4, 12, 18–19; *Suppliant Women* and 65–66, 69; theatrical dimension of 12, 17–18, 22; tragedy and 19, 27, 147–148; vignettes, clinical 18, 38, 63, 91, 114–115, 132–133, 135; *see also specific concept*
Pylades 58, 63, 96–97, 101–102
Pyrophorus (Aeschylus) 126

reality: in *Alcestis* 6, 82, 86–92; in *Antigone* 119–124; barbaric 41, 44–47, 50–51, 53–54; catharsis and 5, 9, 146–148; comprehending, difficulty of 135; crime and 5; denial of 108, 122, 144; dramatic point of view and 11, 13–14, 17–18, 22; external versus internal 1, 3, 11, 13–14, 17–18, 22, 59–60, 68, 70, 79, 113, 142; fantasy versus 5; fear of 5; as finding and creation 1; in *Hippolytus Crowned* 28, 31–33, 37; historic 31–33; illusion and 22; intolerable, facing 2; in *Iphigeneia in Aulis* 106–108, 110–111; in *Iphigeneia in Tauris* 94, 96–97, 101–102; in *Medea* 41, 44–45, 47, 50–51, 53; mythic 31–33; in *Orestes*, fear of impending 5, 57, 59–60, 62–64; in *Philoctetes* 113, 115–117; playing and 18; pleasure principle versus 75; principle 75, 121, 135; in *Prometheus Bound* 132–133; psyche struggles and 2, 5; recognition of 20, 38, 74, 79, 90, 101, 141; in *Suppliant Women* 66, 68–75, 77–79; theatre and 19, 22; tragedy and 19; transformation of 37, 53, 121, 144; trauma of contact with 20; untransformed 12
reality (internal, psychic, external, social) 1, 3, 11, 13–14, 17–18, 22, 59–60, 68, 70, 79, 113, 142

recognition: in *Antigone* 8, 122, 124; Euripides's use of 19; in *Hippolytus Crowned* 27, 34, 36, 38; importance of 146; of infant's experiences 37; in *Iphigeneia in Aulis* 104; in *Iphigeneia in Tauris* 98–101; language and 16, 117; in *Medea* 43, 45, 55; of need to express oneself 2; in *Orestes* 7; physical pain and 117; of reality 20, 38, 74, 79, 90, 101, 141; of stranger 6, 97; tragedy and 7, 13–14, 98, 141, 146; of unconscious processes 119

responsibility: of actor 17; for adolescent development 36; for crime 5, 35, 49; for democracy 65; for fate 60, 104; in *Iphigeneia in Aulis* 104–105, 110–111; in *Iphigeneia in Tauris* 7, 98; for meaning, creating 17–18, 80; in *Medea* 49–50, 53; new political subject and, plea for 136–139; for past 136, 148; for registering own experiences 3; in *Suppliant Women* 65, 69, 72, 74, 77, 79; for traumatic experiences 79

Resurrection 86, 91

revenge 4–5, 42, 45–46, 48–49, 51–52, 57–58, 61, 73, 76, 136, 141–143

Rhetoric 12, 16, 54

rhythm of language 15–16

Richard II (Shakespeare) 60

ritual 73, 76, 143

sacrifice 7, 27, 38, 49, 65, 71, 73, 74, 76, 83, 84, 89, 90, 92, 94–102, 104–111, 119, 122, 123, 144, 148

Salonen, S. 117, 146

Scarry, Elaine 114

Schlesinger, E. 142

Schmidt-Hellerau, C. 114, 116

Secret Sharer, The (Conrad) 110

Seferis, George 76, 122

Segal, C. 36

Segal, H. 86

separation anxiety 15

sexuality: adult 26, 31–32, 34, 36; in *Alcestis* 84; bisexuality and 26, 32, 38, 68–69, 72, 75, 123; child 12, 33; development of 53–54; female 29; in *Hippolytus Crowned* 26–27, 29, 31–34, 36–39; homosexuality and 32; implantation of 36; in *Iphigeneia in Tauris* 98; parental 26, 32, 34, 36; in *Philoctetes* 115; repetition and 36–39;

somatic events and 59; of virgin, young 8

Shakespeare, William 60

Simone, Nina 99

Six Characters in Search of an Author (Pirandello) 18

skene 14, 17; *see also* stage

social bonds 108–109

social institutions 137–138

society 1, 3–4, 6, 37, 59, 65, 68–71, 84, 108, 123–124, 127, 133, 135, 138, 141–143, 146

Socrates 48, 67, 143

Sophocles 2, 57, 121; *see also Antigone; Philoctetes*

space 3, 5, 6, 8, 12, 14, 16–18, 21, 33–36, 42, 51, 52, 54, 59, 60, 62, 63, 65, 66, 70, 71, 74–78, 80, 82, 84, 85, 91, 92, 101, 102, 104, 106, 116, 117, 120, 123, 124, 129, 132, 136, 137, 139, 140

speech, true 16; *see also* language

Sphinx 72

stage 3–4, 12, 14, 17–19, 27, 51–52

stranger, bringing back home 6–7

Superego 32–33, 42, 61–62, 96, 98, 108, 110–111, 130, 133

Suppliant Women (Euripides): bedrock of reality as metaphor in 71; Chorus in 78; death in 66, 71–75, 77; Demeter-Kore (mother-daughter) drama in 73; drives in 6, 68–70, 72–74, 76, 78–79; Eleusinian Mysteries and 73–75; ending of 71; faith in human life in 2; fantasy in 72, 80; fear in 74, 77, 79; femininity in 6, 72–75; guilt in 71–72; history in 71, 76; Hubris in 68, 71, 78; immortality in 71–72, 75; meaning of 65–66; mourning in 6, 70–72; oedipal condition in 70–73; omnipotence in 72, 76, 79; overview 6; plot of 66–68; political order in 75–78; political theory in 65–66, 78–80; political vision of Euripides and 65–66, 69; psychoanalysis and 65, 65–66, 69; reality in 66, 68–75, 77–79; responsibility in 65, 69, 72, 74, 77, 79; scholars' interpretation of 65; staging of 70; tragedy in 68–70; transformation in 65, 68, 70; transitional space in 70–71, 74–77, 80; war and 70–71, 75–76, 78

sympathy 3, 108, 124, 128

talking *see* language
Taplin, O. 21, 147
technology 36, 126, 143–144
Teiresias 122
Thamus 143
Thanatos 89; *see also* death
theatrical space 34–36, 80
Theogony (Hesiod) 143
Theseus 2, 28, 30–31, 33–35, 67, 72, 75–77
Theuth 143
Thucydides 78, 142–143
time 1, 11, 31, 42, 57, 66, 82, 94, 104, 114, 119, 128, 135
Titans 126–127
Topouzis, K. 85
Totem and Taboo (Freud) 18
tragedy: anxiety and 147; Aristotle's view of 13, 20; birth of 2, 13, 53; change in thinking and 1; citizens' activities and 138; commitment to 22; dark side of life and 2; definition of 1; elements of 14–15; emotional content of 20–21; experience of watching 21–22; faith in human life and 2; fear in 53, 147; Freud's understanding of 18; history and 13, 20–22; hypothesis of plot of 148; language in 21; as *mimesis* 20; *mimesis* (imitation) as 20; as mirror of human condition 104; object of 87; omnipotence and, loss of 3, 54, 68–70; persuasion and, art of 12; politics and 120; primal scene of 20; psychoanalysis and 19, 27, 147–148; reality and 19, 22; recognition and 7, 13–14, 98, 141, 146; watching, experience of 21–22; *see also* Greek tragedy, ancient; *specific title*
transference: double 16; hamartia and 136; in *Hippolytus Crowned* 33, 37; in *Iphigeneia in Aulis* 110; in *Medea* 51–52, 55; in *Orestes* 60; in *Philoctetes* 115; psychic staging and 16–17, 19; in psychoanalysis 11; struggle of external/internal reality and 3; tragic plot and 2–3; vignette, clinical 114
transformation: in *Antigone* 121; in *Hippolytus Crowned* 26, 38; internal rationale and 21; in *Iphigeneia in Aulis* 108; in *Iphigeneia in Taurus* 94; in *Medea* 41, 46, 51; mimesis and 20, 140–141, 145; in *Phaedrus* 144; in *Prometheus Bound* 8–9, 126, 130, 132;

psychoanalysis and 12, 16; of reality 37, 53, 121, 144; in *Suppliant Women* 65, 68, 70
transitional space: in *Alcestis* 84–85, 91–92; change in 21, 101; coexistence in 21, 85, 91; development of 8; in *Iphigeneia in Aulis* 104; paradox in 140; of politics 6, 65–66, 77, 116; re-organisation of 54; struggle of external/internal reality in 3; in *Suppliant Women* 70–71, 74–77, 80; of theatre 18, 80
trauma 3–5, 7, 20, 22, 28, 29, 31, 32, 34–37, 41, 49, 51–53, 62, 64, 67, 71, 78, 80, 87, 88, 92, 97, 115–117, 128, 132, 133, 136
triumph in sacrifice 7
Trojan War 57–58, 113
Troy 57, 94, 97, 104, 106, 110–111, 113, 115–116
Trump, Donald 142
truth, knowledge of 144
tyranny, struggle against 139–141

unconscious processes 17, 119

Valery, Paul 21
Vernant, J. P. 116
Vidal-Naquet, P. 116
Virgil 90

war: Asia Minor 76, 102; Athenian 5, 7, 9, 53, 57, 67, 98–99; civil 105, 108–109, 122, 138; Cyprus 122; against drives 29, 31–32, 37; between gods 131; Greek civil 109, 122, 138; *Iphigenia in Aulis* and 104–105, 108–109; Peloponnesian 67, 78, 82; Persian 138; question about 5–6; *Suppliant Women* and 70–71, 75–76, 78; Trojan 57–58, 113
Williams, Bernard 3, 146
Williams, Meg Harris 4, 130–131, 139
Winnicott, D. W. 15, 18, 29, 35, 92, 136, 141, 144
Woodruff, P. 145
words *see* language; logos

Zajko, V. 4, 13
Zeus 8–9, 82–83, 126–127, 129–130, 132–133
Zimmerman, B. 138, 143

For Product Safety Concerns and Information please contact our EU representative GPSR@taylorandfrancis.com
Taylor & Francis Verlag GmbH, Kaufingerstraße 24, 80331 München, Germany

www.ingramcontent.com/pod-product-compliance
Lightning Source LLC
Chambersburg PA
CBHW051401290426
44108CB00015B/2102